W9-CRN-644

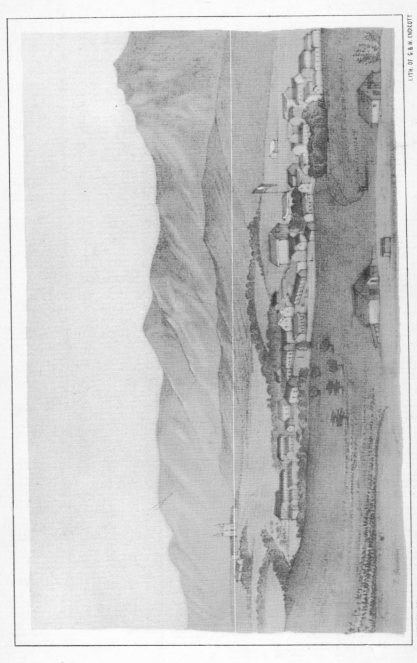

A. ROBINSON DEL

LITH. OF G & W. ENDICOTT

VIEW OF THE "PRESIDIO" OR TOWN OF SANTA BARBARA.

TAKEN FROM A HILL NEAR THE FORT

Life in California

BY ALFRED ROBINSON, *1806-1895.*

A HISTORICAL ACCOUNT OF THE
ORIGIN, CUSTOMS, AND TRADITIONS OF
THE INDIANS
OF ALTA-CALIFORNIA

FOREWORD BY JOSEPH A. SULLIVAN

BIOBOOKS · OAKLAND, CALIFORNIA

1947

CALIFORNIA CENTENNIAL EDITION
Number IX

Contents

Part I

vi

Proclamation of Alvarado—Arrival of an American and a French sloop of war—Consternation of Alvarado—Satisfaction given to the Captain of the St. Louis—Desertion of St. Diego—Consequence of secularization—A ride to the Pueblo—Return of the foreigners—Mines—Anglo-Californian justice—Temblores—Rodeo—Sad incident—Important news—Arrival of a Bishop—His reception—Arrival of Sir George Simpson and Governor McLaughlin.

Part II

ix

Foreword

ON PALM SUNDAY AFTER LUNCH WITH THE hospitable Col. Arthur Stanleys, at Redlands, we proceeded, according to plan, for San Diego.

Our plan was to revisit the Missions from San Diego north. Near Beaumont we picked up No. 79 through Hemet, crossing Captain Anza's trail and traveling south. J.V., "high" over his first bike ride, (the soreness did not come for a couple of days) was leading his mother and the driver in "Zip-a-Dee-*Doo*-Dah" and "Old MacDonald's Farm".

Wildflowers in blossom, lupin, cactus, paint brush, lilac, buttercups, and many we could not name, quail, road runners. The contour road slowing us from 50 to 25 miles an hour, near Sage we caught our first view of Palomar, the new observatory shining in the afternoon sun, as large as the Russ Building on a plateau 6000 feet high and 25 by 30 miles square, dominating an area as large as Connecticut. The scene starting a chain reaction in our mind that has not yet been satisfied, in geology, a gigantic monolith of granite, so large the early Spaniards called it a Sierra, having the most beautiful place name in California, we refuse to accept completely the explanation "dovecot" of Catherine M. Wood, Hill's "Warner's Ranch," excellent on the Missions and the San Jose Valley does not shed light on the mountain's name; Warner's map, however, does show Cañada de Pala. Priestley, "Francisco Explorations in California," has both Pala and Pale. The Indians locally were called Palas. In the old Italian religion was a god or goddess Pales.

The title Palomar has both the Sanskrit Pa and Ma. The Latin tree and sea. The Portuguese and Spanish navigators on the Manila galleons, noted for their picturesque naming, may have marked it, snow clad in winter or green clad in summer, although Wagner's

"Cartography" does not index. Traditionally handed down this could as well be an explanation of such an appropriate name, certainly it would seem homing sailors from the Western Sea seeking a landfall could not have missed this crested giant epaulet near the Southern California Coast. On this Palm Sunday we joined at Temecula that great Shoshone highway that extends from the Columbia ice fields to Coronado, we visited San Luis Rey and several of the missions including San Juan Capistrano, some days later, north to San Miguel, with a very pleasant side trip to San Antonio, the last situated off the present main coast highway in a fascinating flowered unfenced park, spotted with oaks and cattle. The missions bringing the olive and the grape were as well the hospice for the travellers of their day.

This book published by Wiley and Putnam in New York in the decisive year of 1846, author's name not given, was the first book in English by a Californian and according to Layne the most important for its period. In releasing it as number nine in the California Centennial Editions Biobooks is more than ever conscious of the many hands required to make a book.

As the nominater to this series of our author's book we thank Miss Eleanor Reed of Dawson's Book Shop and as this occasion permits, a nod of appreciation to that grand pair of bookmen, Ernest and Glen Dawson, for their continued encouragement. For our text we thank Mrs. Helen Giffen and the Directors of the Society of California Pioneers in permitting us to utilize their copy of the first edition, to our printer for the new font of Fairfield, to Lithographer Merrill Reed for the excellent color illustrations form the Endicott originals. To Padre Geronimo Boscana, born in Mallorca, arriving at San Juan Capistrano in 1814, who wrote the ethnological treatise on the Indians of his Mission. To John P. Harrington for an assist in the present accepted pronunciation of the name of Boscano's work, Chinigchinich (Chi-ñi'ch-ñich) the accent on the second syllable and the *n* in each case having the added *y* sound of the Spanish. Several attempts and all worthwhile have been made at reproductions of this combined book, but of interest this is the only complete reprint of the text since its first printing. We have added an Index for "Life in California" and broken the folios for a little easier reading.

Russell reprinted the first part only ("Zamorano 80" make note). We admire his printing but do not emulate his editorial liberties. Or his subtitle "Before the Conquest". As a matter of historic fact there were at least three great conquerors, Anza for the Spanish and Kearny for the Americans, and both in the shadow of Palomar. For such a precise man as Russell "Between the Conquests" would be nearer a correct descriptive subtitle.

The Fine Arts reprinted Boscano in a magnificent book. Although the Smithsonian Edition may be the more correct translation. All accounts agree that Alfred Robinson was the writer and translator and drew the pictures. Robinson, born in Boston, came to California when 23 years of age as a clerk for Bryant Sturgis & Co. and was a very important factor in the fostering and developing of trade between California and New England. He proved capable, industrious and quite intelligent in his firm's interest, and as the sequence shows, of fine talents. Marrying in 1836 (of which more anon) he carried the first recorded gold from California to the East. Was later Special Agent for Pacific Mail SS. Co. at San Francisco, where he died in 1895. We thank the Oakland Library and especially Miss Mable Thomas and Miss Ethel Blumann for their help on research, and found the most important study so far made of Robinson to be by Adele Ogden and published by the California Historical Society.

Robinson married a daughter of Don de la Guerra y Noriega, the union bringing him at the same time into another well known California family, the Carrillos. They had eight children. Perhaps the best estimate of Alfredo's character is in his own writing published 24 years after his narrative of Early California. We reproduce it here complete.

Jose Antonio de la Guerra

Don José Antonio de la Guerra y Noriega was born in Novales, in the province of Santander, Spain, A.D. 1776. He emigrated to Mexico in 1778, [sic] where, soon after his arrival, he entered the mercantile house of his uncle, Don Pedro Noriega, a wealthy gentleman residing in the capital, with the intention of becoming a merchant; but finding the business unsuited to his taste, and being ambitious of distinction, and desirous of serving his country and sovereign, he obtained, in 1798, the appointment of cadet in the Royal Army. In 1800, he was promoted ensign to the company then stationed at Monterey, Upper California, where he arrived the following year. In 1804, he married the daughter

xiii

of Don Raimundo Carillo, Commandante of the Presidio of Santa Barbara. In 1806, he was again promoted, and received the commission of lieutenant in the company stationed at Santa Barbara. In 1810, he was named "Habitado General" of both Upper and Lower California, and immediately embarked with his family for San Blas, on his way to the city of Mexico. On his landing, he was taken prisoner by the curate, Mercado, a partisan of Hidalgo in the revolution of that time, and carried to Istlan, where he fortunately escaped from the cruel assassination of his fellow-prisoners.

The revolution of Hidalgo having deprived him of his office, he remained some time in Tepic, where he served as Ayudante Mayor in the army there stationed, much to the satisfaction of the government. In 1811, he returned with his family to California. For several years thereafter he held command of the troops quartered at San Diego.

In 1817, he was promoted captain and commandante of the company stationed at Santa Barbara. Thither, in that year, he repaired with his family. In 1819, he again went to Mexico as Habitado General. After a short official service, the revolution of 1821 caused him to return to California.

Upon his return, he forwarded to the Mexican Republican government his resignation. It was not accepted. The President, Guadaloupe Victoria, feeling the great need for his services, continued him in the command at Santa Barbara.

In 1828, he was named Diputado to the General Congress of Mexico, but did not fill the office, in consequence of his seat having been already taken and occupied by the "Suplente," Don Gervasio Arguello. He returned to California the following year, in a vessel which he purchased and loaded with an assorted cargo.

He embarked with him as passengers, Abel Stearns, Sherman Peck, and a Scot named Kinloch. Mr. Stearns' visit to California was to receive a large grant of land which his partner had obtained from the Mexican government, and to make arrangements for opening the same to American colonization.

It was in July, 1829, when they landed at Monterey. Their arrival caused considerable commotion and excitement among the Spanish population which, at that time, inhabited the little town. After passing a few days of feasting and enjoyment among his friends and old companions, Don José took leave of them and started overland for San Francisco, (Yerba Buena). He dispatched his vessel to meet him at the last named place. On his route, he was received at the different missions at which he tarried with all the respect and attention due his rank, by the ringing of bells and firing of guns. In consequence of his great intimacy and friendship with the old Fathers then at the head of the missionary establishments, he was enabled to negotiate very important and satisfactory sales, and soon disposed of his entire cargo.

On reaching San Francisco he found his vessel awaiting him. He immediately discharged his merchandise and set sail for Santa Barbara. His vessel was stranded in attempting to enter the narrow inlet near that port, but all on board were saved and reached their destination.

From that time, Don José lived almost entirely at home in the midst of his family, devoting himself to their welfare and happiness. He took no active part in the political troubles and frequent revolutions of his country, except as a counsellor and mediator, in which capacity, from his great reputation as a man of unspotted integrity, patriotism, humanity and wealth, he wielded immense influence in California.

All the people of Santa Barbara looked up to him as the patriarch of their little community. On every emergency, to him they resorted for advice and succor. Oftentimes, during the periodical visitation of earthquakes in that region, men and women, with their children, would encamp on the square of ground upon which stood his noble mansion, and there remain until their fears subsided, subsisting the while on his hospitality and generosity. It seemed as if they considered his person endowed with supernatural grace. To their simple minds his presence was a sufficient guaranty for their protection.

The children of the little settlement were taught to revere him. As they passed the door of his dwelling they would remove their hats and give the customary obeisance, in the same manner as they did when passing the entrance to their religious sanctuaries.

Don José's family was extensive, and at his death, which occurred in February, 1858, he left behind him *over one hundred descendants.*

Several of his sons made themselves conspicuous in the history of California under the Mexican dynasty. Since its annexation to the United States, Don Pablo de la Guerra and Don Antonio Maria de la Guerra have represented their county in the State Senate. The former is District Judge of the Judicial District comprising Santa Barbara and San Luis Obispo counties. The daughters of the old gentleman were all married to foreigners. The eldest was the wife of Wm. E. P. Hartwell, once a celebrated merchant and connected with the house of John Beggs & Co., of Lima, when considerable traffic was carried on in the country in the purchase of hides and tallow. The second daughter espoused Don Manuel Jimeno, who, at the time of the surrender of the Mexican power, was secretary to the Governor then commanding in California. She afterwards married Dr. James L. Ord, brother of Major General Ord, of the U. S. Army. The third married Alfred Robinson, of Boston, and the youngest married, first, Don Cesareo Laitillade, after whose death she became the wife of Don Gaspar Oreña —both of her husbands being natives of Spain.

Don José's residence was invariably resorted to by strangers who visited California in those early days, when the name of the now prosperous and powerful State was seldom heard spoken beyond her own limits. The excellencies of his table, and the noble hospitality which he extended to his numerous guests, are yet fondly remembered by the few survivors who partook of his bounty.

Doña M. Antonia, his wife, added to the charms of his establishment, and her ladylike manners and amiability of character were admired by all. An American lady who visited California in 1832, in speaking of the many good qualities of Doña Maria Antonia, observed that there were two things supremely exquisite in California—one of which was the grape, and the other the lady of Don José de la Guerra y Noriega.

At times when the political disturbances which agitated the country were most annoying, Don José would frequently exclaim: *"Cuando vendran los*

xv

Americanos para tomar posesion de este pais?—When will the Americans come to take possession of this country?" He had an extraordinary aversion to the Mexican government, and was ready to welcome any change which promised to put an end to the repeated political convulsions harassing the people and ruining the country. Therefore, when war commenced between the United States and Mexico, his ardent love of permanent peace, order and prosperity moved him to call down the blessings of heaven upon the American arms, whose success he predicted. He lived to see the issue of that great conflict, and its happy effects upon the interests and prosperity of his adopted land. It may be said of him, truthfully, paradoxical as the expression may seem, that he was a man of true patriotism, yet beheld his country conquered without regret. When the American flag was unfurled over his own home, he greeted the triumphant banner as the symbol of justice and peace.

At his death, the whole town turned out to do homage to his remains, which were followed to the grave by the largest funeral procession that had ever been seen in Santa Barbara. Many an old veteran, companion of his youth, was seen, whose cheeks were moistened with tears of regret, and whose feeble gait indicated that he, too, would soon be laid by the side of the virtuous and upright old pioneer.

◇ ◇ ◇ ◇

We dedicate this book to a one time resident of Oakland

and a famous Californiac

JOAQUIN MILLER

"He said: 'Sail on! Sail on! and on!'"

xvi   Jos. A. Sullivan

May 1, 1947
Oakland 10, California

Introduction

IN VENTURING TO SUBMIT THE FOLLOWING WORK to public notice, the writer would respectfully state, that it was originally intended as an introduction only, to his translation of Father Boscana's "Historical Account of the Indians of California"; but owing to the increasing interest manifested for the fate of that fair portion of the North American Continent, he has been induced to extend his first views, that he might lay before the reader a simple statement, respecting the country, and its political progress, from the time when Mexico became free from Spanish dominion. It has been his object to confine himself, as much as possible, to those events which came under his own personal observation, and, though possessing but few notes to which he could refer, he has endeavored to connect the historical with the political incidents, so that their dates may be depended upon.

Alta California is called a Territory, and is under the control of the general government of Mexico, which appoints its Governor and subordinate officers. It extends along the border of the great Pacific, which bounds it on the west. On the east, it is bounded by a range of the Cordilleras and the Indian territory. The northern limit is to the forty-second degree of north latitude, and the southern boundary extends to the Presidio of St. Diego, or a little further south.

The writer has gleaned the early history from a celebrated work of Pádre Miguel Vanegas, who says, "The country of which we are to treat, is known on the maps under three distinct names: first, 'California,'—second, 'New Albion'—third, 'Islas Carolinas.' That of California is the most ancient, for we find it in the work of Bernal Diaz del Castillo, a soldier of Hernan Cortez; his companion in the conquest of Mexico, and afterwards his historian." The name of New Albion was given by Sir Francis Drake in 1577, on his second voyage round the world. The name of Islas Carolinas was given a hundred years afterwards in honor of *King Charles the Second of Spain,* when he projected the conquest of California, which at that time was supposed to be an island.

It is thought by some writers, that the name "California" was given by the Spaniards, in consequence of the uncommon heat which they experienced, on their first visit, and was derived from the two Latin words *calida* and *fornax.* Father Vanegas thinks differently; he says, "The name originated accidentally, from a wrong pronunciation, as might have occurred in the sounding of any Indian expression, badly understood by the Spaniards."

The whole of Upper California was left entirely to the control of the Franciscan Friars; while the Dominicans were entrusted with the lower province. From 1769 until 1776, no less than nineteen missions were founded—another in 1817, and one more in 1823, which are all that have ever been established. These were the germs of Spanish colonization, which were advanced under the protection of four *Presidios,* or military fortresses; viz., St. Diego, Santa Barbara, Monterey, and St. Francisco; from whence troops could be marched at any moment, if requisite. The prosperity of these missions was great until the year 1824, since which they have gradually depreciated, and are now almost entirely destroyed.

The shore in some places is lessened by the near approach of a range of mountains toward the sea; but there are spacious openings, which are capable of great improvement. In these openings, or valleys, the missions are located, and are so distanced as to be of great convenience to the traveller.

In the many revulsions suffered by Mexico from political struggles, California has had her share of domestic disturbances; and for years past it has been the scene of numerous conflicts. The natives possess an inveterate dislike towards the Mexicans, which has given rise to sundry revolutions in their government. The time is not far distant when they will cease from such broils, and either become consolidated into an independent form of government, or be the subjects of foreign administration. Immigration will aid the former, while the attractions of its magnificent and giant harbor of St. Francisco may, in a very few years, effect the latter.

Part I

Life in California

Chapter I

NUMEROUS ATTEMPTS WERE MADE DURING the reign of Philip the Second of Spain to colonize the Peninsula of California; but it was not until the reign of his son and successor, "Philip the Third," that the efforts of the Spaniards met with any success. This sovereign, instigated by the same political policy as his father, in the year 1599, despatched orders to the Count de Monte Rey, then commander of the Colony of New Spain, directing him, at the expense of the treasury, regardless of the cost of the enterprise, to use all possible diligence in making new discoveries, and, above all, further entrance into Alta California. Accordingly, the Viceroy, after much deliberation, to ensure the success of a project that excited so much enthusiasm, and caused so many calamities during the previous century, appointed as Captain General of the proposed expedition, "Don Sebastian Viscaino," who had once before commanded on a similar voyage, and who, on this occasion, seemed indefatigable in his endeavors to forward the interests of the enterprise.

Everything being ready, on the 5th of May, 1602, the General made sail from the port of Acapulco. His fleet consisted of two ships and a frigate, together with a small vessel with one mast and drawing but little water, to be used on occasions when the larger vessels would have been impracticable. He was accompanied by three religious Carmelites;

one of whom, Friar Antonio de la Ascension, wrote a long account of the voyage, whereby it appears that Viscaino made actual survey of the coast, up to the latitude of Capes Mendicino and Blanco. They visited a large port near the *"Punta de Pinos,"* which, in honor of the Viceroy, they named "Monterey." St. Diego was also explored, and another port in the neighborhood, which undoubtedly was St. Pedro.

Their hardships, infirmities, and dangers were so great, that to maintain themselves long on the coast was impossible; and, in consequence, they returned to New Spain, after an absence of nearly eleven months, and anchored in Acapulco, in the latter part of March, 1603.

From this time, no particular attention was called to the acquisition and occupancy of Alta California, until the expulsion of the Jesuits, in 1768; when Pádre Junipero Serra, of the order of St. Francisco, was appointed presiding missionary of the Californias. On the 12th of March, 1769, he embarked for Loreto, in company with sixteen others of the same College. They arrived in safety, and immediately commenced operations for a northern enterprise; cattle were driven across the mountains, and a naval and land expedition departed at different periods, for the purpose of uniting at St. Diego, to co-operate in the spiritual conquest. The latter, under the command of the Governor, Don Gaspar Portala, and Pádre Junipero, arrived on the first of July, 1769, and found the ships at anchor, which had arrived nearly two months before them. Mutual congratulations passed between the officers; surveys were commenced; the country was explored; and here, in this wild, uncultivated spot, they erected their first Mission, and named it, in honor of the patron saint of Spain, "St. Diego."

It was not until the succeeding year that San Carlos was founded at Monterey, and in 1771, when other reverend Pádres arrived from St. Blas, they established the Missions of St. Antonio and St. Gabriel. Thus, by occasional succor from the Viceroy of Mexico, the holy enterprise prospered; new Missions were founded, and the missionaries beheld with rapture the success and triumph of the Cross.

More than half a century had passed by. Father Junipero was no more, and the few faithful companions of his pilgrimage to this distant land had, like him, found rest from their labors in the tomb; others had filled their places; and notwithstanding that the subversion of Spanish dominion in Mexico, and subsequent change to a republican form of government, had somewhat lessened their zeal; yet the neophyte was protected, conquests increased, and the abundance of the warehouses and granaries continued to be distributed with the same fostering liberality.

At this period the writer embarked at Boston on a voyage to the north-west coast of America. It was on a beautiful morning in July, 1828, and our noble craft slipped quietly down the bay with a light wind from the southwest. The breeze soon freshened, and the sight of the friends who had accompanied us to the wharf, the buildings, the steeples, and the neighboring hills, all gradually grew fainter and fainter, "till like a dream they passed away."

The pilot left us—and at sunset I stood gazing on the dim outline of our native land, which, like a cloud, appeared slowly fading in the west, till naught remained to gaze upon but the distant horizon. Night passed, and morning came; and with it all the routine of a sailor's life, such as usually accompanies the first few days of a long voyage; clearing decks, stowing cables, securing spars, &c., and then followed, day after day, the same monotonous and tedious scenes, with nothing to relieve them from their wearisomeness, or incident worthy of consideration, till three long months had expired, when we opened upon the Pacific—the great South Sea.

Our ship glides on, and as the mighty wave comes slowly rolling from the west, she, with equal sublimity, rises to the element and then sinks majestically into its course below, as if in courteous recognition of its approach. Wave after wave rolls on, wave after wave is left behind, and thus she pursues unchangingly her destined course. But the scene changes. Thick clouds appear in the horizon, whose quick advance and fearful aspect betoken the coming storm! The ship is prepared to meet its fury—sail after sail is taken in, till from a top-gallant studding sail, and running before the wind, she is lying to, reduced to a close-reefed main-topsail, and mizzen staysail. The storm at length comes—cloud after cloud adds new fury to its blasts—the sea rises, and in its way would seem to engulf all before it—one vast surge comes aboard with heavy crash, and sweeps the deck of boats and spars, the bulwarks, and all that meets its course. The climate changes also; and cold, snow and hail are added to the terrors that surround us. At length, however, the storm abates; sail is made, and we are again in apparent security; but soon it returns with redoubled fury; and the ship is again lying like a log upon the ocean. Thus we proceed, gale succeeding gale! one storm only ceasing, to give place to another—our good ship making but little progress, until, at last, enabled to take a northerly course, and the wind proving favorable, we rapidly leave these tempestuous latitudes. A few days of prosperous gales bring us to anchor in the pleasant bay of Valparaiso.

Our protracted passage of 110 days made it necessary for us to put in here to replenish our water, and after three days' detention we again made sail for the port of Monterey. Three days out, we came in sight of the Islands of St. Felix and St. Ambrose. When about three miles distant from the latter, the mate with a few men started off in one of the boats on a fishing excursion, and returned after a few hours' absence with plenty of fish of different kinds. We next proceeded to St. Felix, which bore N.N.W. of us, distant about fifteen miles, and hove to, between the island and *sail rock,* so called from its singular resemblance to a sail when seen from a distance. This island is much larger than that of St. Ambrose, and easier of access, though equally barren and destitute of vegetation. We found here the ruins of a house which had probably been erected by some sealing-party, for we saw great numbers of seals lying about among the rocks, and killed several ourselves. Seabirds were abundant—fish, also, of which we caught many, and returned on board to pursue our voyage.

From this time no particular occurrence took place until we came in sight of land; and then the weather was such that several days intervened ere we could learn our true position; at length, on the afternoon of the 15th February, 1829, the fog cleared up and we beheld the "Punta de Pinos" bearing east, distant ten or twelve miles. This was the outer southern point of the bay of Monterey, into which we were soon slowly gliding. The breeze now died away, night closed around us, and as we approached our place of anchorage, naught was heard but the occasional cry of the leadsman in the chains, or the dip of the oars as the boatmen towed us slowly into port. Suddenly a flash was seen from the castle, the report followed, and a ball came whizzing across our bow, so near the boat as to throw upon the men the spray, as it glanced over the waters. "Let go the anchor," cried the captain. "Aye, aye," answered the mate, and then followed immediately the splash and the running out of the chain, until the heavy iron instrument had found its resting place in the sand.

A few minutes elapsed when a boat came off from the shore containing an officer of the customs and his assistant; sent by the commandant of the "Presidio." They appeared much pleased when informed that we wished to trade on the coast, and particularly so, when made acquainted with the nature and amount of the ship's cargo. The conversation soon became general, and the more intelligent of the two (Don Manuel Jimeno) gave us an account of the country, its government, missions, and its political condition at that time. He spoke also of the affair of the ship Franklin of Boston, which had a short time previous been detained by the authorities on suspicion of being engaged in contraband trade, causing much excitement throughout the country, and consequent restrictions on commerce. Her flight from the port of St. Diego was thought miraculous, running the gauntlet of a heavy battery within pistol shot of the cannon's mouth, and yet escaping without injury. On she sailed, leaving her enemies in the distance, little heeding their guns, till, once more rolling to the swell of the mighty ocean, she approached Point Loma, when a light cloud was seen to emerge from her side, and the report of her cannon came reverberating among the hills, as if in derision of a government of such weakness and pusillanimity.

The local government, exasperated by this open defiance of their authority, sought by more stringent regulations of trade to prevent in future any fraud upon the revenue; and conscious of its weakness at most of the ports along the coast, laid an embargo upon all, with the exception of the more strongly fortified places of Monterey and St. Diego, at which ports only, foreign vessels were allowed to enter and discharge their cargoes.

The officers bade us *"buenas noches,"* and left us for the shore, leaving us to ruminate upon the events which had passed, and those likely to ensue, with many forebodings of the trials and disappointments which from the recent change in the revenue laws we were probably to encounter. What were we to do? With the exception of Monterey and St. Diego, all the ports were closed, and we were prohibited from discharging at any other. This restriction, if insisted upon, would overturn all our calculations, and in fact ensure a total failure of the voyage.

Our supercargo, Mr. G., was much perplexed in consequence, and resolved to write to the Governor at St. Diego, setting forth the fact of our having fitted out from the United States with the supposition that no change would be made in the regulation of commerce; that the recent alteration had not given sufficient time for the news to have reached us prior to our departure from home, and that consequently, he should take into consideration the embarrassment of our situation and repeal in some way the restrictions of the new law.

Chapter II

THE NEXT DAY, WHEN I WAS TO LOOK FOR THE FIRST time upon those shores which were to become for some years my home, was necessarily one of great excitement, and I hurried on deck much earlier than my usual hour. Before us lay stretched out the shore, and as it curved away toward the northern extremity of the bay, the swell of the ocean, wave after wave, echoed loud and heavily upon its sands. The sun had just risen, and glittering through the lofty pines that crowned the summit of the eastern hills, threw its light upon the lawn beneath. On our left was the "Presidio," with its chapel dome, and towering flag-staff in conspicuous elevation. On the right, upon a rising ground, was seen the "Castillo" or fort, surmounted by some ten or a dozen cannons. The intervening space between these two points was enlivened by the hundred scattered dwellings that form the town; and here and there groups of cattle grazing.

After breakfast, G. and myself went on shore on a visit to the Commandant, D. Mariano Estrada, whose residence stood in the central part of the town, in the usual route from the beach to the Presidio. Its external appearance, notwithstanding it was built of *adobe* or brick, made by the mixture of soft mud and straw, modelled and dried in the sun, was not displeasing; for the outer walls had been plastered and white-washed, giving it a cheerful and inviting aspect. Like all dwellings built in the warm countries of America, it was but one story in height, covered with tiles, and occupied, in its entire premises, an extensive square.

Our Don was standing at his door, and as we approached he, with true Castilian courtesy, sallied forth to meet us, embraced G., shook me cordially by the hand, then bowed us ceremoniously into the *"sala."* Here we seated ourselves upon a sofa at his right, and during conversation "cigarritos" passed freely, and although thus early in the day, a proffer was made of refreshments. We learned from him that the courier was to leave the following morning for St. Diego; and as it was necessary to prepare a petition to the General, we soon took leave of our commandant and proceeded to the house of Lieutenant Rocha, a friend of G., under whose direction the document was to be drawn up.

During the absence of the courier, who left next day with our petition, we determined to prepare the ship for sea, to be enabled to sail immediately in the event of an unfavorable answer from the Governor. Accordingly, the men were employed in replenishing water casks, cutting and embarking wood, packing beef, and other various duties necessary to our departure. Whilst these preparations were going on, I had many opportunities of visiting the neighboring country, and enjoying some friendly intercourse with the inhabitants. Several Englishmen and Americans were residents here, who had been married to pretty Californian women, and had settled down in the peculiar occupations of the country. I became acquainted particularly with Mr. H— and Mr. S—, the former from England, and connected in business with a mercantile house in Lima, having an extensive trade on the coast, and making large contracts with the missions. The latter was a Scotchman, and a partner of H—. A Yankee sea captain from Boston, and several others, were added to the number of my new friends, with whom I enjoyed many pleasant hours.

"El Presidio," or town of Monterey, is situated on the declivity of a beautiful rising ground, the top of which is crowned with stately pines. The gradual ascent to its elevated summit is covered with scattered woods and rich and varied flowers. There are many pleasant locations in the vicinity, where the natives frequently resort to celebrate their festivities or "Meriendas," and many "lagunas" are scattered throughout the neighborhood, that during the winter months are crowded with

8

ducks, whilst the green plains are literally covered with geese. The woods contain an abundance to gratify the sportsman, and a variety to enchant the botanist.

Amongst the many useful herbs whose medicinal virtues have been discovered by the natives, one in particular is held in high esteem, since it is by them considered a specific for the poisonous bite of the rattle-snake. Its peculiar virtues were discovered not long since by an Indian, who seems to have placed the most implicit faith in its power, for he submitted himself to be bitten by a snake upon the arm. His limbs immediately swelled to an extraordinary size, and the poor native seemed just ready to expire, when taking a small quantity of the herb in his mouth and chewing it, he spat upon the wound, and rubbing this into it with his hand, in a short time entirely recovered. It is said by the Indians, that should any venomous reptile eat of the plant, its death would be instantaneous.

Another of their plants of very useful properties, heals the most dangerous wound without the accumulation of *pus,* which is not an unfrequent attendant upon the application of balsam. Another, called the "Canchelagua," is found to be excellent in curing the fever and ague, and may be depended upon in any case, no matter of how long standing. It abounds all over the coast, and in the spring, during the season of flowers, its pretty blossoms add much to the beauty of the country.

At this time the population of the town did not exceed one thousand souls, including all the neighboring "Ranchos"; and although they annually elected a civil magistrate and two inferior officers, yet the general government was a military despotism on a petty scale. The Governor General resided at St. Diego, where the temperature of the climate better agreed with his delicate constitution; so that when any appeal was necessary from the decision of the "Alcalde Constitucional," it was not unfrequently the case that the delay of a month occurred ere the documents were interchanged, and a decisive judgment given.

At length, however, our courier returned. Our petition had obtained only a trivial modification of the law which permitted us to trade at Santa Barbara in addition to the ports before mentioned; but it required the landing of the entire cargo at these places, without any reimbursement of duties in the event of their re-embarkation. This was not suffi-

9

cient encouragement for us to discharge any part of our cargo here, and as G——, in private letters from his friends at the South, had been advised to repair thither, he concluded to make one effort more with the General. Accordingly, after calling upon the Commandant, and taking leave of our friends, we set sail for St. Diego.

We kept the ship close into the land until reaching Point "Almejas," where we stood well over to the northern side of the bay. Here the light wind left us entirely, and our situation became somewhat critical, for the heavy swell from the ocean, which was constantly increasing, threatened to drive us upon the coast. But fortunately, a light breeze springing up from the land, soon wafted us out into the open sea. This is the only danger to be feared in approaching the coast during the night, for the northwest wind during the day usually creates a heavy swell of the sea, which continues to roll in long after the breeze ceases. Several vessels have by this means been entirely lost, and others much endangered, by running too far into the bottom of the bay.

After passing Point "Pinos," we continued our course parallel with the coast, making the most prominent places and islands, until at last we came in sight of the bluff point of St. Diego. Here the ship was hove to, the boat lowered and manned, and G—— went up to the Presidio. Satisfactory arrangements were made with the Governor, the boat returned, and the ship ran in and anchored close under the guns of the low fortification.

Immediately commenced the preparations for a long stay. The long boat was hoisted out, the ship moored, spars were landed, royal yards and masts, and top-gallant yards were sent down, and these and all other surplus rubbish about the decks sent on shore and deposited. Lumber was discharged, and the carpenter commenced building a large house for the storage of hides, which, when finished, served as a place of accommodation for the lighter part of our cargo while under the examination and care of the custom-house officers; for the government as yet had not deemed it important to erect an "*Aduana*" in this port.

Whilst all this was in progress, G—— and myself visited the Presidio, which was about a league distant from the place of anchorage. Horses were sent down to us from Don Manuel Domingues, a brother-in-law of G——. I was unable myself to comprehend the use and necessity of all the trappings connected with the saddle-gear, which appeared to me cumbrous and useless in the extreme; but my companion, who was an old cruiser in these parts, was well acquainted with their convenience and necessity; so with his experience as a guide, we galloped off on our excursion. Our way was barren of interest till we came suddenly to an almost perpendicular descent of some thirty or forty feet into a deep and broad ravine, where formerly some river had flowed, but its bed was now filled with bushes and shrubs. Previous to this we passed a small shanty in an unfinished state, which had been erected some time before as a Custom-House, but owing to its incapacity and situation had been abandoned. We saw also the commencement of a new Presidio, that, on account of the difficulty of procuring water, had also never been completed. These two monuments of the imprudence and want of foresight of the Governor, served as very good evidence to me of the want of sagacity and energy of the government.

A short ride further brought us to the house of our friend Don Manuel. We rode into the "patio," or court-yard, where a servant took the horses. At the threshold of his door we were met by Don Manuel, who embraced us cordially and presented us to the family, his mother, wife, and sister. This was to be our home during the ship's detention, and though its coarse mud walls and damp ground floor did not altogether coincide with the idea I had previously formed of it, yet if their walls were cold and their floors damp, their hearts were warm, and the abundance of their luxurious entertainment more than compensated for any disappointment.

After dinner we called upon the General Don José Maria de Echeandia, a tall, gaunt personage, who received us with true Spanish dignity and politeness. His house was located in the centre of a large square of buildings occupied by his officers, and so elevated as to overlook them all, and command a view of the sea. On the right hand was a small Gothic chapel, with its cemetery, and immediately in front, close to the principal entrance, was the guard-room, where the soldiers were amusing themselves; some seated on the ground playing cards and smoking, while others were dancing to the music of the guitar; the whole was surrounded by a high wall, originally intended as a defence against the Indians. At the gate stood a sentinel, with slouched hat and blanket thrown over one shoulder, his old Spanish musket resting on the other; his pantaloons were buttoned and ornamented at the knee, below which, his legs were protected by leggins of dressed deer-skin, secured with spangled garters.

On the lawn beneath the hill on which the Presidio is built stood about thirty houses of rude appearance, mostly occupied by retired veterans, not so well constructed in respect either to beauty or stability as the houses at Monterey, with the exception of that belonging to our "Administrador," Don Juan Bandini, whose mansion, then in an unfinished state, bade fair, when completed, to surpass any other in the country.

The climate of St. Diego is milder than that of any other port on the coast, and not so much subject to dense fogs as Monterey and St. Francisco. The soil presents a barren and uncultivated appearance, and although several spots dignified by the name of gardens are found upon the banks of a river which flows from the mountains during the rainy season, in which they cultivate a few vegetables, yet nothing can be seen of any agricultural importance except in places at some distance from the town. The hills and glens abound with many kinds of "Cactus," among which the rabbit and quail find shelter when pursued by the sportsman. These are both very numerous, the latter frequently rising in flocks of two or three hundred. Hares are abundant, and here also, as at all other places on the coast during the rainy season, the plains and ponds are crowded with ducks and geese, while thousands of brant cover the extensive bay.

Our accounts with the Custom-House were soon adjusted, and we were prepared to commence our trade. Visitors were numerous, both male and female, who came on board to purchase. Amongst others, the reverend Pádre Antonio Peyri, of the Mission of St. Luis Rey, had expressed a wish to visit his many friends on shipboard, for besides our own, there were two other vessels then in port; the English brig Vulture, under charter by H. D. F., of Massachusetts (whose matrimonial adventures I shall presently relate), and the Mexican brig Maria Ester, from Acapulco. The good old priest was accordingly invited, and the last day of his visit was to be passed with us; other friends came also, and dinner was prepared for the occasion.

As the old gentleman was held in universal respect upon the coast, not only as founder of the Mission over which he presided, but also as a man of great mental energy and capacity; high in favor with the government for these qualities, and being dearly loved by the people for the extreme benevolence of his disposition, we prepared to receive him with "all the honors." Accordingly, as the reverend Pádre descended the gangway, we thundered forth a salute, and proceeded to show him the different parts of the vessel. Particularly did we call his attention to our trade-room, which had been fitted up with shelves and counters, resembling in appearance a country variety store. The amount of his purchases testified how vastly he had been pleased.

On the following morning he departed, and when the boat had reached a short distance from the ship, the men laid upon their oars whilst our guns sounded a parting salute. As the smoke cleared off, I beheld the old man standing in the boat, and gazing towards us with apparent delight, and I thought I could perceive by the glistening of his eye, that future patronage would be the result of this reception.

I soon became acquainted with several excellent families residing at the place, and received from them much attention. The ladies were mostly quite handsome, particularly those of the families of our friends Bandini and Carrillo. The daughters of the former were, though very young, yet very beautiful; those of the latter had attained to womanhood, and it was with the eldest of them that H. D. F. had become enamored. He resolved to marry her if he could prevail upon the chaplain of the Presidio to perform the ceremony without the necessary form of becoming a Catholic. But it was the edict of the Governor, that no foreigner should marry in the country without his special license, and without complying with the regulations established by the church; and though the old friar in his heart wished them married, yet he dared not disobey the injunctions of a superior.

But a plan is soon devised. He resolves to carry her off and marry her in Lima—the idea is proposed, she consents, and parties are appointed to co-operate in the scheme. The day arrives for the brig to sail—F. goes up to the Presidio to take leave of his friends—bids adieu to his betrothed, and departs for the beach. The vessel gets under way—stands out to sea —passes the bluff Point Loma, and hauls on a wind to the west. Night

13

approaches, and a horseman is seen galloping down the road leading to the beach, where a boat is prepared for the reception of some expected visitor—he alights, and assists a lady to dismount, who rode before him— a friend receives her—they hurriedly embark—and the boat, as she skims over the waves for the distant vessel, is soon lost in the gathering dark- ness of the night.

Chapter III

HAVING ACCOMPLISHED OUR BUSINESS FOR the present at St. Diego, the ship sailed for the port of St. Pedro, while G— and myself performed the journey by land. Horses were brought in the evening previous to our departure, and secured for the night in the court-yard, so that when we arose in the morning they were already saddled and impatiently standing at the gate. Little time elapsed ere we were mounted, and coursing our way across the low sandy plain leading from the town to the main road. Don Manuel accompanied us, and his faithful and confidential servant Chulo, who acted usually as a kind of Sancho Panza to his master, but on this occasion led the way, driving before him our extra horses, with the luggage. Away he galloped, swinging and snapping his "lasso," dextrously throwing it amongst them, and singing or whistling the air of some favorite *"jota,"* interrupted by an occasional shout to the animals, to urge them forward.

Thus we proceeded, without any novelty, save the change from a smooth and level road to a rocky and rugged ascent, or a variation in the music of our worthy Chulo, till a few hours' ride brought us to the beautiful little valley of St. Diegito, where we dismounted under a shady grove, by the side of a sparkling stream, spread our blankets on the grass, and waited impatiently, while Chulo prepared our dinner. We had brought provision with us, and a fire being kindled, he soon gave us ample proof of his skill in cookery. A half hour was given to our siesta, and we then resumed our journey to St. Luis Rey.

15

We saw no habitations on the route, and the soil was one continued waste of barrenness, entirely destitute of cultivation. A few scattered trees adorned the road, and now and then a deer was seen running over the hills, or a hare, or rabbit sat basking in the sun, among the low shrubbery. This, with the exception of a passing traveler, or a casual glance of the sea, was all that met the eye during a ride of forty miles. The great number of hills which it is necessary to surmount makes the way very tedious, and to the traveller they seem almost endless, until at length he perceives from the top of one of them, far beneath, in the centre of a beautiful vale, the Mission, with its cultivated grounds and gardens.

It was yet early in the afternoon when we rode up to the establishment, at the entrance of which many Indians had congregated to behold us, and as we dismounted, some stood ready to take off our spurs, whilst others unsaddled the horses. The reverend father was at prayers, and some time elapsed ere he came, giving us a most cordial reception. Chocolate and refreshments were at once ordered for us, and rooms where we might arrange our dress, which had become somewhat soiled by the dust.

This Mission was founded in the year 1798, by its present minister, Father Antonio Peyri, who had been for many years a reformer and director among the Indians. At this time (1829) its population was about three thousand Indians, who were all employed in various occupations. Some were engaged in agriculture, while others attended to the management of over sixty thousand head of cattle. Many were carpenters, masons, coopers, saddlers, shoemakers, weavers, &c., while the females were employed in spinning and preparing wool for their looms, which produced a sufficiency of blankets for their yearly consumption. Thus every one had his particular vocation, and each department its official superintendent, or alcalde; these were subject to the supervision of one or more Spanish *mayordomos*, who were appointed by the missionary father, and consequently under his immediate direction.

The building occupies a large square, of at least eighty or ninety yards each side, forming an extensive area, in the centre of which a fountain constantly supplies the establishment with pure water. The front is protected by a long corridor, supported by thirty-two arches,

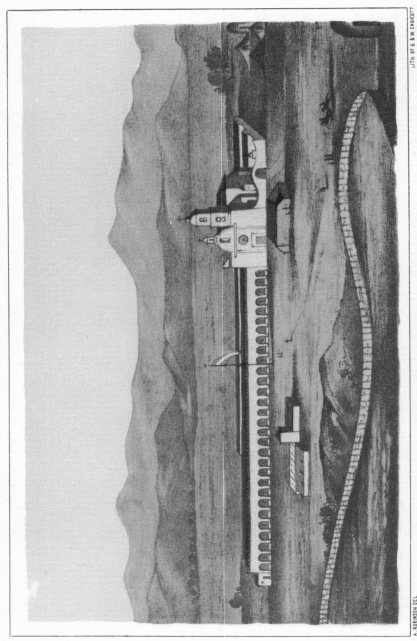

VIEW OF THE MISSION OF Sᵗ LUIS REY.

ornamented with latticed railings, which, together with the fine appearance of the church on the right, presents an attractive view to the traveller; the interior is divided into apartments for the missionary and mayordomos, store-rooms, workshops, hospitals, rooms for unmarried males and females, while near at hand is a range of buildings tenanted by the families of the superintendents. There is also a guard-house, where were stationed some ten or a dozen soldiers, and in the rear spacious granaries stored with an abundance of wheat, corn, beans, peas, &c.; also large enclosures for wagons, carts, and the implements of agriculture. In the interior of the square might be seen the various trades at work, presenting a scene not dissimilar to some of the working departments of our state prisons. Adjoining are two large gardens, which supply the table with fruit and vegetables, and two or three large *"ranchos"* or farms are situated from five to eight leagues distant, where the Indians are employed in cultivation and domesticating cattle.

The church is a large, stone edifice, whose exterior is not without some considerable ornament and tasteful finish; but the interior is richer, and the walls are adorned with a variety of pictures of saints and Scripture subjects, glaringly colored, and attractive to the eye. Around the altar are many images of the saints, and the tall and massive candelabras, lighted during mass, throw an imposing light upon the whole.

Mass is offered daily, and the greater portion of the Indians attend; but it is not unusual to see numbers of them driven along by alcaldes, and under the whip's lash forced to the very doors of the sanctuary. The men are placed generally upon the left, and the females occupy the right of the church, so that a passage way or aisle is formed between them from the principal entrance to the altar, where zealous officials are stationed to enforce silence and attention. At evening again, "El Rosario" is prayed, and a second time all assemble to participate in supplication to the Virgin.

The condition of these Indians is miserable indeed; and it is not to be wondered at that many attempt to escape from the severity of the religious discipline at the Mission. They are pursued, and generally taken, when they are flogged, and an iron clog is fastened to their legs, serving as additional punishment, and a warning to others.

Remaining here but a few days, we then continued our journey towards the mission of St. Juan Capistrano, distant about ten leagues. After taking leave of our hospitable friend, we mounted our horses and rode on without meeting any place worthy of notice till we came to the "Rancho de las Flores," one of the cattle establishments of San Luis. It is situated on an eminence commanding a view of the sea, with the distant islands St. Clemente and Catalina, and overlooking an adjacent level, extending for miles around, covered with thousands of animals grazing. A few inferior gardens are scattered about in the little valleys, cultivated by the Indians, for their own personal benefit, and in which they are permitted to labor when not required to give their time to the interests of the Mission.

Not many leagues further brought us to a beautiful spot in the centre of an opening in the highlands, extending from the beach to the distant mountains. A small river flowed down the glen toward the sea, but the constant action of the surf upon the sand had dammed up its mouth and formed it into a lake. We halted on its margin to partake of the liberal provision supplied us by the father Antonio, and then continued our course along the hard and sandy beach to the Mission. At length we reached an opening between the hills, through which we caught a first glimpse of the establishment; and pushing our horses to a smart gallop, we soon arrived at its entrance. Several straggling Indian boys were seen about the gates, and two or three approached as we alighted; they said nothing, but stood gazing at the great staring eyes of friend G——, which were considerably magnified through the spectacles he wore, till at last a sudden light seemed to break upon their dull comprehensions, and, with a cry of "Cuatro ojos," "cuatro ojos," (four eyes), they darted away. This *soubriquet* we instantly adopted, and G—— was ever known throughout the whole coast by the nickname of "cuatro ojos."

A corpulent old man received us at the door, who bade us welcome, and appeared delighted to see my companion, with whom he had formed an acquaintance in former years. It was the superintendent of the Mission, who, superannuated as he seemed, yet from long experience in the situation, was still capable of fulfilling the duties of his office; he gave us a room within the square, where we proceeded to take possession, and found the furniture, like the building, fast tumbling to

18

decay. Two aged missionary friars resided here, but one alone attended to the temporal concerns of the Mission; this was Pádre Geronimo Boscana; the other, Pádre José Maria Zalveder, though at this time secluded, and apparently weak in mind, once took an active and laborious part in the management of the Missions. This establishment was founded in the year 1776, and, though in early years the largest in the country, yet is now in a dilapidated state, and the Indians are much neglected. There yet remain the ruins of an immense church, which was destroyed by an earthquake in 1812, when many Indians were buried in its fall. It still bears the appearance of having been one of the best finished structures of the country, and the workmanship displayed in the sculpture upon its walls and its vaulted roof would command admiration in our own country.

The arrangement of the mission of St. Juan is similar to that of St. Luis; in fact, all these establishments are formed upon the same plan, and much resemble each other, varying only in their extent and population. In many of the villages the residences consist of straw huts of an oval form, which, when decayed, the Indians set on fire and erect new ones—here, however, they are built of unburnt brick, tiled and white-washed, forming five or six blocks, or streets, which present a neat and comfortable appearance.

It was not until evening (supper time) that we saw the pádres, who were then seated at the table, unconscious of our approach till announced by the old mayordomo. Immediately they arose, embraced us, and welcomed us to their hospitable board. During the meal our conversation turned on the political state of Europe, in regard to which they seemed to be very well informed, and they found an absorbing topic in the prospect of Spanish influence in Mexico.

The following morning we started for St. Gabriel, distant twenty leagues. As we proceeded, our course was through a long and narrow defile between the hills, having before us the high snow-capped mountains of St. Juan, till at length we left them on our right, and a short gallop soon brought us to an extensive plain. The road was level, and "Chulo," elated with the prospect of soon reaching the habitation of his "ladye-love," resumed his whistling and shouting; and dashing forward among the animals, drove them furiously along the track. We followed swiftly in his rear, our horses being unwilling to be left behind, and a few hours brought us to the farm or *rancho* de St. Ana.

The proprietor, "Don Tomas Yorba," a tall, lean personage, dressed in all the extravagance of his country's costume, received us at the door of his house. He came towards us, embraced G. and his *compadre* Don Manuel, took me cordially by the hand, and invited us to enter. Arrangements were soon made for dinner, which, notwithstanding the haste with which it was served, did much credit to the provider, as did our appetites to its excellent qualities.

Don Tomas and friend G. then commencing a business conversation, I got up from the table and retreated to the corridor, where I could study, unobserved, the character and appearance of our host. Upon his head he wore a black silk handkerchief, the four corners of which hung down his neck behind. An embroidered shirt, a cravat of white jaconet tastefully tied, a blue damask vest, short clothes of crimson velvet, a bright green cloth jacket, with large silver buttons, and shoes of embroidered deer skin, comprised his dress. I was afterwards informed by Don Manuel, that on some occasions, such as some particular feast day or festival, his entire display often exceeded in value a thousand dollars.

The day was wearing apace, so we hastened our departure, and mounted again for the journey. Don Tomas had prepared to accompany us to a river that crossed our route, which at some seasons of the year proved dangerous to travellers unacquainted with the pass. This was a thoughtful precaution on his part, and received from us due acknowledgment. We rode along slowly through the sandy soil, till at length we saw the rapid stream, which, by our friend's guidance, was easily forded, and he bade us farewell.

The journey continued across a plain, where thousands of cattle were grazing; and immense herds of wild horses, which fled swiftly to the mountains on our approach. We soon reached the river of St. Gabriel, and having forded this stream, Don Manuel, who had accompanied us thus far from St. Diego, left us to pursue our journey alone to the Mission, which was now just in sight, whilst he proceeded for "El Pueblo de los Angeles," where his wife's family resided, and where he had for some time past made his permanent home.

It was Saturday evening, and as we approached the buildings of the

Mission, the chapel bells tolled the hour for prayer. Hundreds of Indians were kneeling upon the ground, and as the tolling ceased, they slowly rose to retire, and a merry peal announced the coming of the Sabbath.

The director of St. Gabriel was Father José Sanches, who for many years had controlled the establishment, which, through his management, had advanced to its present flourishing condition. Possessing a kind, generous, and lively disposition, he had acquired, in consequence, a multitude of friends, who constantly flocked around him; whilst through his liberality the needy wanderer, of whatever nation or creed, found a home and protection in the Mission.

In the morning, at six o'clock, we went to the church, where the priest had already commenced the service of the mass. The imposing ceremony, glittering ornaments, and illuminated walls, were well adapted to captivate the simple mind of the Indian, and I could not but admire the apparent devotion of the multitude, who seemed absorbed, heart and soul, in the scene before them. The solemn music of the mass was well selected, and the Indian voices accorded harmoniously with the flutes and violins that accompanied them. On retiring from the church, the musicians stationed themselves at a private door of the building, whence issued the reverend father, whom they escorted with music to his quarters; there they remained for a half hour, performing waltzes and marches, until some trifling present was distributed among them, when they retired to their homes.

As is usual on all their "dias de fiesta," the remaining part of the Sabbath is devoted to amusements, and the Indian generally resorts to gambling, in which he indulges to the most criminal excess, frequently losing all he possesses in the world—his clothes—beads, baubles of all kinds, and even his wife and children! We saw them thus engaged, scattered in groups about the Mission, while at a little distance quite an exciting horse race was going on; the Indians betting as wildly on their favorite animals as upon the games of chance, which found so many devotees.

There are several extensive gardens attached to this Mission, where may be found oranges, citrons, limes, apples, pears, peaches, pomegranates, figs, and grapes in abundance. From the latter they make yearly from four to six hundred barrels of wine, and two hundred of brandy;

21

the sale of which produces an income of more than twelve thousand dollars. The storehouses and granaries are kept well supplied, and the corridor in the square is usually heaped up with piles of hides and tallow. Besides the resources of the vineyard, the Mission derives considerable revenue from the sale of grain; and the weekly slaughter of cattle produces a sufficient sum for clothing and supporting the Indians.

The two *"ranchos"* of St. Bernardino and Sta. Anita are included in the possessions of the Mission; the former of these has been assigned by the pádres for the sole purpose of domesticating cattle, and is located some leagues distant, in a secluded valley among the mountains; the latter is for cultivation, and is one of the fairy spots to be met with so often in California. On the declivity of a hill is erected a *molino,* or grist-mill, surrounded with fruit trees and flowers. A beautiful lake lies calm and unruffled in front, and all around fresh streams are gushing from the earth, and scattering their waters in every direction. It would be a magnificent spot for a summer retreat, and much reminded me of many of the beautiful locations to be met with in the vicinity of Boston.

The Mission of St. Gabriel was founded in the year 1771, and its population, including the two *ranchos* before mentioned, now numbered from twelve to fifteen hundred. It was thought at one time to possess from eighty to over a hundred thousand head of cattle, besides horses, mules, and sheep, and countless numbers which run at large. No advantage is derived from them beyond the value of their hides and tallow, and thus thousands of dollars are yearly left to perish on the field.

While here, I met with a Yankee from the interior of New England, who had been a resident in the country for many years, and who had become, in manner and appearance, a complete Californian. One peculiarity, however, he retained—the spirit of trade, which had lost none of its original power, and to which I owed thus early my acquaintance with him. He was married, and living in Santa Barbara, where he was engaged in business in a small way, and learning that we were on our route up the coast, he had come all the way to meet us, in order to gain some trifling advantage over his competitors in trade.

Our next destination, after concluding our business with Father Sanches, was St. Fernando, situated only about eight leagues further up the coast. We accordingly set out, on being rejoined by Don Manuel

22

and his "Sancho Panza," who once more took the lead, and we followed close in his rear. Our horses were in fine condition, and we arrived at the Mission in little more than three hours. The road generally was good, and the scenery for the first few leagues was a continuation of the beautiful grounds of *Sta. Anita,* with a fine view, on the right, of one of the ridges of the lofty Andes.

St. Fernando was founded in the year 1797, and at this time was governed by the reverend Father Francisco Ybarra; a short, thick, ugly-looking old man, whose looks did not belie his character. In his own opinion no one knew so much as himself; nothing was so good as that which he possessed; and, being at the head of his establishment, no one ever presumed to call his sentiments into question. The niggardly administration of this place, compared with the liberality and profusion of the other missions we had visited, presented a complete contrast; and the meanness and unpopularity of our host had gained for him the nickname of "cochino" or "hog." At supper I was amused at the economy displayed in the arrangement of his table, which seemed perfectly in accordance with the narrowness of his mind. A door, hinged at the bottom, which served to close a recess in the wall, used as a cupboard, was let down upon the occasion; and on this was placed our repast. The dimensions were only sufficient to admit of four persons comfortably seated; and, when the number was larger, to accommodate them all, recourse was had to a dirty-looking bench which stood in one corner of the apartment.

Distrustful of every one who wished to purchase his tallow or hides, he had accumulated an immense amount in his storehouses, where many of the latter had been destroyed by the length of time they had remained deposited. The tallow he had laid down in large, arched, stone vats, of sufficient capacity to contain several cargoes.

In the morning we left, and pursued our course across the valley of St. Fernando, towards the glen of Cowwanga, and a short gallop over the hills brought us in sight of the "Pueblo de los Angeles," situated about three leagues from St. Gabriel, and about twenty miles from the bay of St. Pedro. The population of this town is about fifteen hundred; and has an alcalde, two regidores, and a syndico, who compose its *"Ayuntamiento"* or Town Council. In the vicinity are many vineyards

23

and corn-fields, and some fine gardens, crossed by beautiful streams of water. The lands being level and fertile, are capable of great agricultural improvement; and several Americans, taking advantage of the resources of the place, are living here, having storehouses, and are engaged in business. After passing the night here, we resumed our journey to St. Pedro. The ride was over a long plain through the farm of Don Manuel, called "El rancho de Dominguez," where we stopped a while to rest, and having taken a final leave of our friend, pursued our way to the beach.

We found the ship at anchor, having performed the passage in three days and a half, and was then waiting our arrival. On board were our friend Yorba, from Sta. Ana, the old mayordomo from St. Juan, and several others waiting for goods, whom we immediately despatched, and then made preparations for the numerous friends whom we expected to arrive in the morning.

Having imprudently left St. Diego without passports, we found a letter from the "Comandante" of the place, reproving us for having presumed to travel in the country without these necessary documents. We met with no difficulty, however, on our route without them, which we attributed to the fact of our being "pretty well known upon the road, as the saying is." The necessity of procuring passports is not confined to foreigners alone, but also to the country people, who, when even going to their farms, or to the neighboring villages, are required to obtain permission from the authorities. The rigid performance of this custom, although oftentimes extremely inconvenient, still had its advantages; inasmuch as the escape of a criminal was next to impossible, for he was most generally sure to be detected at the missions or outposts.

The harbor of St. Pedro is an extensive bay, and, although not considered a safe anchorage during the winter months, when the southeast wind prevails, yet vessels frequently embark and discharge their cargoes here at all seasons of the year. The best anchorage is close under the northwest point of the bay, about three quarters of a mile outside of a small and rocky island; and the same distance from the beach. There is a house at the landing-place, which generally serves as a land-mark, in connection with the preceding locations, and vessels usually, in the mild season of the year, bring this to bear W.N..W., whilst the point lies

S.W. by S., and the island N.½E. From the month of October till the beginning of May, vessels anchor at least a mile outside of these bearings, and ships are necessarily prepared for slipping their cables, and getting under way, should the wind, as is often the case, chop in suddenly from the S.E. The holding ground is good; of stiff mud, in four and a half to nine fathoms.

As we anticipated, our friends came in the morning, flocking on board from all quarters; and soon a busy scene commenced, afloat and ashore. Boats were plying to and fro—launches laden with the variety of our cargo passing to the beach, and men, women, and children crowding upon our decks, partaking in the general excitement. On shore all was confusion. Cattle and carts laden with hides and tallow, "*gente de razon,*" and Indians, busily employed in the delivery of their produce, and receiving in return its value in goods; groups of individuals seated around little bonfires upon the ground, and horsemen racing over the plain in every direction. Thus the day passed; some departing, some arriving; till long after sunset the low white road leading across the plain to the town, appeared a living panorama.

Due north from the place of anchorage is a narrow creek, communicating with a shallow basin, operated upon by the tides, where at this time thousands of hair-seal might be seen at low water, basking on the sand-banks. The channel here when at full flood has ten feet of water over the bar; so that, in moderate weather, vessels drawing nine feet can easily pass over, and anchor sufficiently near the shore to discharge their cargoes without the aid of launches. With very little expense it might be made a place of anchorage for large ships, either by digging out and deepening the present channel, or by closing up another outlet to the north of the island, which would bring the whole strength of the current through one passage, and thus wash away its sandy bottom.

Chapter IV

HAVING COLLECTED IN ST. PEDRO MORE PRO-
duce than could be well received on board at that time, we resolved to
deposit it in the storehouse on shore, while the ship proceeded to some
of the northward ports. The anchor was weighed; the vessel hauled on a
wind, and stood over towards a low gap in the island of St. Catalina,
and then back again to the main; tacking off and on shore during the
night, so that when daylight broke, we found ourselves between Point
Dume and Point Conversion. The wind was very light, hardly sufficient
to keep steerage way; but soon the sea breeze began to blow, and a
cracking westerly wind enabled us during the day to beat up off the
mission of St. Buenaventura. Here the shore is bold, and there is good
anchorage for all classes of vessels; but it is seldom visited on account of
the high surf. The country as we proceeded northward assumed a more
cultivated and beautiful appearance; the hills, however, seemed bleak
and barren, but the valleys presented the highest degree of fertility.
From the mission, we stood over for some small and rocky islands at the
southeast point of Sta. Cruz; and on the following morning, close under
our lee, we beheld the beautiful vale of Sta. Barbara.

Seen from the ship, the "Presidio" or town, its charming vicinity, and
neat little Mission in the background, all situated on an inclined plane,

rising gradually from the sea to a range of verdant hills, three miles from the beach, have a striking and beautiful effect. Distance, however, in this case, "lends enchantment to the view," which a nearer approach somewhat dispels; for we found the houses of the town, of which there were some two hundred, in not very good condition. They are built in the Spanish mode, with *adobe* walls, and roofs of tile, and are scattered about outside of the military department; shewing a total disregard of order on the part of the authorities. A ridge of rugged highlands extends along the rear, reaching from St. Bonaventura to Point Conception, and on the left of the town, in an elevated position, stands the *Castillo* or fortress.

The port of Santa Barbara is completely sheltered from the northwest and westerly winds, but somewhat exposed to those from the southeast. The anchorage is hard sand, abounding in sea-weed, where the ship came to, in six and a half fathoms. The sails were furled, the boat lowered and manned, and we proceeded to the shore.

A heavy westerly wind during the night had "knocked up" considerable swell, which continued to roll in and fall heavily upon the sand. Our men pulled lustily till ordered to lay upon their oars, when we effected our landing. In approaching the shore through the surf, more depends upon the judgment of the person steering the boat than upon the rowers. Usually, there are three consecutive rolls, and then follows a temporary recession; and to land safely, it is necessary to proceed with caution, wait an opportunity by observing the swell; pull in strong on a third roller, and the moment the boat strikes the sand, the oars should be cast on either side, while the men jump out and prevent her being carried back by the retiring surf.

At the landing we found our Yankee friend Daniel H——, and a few others who had come down to greet G——. As the town was three quarters of a mile distant, I accepted Daniel's offer of his fine saddled mule, and he getting up behind me, we rode along slowly, until we reached a small descent, where flowed a stream which recent rains had swollen beyond its usual bounds. Here the stubborn animal stopped, and seemed disinclined to proceed, but repeated application of the spurs at last urged him forward, and he forded the stream. Ascending the opposite bank, he again stopped, and giving a sudden fling in the air with his

27

heels, sent us both rolling down towards the water. Fortunately we were neither wet nor hurt, but after so decided a manifestation of the creature's abilities, I declined remounting. Daniel, however, nowise disconcerted, mounted the beast and rode off alone.

As was requisite, we first visited the Commandant, in order to leave with him the ship's roll. This is a compliance exacted from all vessels arriving at ports in California, and usually their captains are obliged to deliver their documents in person.

The most stately house in the place at this time was that of the *diputado* to Mexico, Don José de la Guerra y Noriega. G— having in his possession some presents for the family, we proceeded thither at once. Here we partook of chocolate with the lady of the house, Doña Maria Antonia, whilst her daughters eagerly distributed the several gifts. The old lady, a fine, motherly, good woman, had acquired by her deportment and affectionate manner toward strangers the esteem of all who knew her. Her father was an officer in the royal command, previous to the success of republicanism in Mexico, and her brothers, all but one, were then officers in the army. An American lady once observed to me, that there were in California two things supremely good, La Señora Noriega, and grapes!

During the afternoon, we visited the house of our friend Daniel. He was standing at the door anxiously awaiting our approach; and two or three children were playing in the corridor before him. As we drew near, the little ones retired, and chairs were brought outside, that we might enjoy the fresh air. Here we were to remain for the night, and arrangements were made accordingly. Supper was soon announced, when we had the pleasure of seeing the lady of the house, a fine healthy-looking female, with splendid eyes and beautiful black hair; but she said but little, and soon retired with her children.

The Presidio of Santa Barbara consists of a large square of buildings, surrounded by high walls, in plan similar to that of St. Diego, and contains a chapel, cemetery, prison, and storehouses. The Commandant, Don Romualdo Pacheco, is a Mexican, who came to the country in the year 1825, with the present Governor, Echandia. The number of men garrisoned under his command does not exceed forty.

In the morning we walked to the mission, distant from the town about half a league. The road was pleasant, through scattered oaks; and groups of cattle were seen grazing upon the grassy plains. On the right were spacious wheat fields; at length, through a narrow way, amid immense rocks scattered over the ground, we reached the establishment. The stone church, with its two towers and extensive wing, its artificial clock, tiled roofs, arched corridor, and majestic fountain, was before us. On the right were various buildings for superintendents, a guard-house, tannery, and a dilapidated grist-mill; on the left, the spacious garden, with its fruit trees and flowers, and several rows of low buildings. Father Antonio Jimeno, the missionary, received us in a small but tastefully arranged apartment; the floor of which was of colored cement, and the walls painted and hung round with pictures of saints. Two or three sofas, a long table and bookcase, comprised its furniture. He welcomed us kindly, and after a short conversation, we walked into the *"patio,"* or square, where carpenters, saddlers, and shoemakers were at work, and young girls spinning and preparing wool for the loom. We next entered the vestry, which was carpeted and hung round with looking-glasses and fine paintings. Adjoining this was a small, but convenient dressing-room, where were arranged the numerous dresses and ornaments used in the church services, some of them rich and of the most costly description. From this, a door led into the church, where we beheld a gorgeous display of banners, paintings, images, and crucifixes of gold and silver. The musicians attached to the choir were practising, and played some very fine airs; rather unsuitable, however, to the place. It was not unusual, both there and at the churches of other missions, to hear during the mass the most lively dancing tunes. Another door of the church opened upon the cemetery, where were buried the deceased Christians of the Mission and Presidio, surrounded by a thick wall, and having in one corner the charnel house, crowded with a ghastly array of skulls and bones.

In the rear, from a slight elevation, might be seen large fields of wheat and corn; and the little valleys among the hills, filled with fruit and vegetable gardens. A foaming stream rushes down the mountain, from which is carried in an open aqueduct along the brow of the hill, a supply of water for a spacious reservoir of beautiful masonry.

We returned to town, and at the beach found a lively and busy scene.

Our men were passing through the surf to the launch bearing hides upon their heads, while others landed, from smaller boats, portions of the ship's cargo. It was a merry sight, and their shouts mingled with the sound of the waves as they beat upon the sand. We embarked on board ship, where soon our decks were crowded with men and women of all classes; many coming to purchase, some to see the vessel, and others to accompany their friends, so that it was not unusual for us to have a party of twenty or thirty at dinner.

The dress worn by the middling class of females is a chemise with short embroidered sleeves, richly trimmed with lace, a muslin petticoat flounced with scarlet, and secured at the waist by a silk band of the same color, shoes of velvet or blue satin, a cotton *reboso* or scarf, pearl necklace and ear-rings, with the hair falling in broad plaits down the back. Others of the higher class dress in the English style, and instead of the *reboso* substitute a rich and costly shawl of silk or satin. There is something graceful in the management of the *reboso* that the natives alone can impart, and the perfect nonchalance with which it is thrown about them and worn, adds greatly to its beauty.

Very few of the men have adopted our mode of dress, the greater part adhering to the ancient costume of the past century. Short clothes, and jacket trimmed with scarlet, a silk sash about the waist, *botas* of ornamented and embroidered deer skin, secured by colored garters, embroidered shoes, the hair long, braided and fastened behind with ribbons, a black silk handkerchief around the head, surmounted by an oval and broad-brimmed hat, is the dress universally worn by the men of California.

The following morning, intending to visit the northern missions of Santa Ynes and Purissima, we started off about eight o'clock accompanied by our friend Daniel. We rode through a woody pass, crossed a small plain and many hills, till we at length reached a place called, from the innumerable bogs and quagmires with which it abounds, "Las Cenegitas"; yet we found here several gardens and two or three fine maize fields. Continuing our course from this place, nearly parallel with the coast; passing several small farms attached to the Mission, and many pleasant little valleys, through which rivulets flowed down to the sea; a ride of about two hours and a half brought us to the "Rancho del Refugio," generally termed "Ortega Farm." It consisted of three or four large buildings, several gardens or vineyards, and a few fields of corn, wheat, and beans. Daniel informed me it was once a large place, and, under the supervision of its proprietor, Don José Maria Ortega, appeared like a little mission; but that in the year 1819 it was visited by a piratical vessel, under the command of Buchard, who nearly destroyed it, since when it has never regained its once flourishing condition.

Here commences the *Cuesta* or pass across the mountains. It is a winding road, in many places only of sufficient width for one animal to pass, and almost blocked up with loose stones. From the level summit to which we slowly ascended, we had on one side an extensive view of the shore from Point Conception to Santa Barbara, comprising more than sixty miles of sea-coast, and on the other a fine open country covered with woods and abounding in excellent pasturage. Here we rested a few moments to give our animals breath, and then commenced our gradual descent. This we found even more tedious, and oftentimes, from the immense numbers of worn rocks and loose stones, more dangerous than had been our ascent. We accomplished the task, however, and soon beheld, upon a distant elevation, the Mission of Santa Ynes. The fording of a river and a short gallop soon brought us to its door.

This Mission, founded in 1797, was governed by Father Blas Ordas, who received us with the accustomed cordiality of his hospitable order. The building we found much like that of Santa Barbara, differing only in the appearance of the church and the cleanliness of its apartments. In front was a large brick enclosure where the females bathed and washed; to the right the gardens, filled with choice fruit trees, and on the left a few clusters of Indian huts and tiled houses. The storehouses were well stocked with grain, and the domesticated cattle numbered nearly nine thousand.

In the morning we rode over to the Purissima, where we found two reverend friars, Fathers Victoria and Juan Moreno. This mission was originally established in 1787, at a place now known as "La Mision Vieja"; but has since been rebuilt in its present location, and though possessing abundant wealth, in cattle and planting grounds, yet it has been much neglected, and the Indians generally are ill clothed, and seem in the most abject condition. We remained here but a short time, and returning to Santa Ynes, slept there that night, and the next day reached the ship.

The morning after, we set out on an excursion to St. Buenaventura. The road thither is partly over the hard sandy beach, and at times, when the tide is low, it is possible to perform the whole journey over this smooth level. We were not over two hours on the road, and arrived before dinner, finding the reverend Father Francisco Uria closely wrapped up in his studies, in his sitting apartment. He was the Pádre of the Mission which was founded in 1782, and which is situated near the sea-shore, at the entrance of a valley leading into the interior among the mountains. It possesses about six thousand cattle and some splendid locations for cultivation. Besides the church attached to the main building, there is a small chapel towards the beach, in which mass is at no time performed except on extraordinary occasions.

At dinner the fare was sumptuous, and I was much amused at the eccentricity of the old Pádre, who kept constantly annoying four large cats, his daily companions; or with a long stick thumped upon the heads of his Indian boys, and seemed delighted thus to gratify his singular propensities.

After concluding our meal, we walked with him to the garden, where we found a fine fountain of excellent water, and an abundance of fruits and vegetables. In their proper seasons they have apples, pears, peaches, pomegranates, tunas or prickly pears, and grapes. Along the margin of the river St. Buenaventura are many small gardens belonging to the Indians, where they raise fruit and vegetables, which are taken to the town and disposed of. The whale ships that touch at Sta. Barbara are from them frequently supplied with provisions. The small streams in the vicinity abound with fish, and salmon of excellent quality are sometimes taken in the river.

In the morning we departed early for the town, where, on our arrival, the ship was immediately prepared for her return south. The wind was favorable; the passage short; and twenty-four hours after weighing anchor at Sta. Barbara, it was cast a second time in the bay of St. Pedro. Here we embarked the hides and tallow we had deposited, and then proceeded for the port of St. Diego.

The ship arrived there after a passage of two days, came to, and was

A. ROBINSON DEL.

VIEW OF THE MISSION OF Sᵗ GABRIEL.

LITH. OF G. & W. ENDICOTT

anchored within pistol-shot of the shore, immediately opposite the store-house, so as to be conveniently located for landing hides. Then commenced a busy scene. Boat after boat, launch after launch was laden and discharged on the beach, where men were stationed to receive and pile them upon large spars for protection from the dampness of the ground; some secured together by ropes were placed at low water-mark to soak, and two large vats which had been made by the carpenter during our absence, were filled with sea-water, into which large quantities of salt was thrown to increase its strength for a second immersion which the hides underwent to prepare them for shipping.

Señor Bandini had his house *bendecida,* or blessed, during our stay here, and G. and myself were invited to attend. The General, his officers, with many friends and their families, were present. The ceremony took place at noon, when the chaplain proceeded through the different apartments, sprinkling holy water upon the walls, and uttering verses in Latin. This concluded, we sat down to an excellent dinner, consisting of all the luxuries the place afforded, provided in Don Juan's best style. As soon as the cloth was removed, the guitar and violin were put in requisition, and a dance began. It lasted, however, but a little while, for it was necessary for them to spare their exertions for the evening *fandango.* So *poco a poco,* all gradually retired to their homes.

At an early hour the different passages leading to the house were enlivened with men, women, and children, hurrying to the dance; for on such occasions it was customary for every body to attend without waiting for the formality of an invitation. A crowd of *leperos* was collected about the door when we arrived, now and then giving its shouts of approbation to the performances within, and it was with some difficulty we forced our entrance. Two persons were upon the floor dancing "el jarabe." They kept time to the music, by drumming with their feet, on the heel and toe system, with such precision, that the sound struck harmoniously upon the ear, and the admirable execution would not have done injustice to a pair of drumsticks in the hands of an able professor. The attitude of the female dancer was erect, with her head a little inclined to the right shoulder, as she modestly cast her eyes to the floor, whilst her hands gracefully held the skirts of her dress, suspending it above the ankle so as to expose to the company the execution of her feet. Her partner, who might have been one of the interlopers at the door, was under full speed of locomotion, and rattled away with his feet with wonderful dexterity. His arms were thrown carelessly behind his back, and secured, as they crossed, the points of his *serape,* that still held its place upon his shoulders. Neither had he doffed his "sombrero," but just as he stood when gazing from the crowd, he had placed himself upon the floor.

The conclusion of this performance gave us an opportunity to edge our way along towards the extremity of the room, where a door communicated with an inner apartment. Here we placed ourselves, to witness in a more favorable position the amusements of the evening. The room was about fifty feet in length, and twenty wide, modestly furnished, and its sides crowded with smiling faces. Upon the floor were accommodated the children and Indian girls, who, close under the vigilance of their parents and mistresses, took part in the scene. The musicians again commencing a lively tune, one of the managers approached the nearest female, and, clapping his hands in accompaniment to the music, succeeded in bringing her into the centre of the room. Here she remained a while, gently tapping with her feet upon the floor, and then giving two or three whirls, skipped away to her seat. Another was clapped out, and another, till the manager had passed the compliment throughout the room. This is called a *son,* and there is a custom among the men, when a dancer proves particularly attractive to any one, to place his hat upon her head, while she stands thus in the middle of the room, which she retains until redeemed by its owner, with some trifling present. During the performance of the dances, three or four male voices occasionally take part in the music, and towards the end of the evening, from repeated applications of *aguardiente,* they become quite boisterous and discordant.

The waltz was now introduced, and ten or a dozen couple whirled gaily around the room, and heightened the charms of the dance by the introduction of numerous and interesting figures. Between the dances, refreshments were handed to the ladies, whilst in an adjoining apartment, a table was prepared for the males, who partook without ceremony. The most interesting of all their dances is the *contra danza,* and this, also, may be considered the most graceful. Its figures are intricate, and in connection with the waltz, form a charming combination. These *fandangos* usually hold out till daylight, and at intervals the people at the door are permitted to introduce their *jarabes* and *jotas*.

G— and myself retired early, and in the morning hastened to the beach. Ten days had now elapsed since our departure from St. Pedro, and we were at last ready for sea. The launch was hoisted in, the ship unmoored, and the day appointed for our departure, which was to be the following.

Chapter V

AT NOON THE COMMANDANT MADE HIS appearance on board with the ship's roll, and we got under way, and stood out of the bay till well clear of the shoal, off Point Loma, where we hauled to the wind, and stood off to the west. Unfavorable weather carried us much out of our course, and it was with difficulty that we could make a northerly direction, so that twenty-two days elapsed ere we had obtained our point of latitude. Finally, we saw the rocks called the *Farallones,* bearing northeast, distant from us eight or nine miles. We soon passed the largest and southernmost one, which was still occupied by the Russians; and could distinctly perceive among the huts ten or twelve persons, who were living there for the purpose of catching fur seal, which were so abundant in former years, that my friend G— assured me he had assisted in collecting during one season, over eighty thousand skins from this same island. Four or five hours more brought us to the entrance of the port of St. Francisco, but as it was then quite dark, I could not discern the appearance of the land. As we passed the castle point, the water became less acted upon by the ocean's swell, and the only ripple visible was caused by the course of our ship, as she drew near her place of anchorage. Leaving the Presidio on our right, we continued our course for Yerba Buena, where we came to, in six and a half fathoms.

When morning came, I found we were in a small bay, close to the shore; on one side of which were steep rocks, and on the other a smooth sandy beach. Outside of us was the island of Yerba Buena, and beyond this, on the other side of the bay of St. Francisco, the highlands of St. Antonio. At ten o'clock we were visited by the Commandant, Don Ignacio Martinez, who remained to dine; a Mexican by birth, though more of a Spaniard in feeling. In his conversation, it would have been difficult for a stranger to designate his nation, for having learned a few words in English, Russian, and French, he had formed a jargon which no one could understand but himself. As soon as dinner was over, we accompanied him to his house. It was a short ride over the hill, in the direction of the *castillo*, or fort. We soon caught a glimpse of the low buildings, with their dark tiled roofs, resembling prisons more than dwelling houses, and the residence of our Commandant was the most conspicuous amongst them. This was the Presidio. In its plan, it is similar to those already described, but is in a most ruinous state. There are a few framed houses scattered about outside the square, and a short distance beyond, upon the extreme point of the little bay, is the fort, which, on account of its elevated position, is used as a "look-out place."

In the morning, G— went to the Mission of Dolores to visit the pádre, and engage horses for our contemplated journey to Santa Clara, and returned on board in the afternoon. On the following day, at an early hour, our animals were on the beach, in charge of a *vaquero*, who was sent to accompany us as a guide in the journey. This was an accommodation universal with all the good old friars, for which they accepted no compensation. We mounted speedily, and commenced our route through a dense thicket, where the path was narrow, and where the trees so intersected their branches, as to endanger our heads as we rode along. Thus we went on; sometimes crossing little valleys, where the fox-like *coyote* prowled, and sometimes rising sandy eminences, where a glimpse was had of the neighboring bay. Through the woods resounded the wolf's howl, and the heavy track of the grizzly bear lay printed in our course. At length, through an opening in the woods, we saw the Mission of Dolores. Its dilapidated walls, and dark tiled roof, well accorded with the bleak and cheerless scenery with which it was surrounded; for the cold, blustering sea winds, as they sweep over the hills, chill and destroy vegetation. As we approached the building, we saw in the long corridor the old friar and his *mayordomo,* to whom he appeared

37

to be giving some directions, for the latter, hat in hand, attentively listened. Some Indians were employed in throwing out hides from one end of the building, and he was evidently giving orders for their transportation to the beach. "*Como les van amigos? pasan vmds.*" "How are you, friends? walk in," he shouted, at the top of his voice, as we entered the hospitable mission, and his extended hand was warmly closed on mine, in earnest of the sincerity of his invitation.

After a short conversation we remounted our horses and proceeded on our route for Sta. Clara. The first two or three leagues of the journey were over a succession of hills and small valleys, where the strong westerly gales came with such force that the progress of our horses was somewhat impeded, in consequence of the violent effect of the wind on the large leather trappings attached to our saddle-gear. We passed on the road a large inclosure, called *El potrero*, used for the rearing of horses, the walls of which were of loose stones, piled up to the height of about four feet.

Passing this, we opened upon the grazing grounds of the Mission, where thousands of cattle were scattered about in herds. On our right, the land was elevated, and as it continued in the distance, its top was covered with pines. To the left lay the smooth and spacious bay, extending in a southeast direction, full thirty miles from the ship's place of anchorage, bounded on the opposite side by the highlands of St. Leandro and St. José. Our ride was charming, and now and then a distant farm-house, or Indian hut, with its little garden, would come in sight; and numerous rivulets winding their way towards the bay, adding much to the picturesqueness of the scene. A few leagues brought us to the sheep-farm of St. Mateo, situated in the midst of a small wood. The building, occupied by the *mayordomo* and servants, is spacious and covered with burnt tiles. Here we alighted, and, after a short rest, remounted and resumed our journey. "El Rancho de las pulgas" was the next place of any importance in our route, and is situated a little retired from the road, at the foot of a small rising ground. It is the property of Doña Soledad Ortega, widow of Don Luis Arguello, formerly governor of California. I found her a beautiful woman, and the mother of three or four fine children. She was very lady-like in her manner, and treated us with the utmost courtesy. After dinner, we bade her adieu, and again proceeded on our way, which was uninterrupted, till, far distant, in the centre of a spacious plain, we beheld Santa Clara and its numerous buildings.

It was three o'clock when we arrived at this Mission, having performed the journey of eighteen leagues in about eight hours. Father José Viader was director of the establishment; a good old man, whose heart and soul were in proportion to his immense figure. This institution was founded in the year 1777, and formerly stood a few rods beyond its present location. Like the other Missions in the neighborhood of St. Francisco, its resources were immense, from the annual production of grain; and, possessing large stocks of cattle, it was enabled to make liberal "matanzas," of which the abundant proceeds were usually heaped up, under the corridor in the square of the main building. A large garden of choice fruit-trees adorned its right, whilst another of greater magnitude occupied a space in front. The hills of St. José were visible beyond, and betwixt the trees that covered the plain we obtained a distant view of the town of that name.

Our stay of several weeks in the neighborhood gave ample time for observation, and I had various opportunities to visit among the inhabitants, from whom I received great kindness and hospitality. Business required several trips to and from the ship, which were performed sometimes on horseback, and sometimes by means of a launch belonging to the Mission of Dolores. The latter mode of conveyance was preferable by far, and the more expeditious when aided by the tides, which here rise and fall some five or six feet.

San Francisco has one of the largest and most valuable harbors in the world. Nature has so defended its narrow entrance, that with but little expense it might be made perfectly impregnable. Its steep and lofty cliffs, on either side, combined with other prominent locations within, might be so fortified as to bid defiance to the most powerful and determined foe. The soundings are deep, and, in mid-channel, may be found in from forty to forty-five fathoms. The course for vessels coming in from sea, is generally midway between the bluff points of land.

There are five missionary establishments located upon the sides of the bay, called the Missions of Dolores, Santa Clara, St. José, St. Francisco Solano, and St. Rafael. These have a population of over five thousand

Indians, and only about two hundred whites. The whole number of cattle, domesticated, is more than forty thousand, exclusive of horses, mules, and sheep. The rivers and creeks are supplied with an abundance of salmon and other fish; game is plentiful, and bears, wildcats, wolves, and coyotes, are often met with. On the northern side of the bay are found the American elk and antelope, and great quantities of deer; the first of these is hunted for its tallow, which is preferred to that taken from bullocks. The islands and neighboring lands afford abundance of wood and timber. The soil is excellent, and perhaps in no part of the world more yielding, particularly for wheat; as an instance of its immense fertility in this respect, the following circumstance was related to me by the mayordomo of the mission of St. José. Eight fanegas, equal to twelve bushels of wheat, were sowed, which yielded twelve hundred fanegas or eighteen hundred bushels; the following year, from the grain which fell at the time of the first harvest, over one thousand bushels were reaped; and again in the succeeding year three hundred bushels. The average production of wheat is one hundred fanegas for one sowed. In many parts of the country irrigation is necessary, but here, owing to the heavy dews which fall at night, the earth becomes sufficiently moistened for cultivation.

Having accomplished our business for the present at St. Francisco, we got under way and proceeded along the coast to Monterey. During the night a strong current swept us down below Point Pinos, so that we did not arrive till the third day after our departure. We found at Monterey two new comers; an American schooner from the Sandwich Islands, and a Mexican vessel belonging to Don José de la Guerra y Noriega, late "diputado" to Mexico, who had just returned after an absence of two years. He brought with him, as passengers, two American gentlemen who had received large grants of land from the general government, and had come to the country for the purpose of making arrangements for colonization.

Remaining here but a short time, we continued our voyage to Santa Barbara, where we arrived after a protracted passage; the same strong current from the north having carried the ship a second time beyond her port of destination. Here we left the ship for a short excursion across the country, proposing to meet her again at St. Pedro, and starting early in the morning, arrived about noon at the mission of St. Buenaventura, where we remained till evening, and then resumed our journey upon the same horses. A fine moon had risen just as we set out, and so brilliantly was the whole country lighted up, that our way lay before us as clearly as at noonday. The clear heavens; the bright moon; the beautiful country stretching far away into the blue distance, and basking in the moonlight; the deep silence, unbroken save by the footfalls of our horses, or the cries of some wild night-bird; all formed a scene of such rare beauty that the impression still lingers in my memory. At midnight we reached the "Rancho de Simi," some fourteen leagues from the Mission. The good people who inhabited this lonely spot we found were fast locked in sleep, so that we were obliged to take up our quarters upon the ground, in the open air. The "mochillas" and "armas" attached to our saddle gear were spread for a bed, to secure our bodies against the dampness of the earth, whilst our "serapes" served as coverlets, and our saddles as pillows. We slept soundly in spite of the rudeness of our beds, and awaking at daylight much refreshed, pushed on for Los Angeles, which we reached at noon. We stopped at the house of Don Tiburcio Tapia, the "Alcalde Constitucional" of the town, once a soldier in very moderate circumstances, but who by honest and industrious labor had amassed so much of this world's goods, as to make him one of the wealthiest inhabitants of the place. His strict integrity gave him credit to any amount, so that he was the principal merchant, and the only native one in El Pueblo de los Angeles. A short ride brought us to the beach at St. Pedro, where we embarked for St. Diego. The ship was soon under sail, and forty-eight hours' run brought us to our place of anchorage.

The consequent bustle of disembarkation commenced. The hides were landed, tallow bags whitewashed, ship smoked, and every thing again prepared for her departure. During her trip to the northward I was to remain a resident at St. Diego, and quantities of goods were landed, and a store fitted up in the house of the mother of our old friend Don Manuel Dominguez. The day for the ship's departure arrived. I bade adieu to G——, and proceeded to take charge of my future occupation and residence.

Chapter VI

THE FAMILY IN WHICH I NOW RESIDED AT ST. DIEGO consisted of the old lady Dominguez, Don José Antonio Estudillo and his wife, Doña Victoria, with two children, and three servants. My first week's residence proved rather dull, and I found it necessary to make frequent hunting excursions in the neighborhood, with an occasional ride to our dépôt at "Hide Park," in order to wear away the time, and break up the monotony of our little village.

My new lodgings unfortunately had no direct communication with the street, except by a small window, so that my customers were compelled to pass through the *sala,* and a sleeping apartment, ere they could get access to my place of business. On the third or fourth night I was aroused by a rap at the little window and requested by an old woman to go with her and prescribe for her daughter, who was taken suddenly ill and was suffering most violent pain. Fearful of exposing myself to the night air and endangering the safety of the property under my charge through such indiscretion, I concluded not to accompany her, but advised her to give her daughter a few drops of laudanum. She then left me, but on the following morning returned to express her thanks for the wonderful cure I had so accidentally performed. This was enough to establish my fame as a *medico* throughout the town, and had I been so inclined I might (by providing the medicine) have become quite a proficient in the art of killing.

42

There are no physicians in the country, and every foreigner is supposed to possess some knowledge of the practice of medicine. I recollect a circumstance which will serve to illustrate the fact. One of our sailors, who had absconded from the ship at one of the neighboring ports, found his way to Santa Barbara and set himself up as a doctor. It was not difficult to impose upon the poor credulous creatures of the lower class, and thus he managed to get as much liquor as he wanted during his stay by administering his remedies in *"aguardiente,"* of which he partook freely, himself, to prove their simplicity.

In a short time I became acquainted with many of the inhabitants of the place, whose frequent visits to the house established between us a familiarity which resulted in many a pleasant pastime. Señor Lugo was one who nightly made his appearance, and amused us by his stories and eccentricities. One evening he came prepared to play off a practical joke upon me. He had loaded a paper cigar with gunpowder and placed it amongst his *cigarros*. During his visit he repeatedly asked me to smoke, but fortunately I missed the one he prepared, until finally, from the lateness of the hour, he withdrew. In the course of the night, after retiring, he awoke, and feeling a desire to smoke, selected from his bundle, quite forgetful of the evening's amusement, the very cigar he had prepared for me. Having lighted it, he returned to bed and extended himself by the side of his fair *esposa*. The cigar was about half consumed and he more than half asleep, when a sudden explosion carried away the better part of his moustache, and so thoroughly frightened his poor wife, that I venture to say the event will never be forgotten.

Don José Antonio was equally amusing in his character, and was ever on the alert seeking for some new device for my gratification. It was nearly time for the religious festival of "la noche buena," and he directed the customary exhibition of the *"pastores."* They were rehearsing night after night, till at length Christmas arrived, and I had an opportunity of beholding the ceremony of midnight mass and the subsequent performances.

At an early hour illuminations commenced, fireworks were set off, and all was rejoicing. The church bells rang merrily, and long before the time of mass the pathways leading to the Presidio were enlivened by crowds hurrying to devotion. I accompanied Don José Antonio, who procured for me a stand where I could see distinctly everything that took place. The mass commenced, Pádre Vicente de Oliva officiated, and at the conclusion of the mysterious *"sacrificio"* he produced a small image representing the infant Saviour, which he held in his hands for all who chose to approach and kiss. After this, the tinkling of the guitar was heard without, the body of the church was cleared, and immediately commenced the harmonious sounds of a choir of voices. The characters entered in procession, adorned with appropriate costume, and bearing banners. There were six females representing shepherdesses, three men and a boy. One of the men personated Lucifer, one a hermit, and the other Bartolo, a lazy vagabond, whilst the boy represented the archangel Gabriel. The story of their performance is partially drawn from the Bible, and commences with the angel's appearance to the shepherds, his account of the birth of our Saviour, and exhortation to them to repair to the scene of the manger. Lucifer appears among them, and endeavors to prevent the prosecution of their journey. His influence and temptations are about to succeed, when Gabriel again appears and frustrates their effect. A dialogue is then carried on of considerable length relative to the attributes of the Deity, which ends in the submission of Satan. The whole is interspersed with songs and incidents that seem better adapted to the stage than the church. For several days this theatrical representation is exhibited at the principal houses, and the performers at the conclusion of the play are entertained with refreshments. The boys take an enthusiastic part in the performance, and follow about, from house to house, perfectly enraptured with the comicalities of the hermit and Bartolo.

About this time, the general received information of an insurrection in the north, headed by a person named Soliz. The town of Monterey had surrendered to his forces, the garrison having been surprised during the night and overpowered without the shedding of blood; and he was now on his way south, to cope with Echeandia. Accordingly, the busy preparations for war commenced. Old rusty guns were repaired, hacked swords were sharpened, rude lances made, and all the force that could be mustered was soon on its way to meet the enemy.

At the commencement of this revolution, there were in the hands of the commissary about three thousand dollars, which were seized upon by Soliz. A contribution also was levied upon the inhabitants for the support of the new government. Their manifesto declared that they only contended for their rights; that they would not interfere with foreigners, nor in any way interrupt the commercial interests of the country. Soliz was elected President, and had under his command over one hundred well-armed men. This was considered a powerful force in California, and it was generally believed that Echeandia would have considerable difficulty in quelling the disturbance.

Several weeks elapsed ere we received information of the success of the government party. They had defeated the rebels, and the ringleaders were taken to St. Blas. An old friar of the Mission of St. Luis Obispo was charged with having aided the insurgents, and after undergoing a strict examination before the general and his officers, he was embarked on board a merchant ship, and sent out of the country.

The population of St. Diego being somewhat reduced in consequence of the departure of the troops, the town was dull in the extreme, so that I was compelled to make daily use of my fowling-piece, and resort with greater frequency, to the scene of hide curing at "Hide Park." On one of my visits, I was informed by our officer in charge, that for several days he had missed hides from the number put to soak; that the night previous he got up in consequence of some unusual noise among the dogs, and seizing his gun, sallied forth to discover the cause. He soon perceived a dark object moving along, a little above the surface of the water, at which he immediately fired. It dropped at once, and a tall figure sprang from the water to the shore, and rushed from the beach by one of the pathways leading to the hills. It was an Indian, who had swam to the hides, and, having succeeded in abstracting one of them, was returning to the shore with it upon his head.In this way he had stolen about a dozen, which were subsequently found secreted among the bushes.

During the absence of friend G——, I had received from him but two letters, which were of a date prior to his leaving Santa Barbara for the north, so that I had no specified time to look for his return; but, at length, after an absence of three months, the ship was reported in the offing, and to my great joy, she soon appeared coming round Point Loma. I immediately started for the beach, and, putting spurs to my horse, reached our *barraca* just as she came to, when a boat was dispatched to convey me on board. I found as passengers in the ship several of the officers who were liberated at Monterey, in consequence of the success of Echeandia. The ship had made a fortunate trip, and had gathered nearly enough hides to make a homeward cargo, and only one visit more to the north was to be made ere she would leave for the United States. This was gratifying to the crew, and to all concerned, and the labor of discharging went on so briskly, that soon every thing was in readiness for our departure. The store was abandoned, the goods unsold re-embarked, and again we made sail for the port of St. Francisco.

A tedious passage of twenty-one days brought us to the place of anchorage at Yerba Buena, where we found several American vessels, and a large Russian ship from Sitka, which had come for a cargo of wheat and beef-fat. The next morning after our arrival, I took an early ride to the Mission of St. Clara, and from thence, after dinner, visited the Pueblo de San José, about three miles distant. The road, which is level and shaded on each side by large and stately trees, is called the "Alameda." It is frequented generally on the Sabbath or feast days, when all the town repair to the church at Santa Clara. On a Sunday may be seen hundreds of persons, of both sexes, gaily attired in silks and satins, mounted on their finest horses, and proceeding leisurely up the road. No carriages are used, and, of course, the scene is divested of all the pomp and splendor which accompanies church-going in the larger places of the republic, yet, in one respect it excels them all, that is, in the display of female beauty. No part of Mexico can show so large a share of bright eyes, fine teeth, fair proportions, and beautiful complexions.

The town of St. José consists of about one hundred houses; it has a church, court-house, and jail. Its civil authorities are an Alcalde, two Regidores, &c., as in the town of Los Angeles, at the south. Their decisions in important law cases are subject to the confirmation of the Comandante General, ere they can be acted upon. In all capital offences, the delinquents, after an investigation of their cases by the Alcalde, are sent to the supreme government, unless the arbitrary general sees proper to take upon himself the execution of the law, which has been the case in some few instances.

Many little gardens of fruit trees are attached to the houses, also some fine fields, where are raised large quantities of wheat and corn. A small stream of water supplies the means of irrigation, and serves as the power to a profitable grist-mill. The men are generally indolent, and addicted to many vices, caring little for the welfare of their children, who, like themselves, grow up unworthy members of society. Yet, with vice so prevalent amongst the men, the female portion of the community, it is worthy of remark, do not seem to have felt its influence, and perhaps there are few places in the world, where, in proportion to the number of inhabitants, can be found more chastity, industrious habits, and correct deportment, than among the women of this place. This observation may be applied to the country, generally; which is rather surprising when we consider the want of distinction observed between those of virtuous and immoral habits: for it is not unusual to see at public assemblages the most perfect familiarity between the two classes. This often misleads strangers, who form, in consequence, incorrect opinions. In time, when the country becomes more settled, a necessary distinction will prevail among the various classes; and society will be found more select, as in places of greater civilization. Their adherence to the faithful observances of the church, as in all Catholic countries, is truly firm; and the most trifling deviation from its commands is looked upon with abhorrence. The extreme veneration shown towards the holy teachers of their religion, and the wonderful influence exercised by them, even in the affairs of their every-day life, may account for any virtue they may exhibit. The friar's knowledge of the world, and his superior education, give him a station far above the unenlightened state of the laity, and place him in a sphere to inculcate good or disseminate evil. Fortunately, however, for the country, the original founders of Christianity in California were truly pious, excellent men, and their successors, generally, have endeavored to sustain their honorable character.

Commerce is very limited, being confined to only four or five merchants in the place, who are principally foreigners, so that my business here was soon accomplished; but, ere returning to the ship, I concluded to ride to the Mission of St. José, about ten leagues from the town. My guide took the lead, and we galloped along, over a grassy plain, till we reached the banks of quite a large river. It was deep, and rapid, and I felt somewhat reluctant to follow my companion, who plunged in, regardless of danger, and was soon on the opposite side. Seeing that I had not kept behind him, he returned to encourage, and show me how to proceed. Our horses simultaneously stepped in, and I was soon in the middle of the stream, with my legs crossed above the saddle, for the water in some places was so deep from recent rains, that our steeds were obliged to swim. Having succeeded in reaching the opposite bank in safety, although pretty thoroughly wetted, we resumed our gallop, till we came to a cluster of hills, where the road was somewhat miry, from the continued flow of a neighboring hot spring. The Mission was situated a little beyond this, and, as we reached the summit of the last hill, we saw distinctly its long buildings, and singular church.

The pádre was at home when we arrived, and immediately ordered chocolate and refreshments. This was father Narciso Duran, a venerable, old man, who had spent the most valuable part of his life, in incessant labor, to promote the advancement of his holy religion. Generous, kind, and benevolent, the natives not only revered him, as their spiritual father and friend, but seemed almost to adore him. He was universally beloved, and the neighboring village bore testimony to his charitable heart, while many a transient traveller blessed him, and thanked God, that such a man existed among them.

The Mission of St. José was founded in 1797, and had, at this time, a population of about two thousand Indians. It possesses some of the best lands in the country for agricultural purposes, from which is obtained an immense quantity of grain. It frequently supplies the Russian company, who yearly send three or four large ships for stores for their northern settlements. In the rear of the establishment is a large reservoir of excellent water, which is carried, through pipes, to the gardens, and other parts of the Mission. In front of the church is a very neat fountain, and also conveniences for washing and bathing. In point of beauty, the buildings here were very inferior to those of the southern missions. Durability and convenience alone seem to have been consulted in their construction, and they mostly presented a very ordinary appearance.

Time passed swiftly during my stay with the old friar, and I left him with regret. It was late in the day, and the sky was clouded; yet fearing no danger from a storm, off I galloped to the landing-place, where I embarked in a small boat, with four Indians to row me to the ship. Arriv-

VIEW OF THE PRESIDIO OR TOWN OF SANTA BARBARA.

ing at the mouth of the creek, we tarried there until the tide had risen, to take advantage of the entire ebb, and to put off as soon as the water slackened. The wind blew fresh from the southeast, the rain drizzled, and everything foretold a disagreeable night. However, we pushed off; but by the time we had reached the middle of the bay, the rain increased, and darkness closed around us. As the wind was favorable, we rigged the boat-hook for a mast, and taking the blanket of one of the Indians for a sail, we in this way proceeded admirably; but my oarsmen soon stretched themselves in the bottom of the boat, leaving me to accomplish the voyage under my own management. Unable to perceive any object beyond the boat's head, and without a compass, I was obliged to steer by the wind, and trust to the chance of its steadiness. In this dilemma, I remained for some hours in extreme doubt as to my whereabouts, often imagining I felt a gradual increase of the swell, which betokened an approach to the sea. At last, I caught a glimpse of the land. This gave me encouragement to proceed, and though ignorant of the localities of the place, yet presuming this to be the "Mission Point," I bore away for the ship's anchorage. A few minutes of great anxiety passed, when a sudden shock fully determined the fact. Our boat had struck the vessel amidships, luckily however without sufficient force to do us injury. The Indians, supposing we had struck a rock, started up in terror, but how great was their surprise, when, on looking up, they beheld the side of our noble ship. The night-watch assisted us in securing the boat alongside, and I speedily ascended to the deck. We had been four hours performing a distance of thirty miles, with a fair wind and favorable current. Had we been so unfortunate as to have missed the ship, we must have been carried out to sea, which would most probably have been the last of us, but something better, or worse, was reserved for our destiny.

A few days, only, passed ere we were once more, and for the last time, on our way to the port of Monterey. As we beat along down from the anchorage to "Castle Point," the breeze gradually died away, and when we reached the very entrance, and narrowest portion of the bay, it ceased entirely, leaving us to the force of the stream, the strength of which in the centre of the channel is from four to six knots an hour. On both sides are very strong eddies, and the junction of the waters from

49

the northern and southern basins forms a multitude of whirlpools of such strength that vessels when becalmed are frequently driven by them upon the rocks. In such cases one or two boats in advance of the ship, to keep her in range with the current, is of the utmost importance. After passing the low point south of "Whaler's Harbor," where may be seen a few rocks, no danger need be apprehended of striking the northern shore, for the course of the current will take every thing clear of the rocks, and the soundings are deep. We passed so near with our ship, of four hundred tons, that I could have jumped upon the projecting points. Five miles outside of the castle, the soundings lessen considerably, and good anchorage may be found in from five to ten fathoms. Here we came to, and waited for a breeze, as there is danger along the shore at the south of the port, unless the vessel has a good offing, for the swell sets directly upon the land. We did not wait long. The sea breeze soon set in, we continued our course, and the next morning found us busily employed at Monterey.

Having progressed thus far on our voyage, it was necessary to make arrangements for the disembarkation and storage of our cargo remaining unsold. Santa Barbara, on account of its central situation and quiet character of its population, was determined upon as the most suitable location, but it was necessary to ascertain if a building could be procured of sufficient capacity. For this reason I was obliged to proceed thither with all possible haste, G— accompanying me as far as the Mission of La Soledad.

It was about nine o'clock in the morning when we started, and a few leagues of pleasant riding, mostly through dense woods, brought us to Buena Vista, the farm of Don Mariano Estrada. Here we alighted, and found the old gentleman at dinner. He had just commenced, and was tasting "la tasa de caldo," a bowl of soup. His invitation to partake of his cheer we accepted, and seated ourselves at the table. We found him rather a lover of good eating, and, indeed, one would suppose that this remark might apply to all Californians, for the lowest personage must have his three or four different dishes. Their *olla, azados, guisados,* and *frijoles,* are found at every board. Dinner concluded, we took leave of Buena Vista and continued our journey. Our road was quite level the whole distance, and wound along the base of a long range of hills, which run parallel with the sea-coast. A river flowed through the valley, emptying into the bay of Monterey, upon the bank of which was a farmhouse belonging to the Mission of Carmelo; this, and a few small huts scattered in our route, were the only buildings we passed in our ride. It was near sundown when we arrived and dismounted at the door of La Soledad. The gloomiest, bleakest, and most abject-looking spot in all California!

This mission was founded in 1791; and, although it presents a very unpromising aspect to the traveller from the gloominess of its exterior, its interior exhibits a striking contrast. A pious old man controls its concerns, and pours out to his guests with free hospitality the abundance thereof. His charities, his goodness, and meekness of character are proverbial; and to have known the old Pádre Seria was a happiness indeed. For many years he was Prefect of the Missions, and still exercised this function while attending to the spiritual, as well as the temporal affairs of his own establishment. In the kindness of his heart, he gave me a letter of introduction to the priests of the other Missions, requesting their assistance and hospitality during my journey.

The next day I took leave of G—— and set out for the Mission of St. Antonio, ten leagues distant from La Soledad. A *vaquero* accompanied me as guide. We travelled slowly, owing to our miserable horses, and the almost impracticable state of the road which in many places extended across the mountains in narrow pathways, and was so obstructed with rocks, that I was obliged every few moments to dismount and walk. Thus we toiled on; and in this way we performed the greater part of our journey until we arrived at the top of the mountains and began to descend on the other side. The descent was so gradual that we put our horses to the gallop without danger or fear of their stumbling. This soon brought us to the neat little Mission of St. Antonio, which was the first mark of civilization we had met with during the ride. It is built of brick, with an arched corridor similar to the other missions, and was established in the year 1771. Pádre Pedro Cabot, the present missionary director, I found to be a fine, noble-looking man, whose manner and whole deportment would have led one to suppose he had been bred in the courts of Europe, rather than in the cloister. Everything was in the most perfect order: the Indians cleanly and well dressed, the apartments tidy, the

51

workshops, granaries, and store-houses comfortable and in good keeping. Whilst taking chocolate, my host sent for the *vaquero* who was to accompany me in the next day's journey, to give him some instructions; and I took occasion to slip out after him, to urge the procuring of good horses, and the necessity of having them ready at early dawn. Soon after supper I retired to my quarters, and having arranged everything for an early start, getting my saddle, luggage, &c., conveniently together, sprang into bed, closed my eyes, and slept till aroused by a rap at the door and a voice calling "Señor! Señor! it is daybreak." As I went forth the light was just peeping over the eastern hills, and our horses stood impatiently pawing the ground in the courtyard. I sprang into the saddle, and hastened our departure; for I intended to perform, if possible, a two days' moderate journey in the next twelve hours.

Our horses were excellent; and we galloped briskly over a smooth and level road for several leagues, without checking their speed, except to ford a small river, or ascend a few hills in the vicinity of the Mission of St. Miguel. From the tops of these we saw spread out before us a charming valley, through which our course lay. It was near mid-day when we descended the last hill, and rode up to the house. Father Juan Cabot, its director, was absent, having gone to pass a few days with the pádre of St. Luis Obispo. So I repaired to the mayordomo, presented my letter, and requested immediate despatch. As it was necessary to send some distance for his horses, the delay of a couple of hours, ere they were procured, gave me ample time to look about the Mission. Like that of St. Antonio, it possessed few resources, owing to its distance from the sea-coast, and the moderate extent of its domains. It was founded in the year 1797; and is built near the extremity of a small pass through the hill, where the sun casts its burning heat in a degree almost insufferable. They say there, in proof of the warmth of the Mission, that the fleas cannot endure the summer months, and during the heat of the day may be seen gasping upon the brick pavements! At the distance of about five leagues is a beautiful little bay called St. Simeon. Its anchorage is safe, and well protected from the winds, yet it is seldom visited by navigators.

Having already ridden fourteen leagues, I felt little inclined to extend my journey farther, for my whole frame seemed as if it had undergone a severe pummeling, but ambitious to achieve my morning's undertaking, I again set off, following close at the heels of my guide. Shortly after our departure we reached a place where a sulphurous hot spring boiled up from the ground, and formed a little rivulet which crossed the road. Father Juan had erected a small house over the spot for the purpose of shelter, and convenience for bathing, and it was resorted to by many persons, suffering with rheumatic disorders, who generally obtained immediate relief. We afterwards stopped at the sheep farm belonging to the Mission of St. Miguel, where were two large houses and a number of straw huts. Gardens were attached to them, in which a variety of vegetables were cultivated by the Indians, who were there as keepers of eight or ten thousand sheep. Some distance off, on the other side of the valley, was a vineyard of excellent grapes, from which were annually made considerable quantities of wine and brandy. Further on, some three or four leagues, we reached "el rancho de Santa Margarita," a place used for the cultivation of grain, where, on an eminence that overlooked the grounds, an extensive building was erected. It was divided into store-rooms for different kinds of grain, and apartments for the accommodation of the mayordomo, servants, and wayfarers. At one end was a chapel, and snug lodging-rooms for the priest, who, I was informed, frequently came and passed some weeks at the place during the time of harvest; and the holy friars of the two missions occasionally met there to acknowledge to each other their sins.

Here our horses were changed, and a smart gallop through forests of pine and oak brought us soon to the ascent of a rough-looking hill, called "la cuesta de St. Luis."

Notwithstanding its rugged appearance, we easily surmounted it, and arrived at the Mission of St. Luis Obispo, situated just beyond it. The sun was yet high above the hills, and we had journeyed, since morning, over eighty miles. I was of course much fatigued, and as the Pádres Joaquin Jimeno and Cabot were taking a walk in the gardens, I had a short time for repose ere they returned. The former of these was a young man, of not more than twenty-four years of age, born in Mexico, from whence he had recently come, and was now missionary of St. Luis Obispo. The other, Father Cabot, was a native of Spain, and brother to Father Pedro Cabot of St. Antonio, but as unlike him in character and appearance as he could possibly have been. He was a tall, robust man of over fifty years, with the rough frankness of a hardy sailor, differing widely from the soft and pleasing manners of his brother, and celebrated for his good-humor and hospitality.

This Mission, though formerly a wealthy establishment, is now of little importance. The buildings are in a decayed state, and every thing about them appears to have been much neglected. It is surrounded by high and rocky hills, the soil of which bears the appearance of containing ore of some kind. In the vicinity are to be found the peculiar indications of gold and silver mines. Within a short ride is the harbor of St. Luis, where, in former years, during the monopoly of the Spanish government, the old friars sometimes secretly purchased goods of the American trading ships. The Mission possesses excellent horses, and a great many good mules; but, owing to want of attention, many of them are permitted to stray away, and mix with the wild cattle of the mountains.

The next morning, I started at daybreak with an excellent *vaquero* and fine horses. The road continued along the Mission valley for some distance, when it suddenly changed its course for the hills, and, passing over their woody summits, descended to the sea-coast, and opened upon a smooth, sandy beach, that extended for miles to the south. Here we raced along at a rapid rate, full three leagues, till it was necessary to strike off for the interior, through numerous sand-hills. Passing these, we reached an extensive plain, in the midst of which lay the cattle farm of "La Purissima," called "Guadaloupe."

We found the Indians busy at their annual "matanzas" or cattle killing. Numbers of the poor animals lay stretched upon the ground, already slaughtered; others, just suffering under the knife of the butcher, whilst, in a spacious enclosure, hundreds were crowded for selection. The *vaqueros,* mounted on splendid horses and stationed at its entrance, performed by far the most important part of the labor, When the mayordomo pointed out the animal to be seized, instantly a lasso whirled through the air, and fell with dextrous precision upon the horns of the ill-fated beast. The horse, accustomed to the motion, turned as the lasso descended, and dragged him to slaughter. Another lasso was then thrown, which entrapped his hind leg, and threw him prostrate on the ground. In this position he was dispatched, and the horsemen returned for another. Sometimes it happened that one would escape and make off for the fields, pursued by the "vaqueros," who, as they rode close in full chase, swung their lassos above their heads, and threw them upon the animal's horns and neck, giving their well-trained horses a sudden check, which brought him tumbling to the earth; or some one of the more expert would seize upon him by the tail, and, putting spurs to his horse, urge him suddenly forward, overthrowing the bull in this manner.

Leaving Guadaloupe, we continued on for several leagues through the plain, then across a range of elevated hills, arriving at La Purissima before twelve o'clock; thus accomplishing the distance of fifty-four miles in seven hours. I made arrangements for our horses, and we started immediately after dinner for "St. Ynes," where we arrived in about three hours. Pádre Blas was alone, and could not accommodate me with horses till the following morning; but ambitious to extend the ride to Santa Barbara, I prevailed upon my "Purissima" guide to take me to the other side of the mountain. Our horses held out very well till we reached its base, but here began to fag a little, and with great difficulty bore us up the ascent, so that it was quite late when we reached a small hut. Being completely exhausted, I halted here for the night, and in the morning proceeded to Santa Barbara, where every thing succeeded as I wished. Within two days after my arrival I had made arrangements for the purchase of a spacious building, and was on my way back to Monterey.

I had been absent but nine days when I arrived there, and dismounted at the house of friend C——. In an enclosure in the rear, a party of hunters were practising target-shooting with rifles, and appeared to have had considerable sport. A tall, gigantic Kentuckian, named Galbraith, was retiring from the scene as I entered, with extravagant boastings of his superior skill. When dinner was over, they gaily resumed their amusement, and G—— and myself were invited to take part in the sport. The mark was a small, square piece of paper, of the size of a dollar, secured to a board by a pin through its centre. I took my stand at forty paces, fired, and a loud shout followed. The mark was hit! My ball had struck the pin fairly upon its head, and driven it through the board. My triumph, however, seemed to create no little jealousy on the part of our Kentuckian, who challenged me to a second trial. But this was enough for me; a chance shot had gained my victory, and I had no idea of losing my credit by a second attempt, particularly with a person who ·

55

amused himself daily by shooting off the heads of little "chenates" (blackbirds) at the distance of twenty paces.

In the course of a week we got under way and sailed for Santa Barbara, where we arrived safely, and immediately commenced landing our cargo. Many of our packages were bulky, and it required considerable care to get them through the surf without damage; and owing to the distance of the ship from the shore, and the rough state of the beach at times, a fortnight elapsed ere everything was disembarked. At length the last load was deposited in the house, and the men were employed in getting on board wood and water; this having been accomplished, the ship made sail, and stood out of the bay, on her way to St. Diego, where she was to take in her home cargo. The breeze was fair, and a few hours carried her beyond the reach of our glasses.

So, now I was a resident again on shore—a "comerciante de Santa Barbara." My house was a building of one story, containing one large room some fifty feet square, and four smaller ones. The large one was filled to the roof with bales and boxes, leaving a narrow passage only for communication with the other apartments, which were differently occupied. One of these was fitted up with shelves and a counter, serving as a show-room, and another I had transformed into a bed-chamber. I slept in a cot suspended from the cross-beams of the roof; and, besides the necessary furniture of chairs, tables, looking-glass, &c., I had, displayed against the wall, two old muskets newly brightened up, two pair of pistols, and a very terrific sword. The sight of these appalling instruments was ample security against the rogues, who were generally lounging about the door, leading from the corridor to the street. I had but one companion, a servant, who had lived for many years in my father's house, and had followed me in my wanderings. Poor David! he was a good, honest fellow, officiating in many capacities, and often remaining in sole charge of a valuable amount of property; but he was fated to meet a watery grave a few years afterwards, in crossing the passage from Santa Barbara to St. Buenaventura.

The house united with that of my friend Daniel, whose immediate vicinity I found of great convenience, for we took our meals together; and he was often of much assistance to me in matters of business. In fact, Daniel was a sort of *factotum* for the whole town, and was carpen-

ter, or mason by turns, as his services were wanted; for his natural ingenuity made him useful in either capacity. For our better security, I
made some additions to the house, which needed also some repairs and
painting, so Daniel's aid was required. A large cookhouse was built in
the rear, surrounded by a high wall of brick, and the windows at the
end of the house were barricaded. David attended to the painting, and
very soon we had the best-looking establishment in the place.

While our arrangements were going on, G— was at St. Diego with
the ship, superintending the stowing of the cargo. I had several letters
from him, one of which informed me of the arrival, from St. Blas, of
the ship Harriet, Captain F—, whose elopement, and flight with his
betrothed, I have mentioned in a previous chapter. His wife, whom he
had married immediately on his arrival at Lima, he had brought with
him. Don José Maria Padrés, the new Inspector General, was passenger
with his family, besides over fifty prisoners, who had been sent by the
Mexican government; making another Botany Bay of the fair fields of
California. Padrés expected to have found there the new Governor,
Don Manuel Victoria, who was on his way, by land, from Lower California, and who, it was reported, would again close the ports against
foreign flags.

G—, who had been complaining for some time of ill health, was resolved to return home in the Brookline, to obtain medical advice, and
had notified me of the determination, that I might be prepared, on his
arrival, to remain alone in charge of the business. A few days after, the
ship was seen in the offing. As soon as she came to, G— landed and
came up to the house. She had put into St. Pedro on her way up, and
more hides had been embarked, which were to be cured. The old house
at St. Deigo had been taken down, and brought up to be erected at
Santa Barbara. The carpenter immediately commenced operations, in
laying vats, &c., so that in a few days the same busy scene of hide salt-
ing was going on here that had been so long in process at St. Diego. At
last, the hides being all cured and embarked, the day arrived for the
ship's departure. With a heavy heart, and swimming eyes, I took leave
of G—, the officers, and all hope of seeing my home, my "native land"
again for years.

57

Chapter VII

THE SHIP HAD GONE, AND A BRIGHT SUNDAY MORN-
ing succeeded her departure. The bells were already ringing their first call to mass, when Daniel appeared, busily employed in making ready his wagon for a ride to the Mission. We had but time to snatch a hasty breakfast, for Father Antonio, being of delicate constitution, could not suffer a long detention from his chocolate, and until Mass had been said, he was forbidden to partake of any nourishment whatever. In consequence, the whole population was in motion as early as sunrise, on their way to the church. At Daniel's invitation I accompanied him, and jumping into the vehicle, I seated myself by his side, and off we started.

Our wagon, once a handcart, through the ingenuity of Daniel had been converted to its present use, and was one of the many specimens of his cleverness. He had put springs to it, and contrived it that it might be drawn by one or two horses, with accommodations for four passengers. Several Jersey wagons accompanied us on the road, and one very fine-looking barouche, but none of them went off with the spirit of our own. The others were drawn mostly by mules, led along by a person on horseback, making rather a ludicrous appearance in comparison with the free movement of our carriages at home.

The distance being short, we soon arrived at the Mission, and after securing our horse to the railing of the corridor, we ascended the steps into the private apartment of the priest. Pádre Antonio had retired for the purpose of preparing for the Mass, but we found a number of the chief men of the town, and officers of the army, seated around in familiar conversation. Among them were the Comandante, Pecheco, dressed in full uniform, Don José de la Guerra, a retired veteran, dressed in citizen's clothes, with two gold epaulettes, and Lieutenant Antonio Maria Vallé, a little dried-up piece of vanity, who made up in boastful words what he lacked in physical proportions. I was a stranger to the party, and received a formal introduction to the two first mentioned. The seats were all occupied, and I saw no place for me to sit, but by lifting from the sofa the hat of Vallé, which I handed to that august personage, and squeezed myself in by his side. This was sufficient to wound his pride, and call forth a demonstration of his dissatisfaction; but perceiving I paid no attention to his indignation, his rage began to increase, when the tolling of the bell, announcing the commencement of the ceremony, put an end to the scene, and we passed into the church to take part in the devotion. After Mass we again repaired to the apartment of Pádre Antonio, where breakfast had been prepared, and served upon a long table. All were kindly invited to partake, but as Daniel and I had already breakfasted, we declined, and taking our leave, returned home.

As we rode along we had an excellent opportunity of seeing the different varieties of riding, common in the country. The universal mode of travelling, with both males and females, is on horseback; the latter generally ride with a person behind them, who guides the horse. In this way many were returning from the Mission. Now and then we passed a poor broken-down horse with three lazy vagabonds astride him, who unfeelingly beat and spurred him onward. A few old men came trotting along, who from their firm manner of riding with their legs clinging to the sides of their horses, seemed almost to have grown to them. More amusing still, we saw many children of not more than three or four years of age, two or three together on one horse, who appeared as secure in their seats as the old men who had lived all their lives in the saddle. The young commence thus early their lessons in horsemanship, and when despatched by their parents on some errand, the two more expert riders seat the youngest between them, and go tearing across the country without the least apprehension, not unfrequently with a bullock's hide dragging over the ground behind them. Both young and old are passionately fond of riding, and rarely go from one house to another, no matter how short the distance, except on horseback. Many take their meals in the saddle, and the poor animal is fortunate if he gets either food or drink till late at night, when his master quits his back for his bed and retires to repose.

I sat down at my door on my return, to enjoy the following lively scene. In the front of the house was a large square, where the Indians assembled on Sunday afternoons, to indulge in their favorite sports and pursue their chief amusement—gambling. Here numbers were gathered together in little knots, who appeared engaged in angry conversation; they were adjusting, as Daniel informed me, the boundary lines for the two parties who were to play that afternoon at ball, and were thus occupied till dinner time. When I returned from dinner they had already commenced, and at least two or three hundred Indians of both sexes were engaged in the game. It was the "Presidio" against the "Mission." They played with a small ball of hard wood, which, when hit, would bound with tremendous force without striking the ground for two or three hundred yards. Great excitement prevailed, and immense exertion was manifested on both sides, so that it was not till late in the afternoon that the game was decided in favor of the Indians of the Presidio.

Many of the Indians retired afterwards to the enjoyment of their *Temescal* or hot air baths, which is their usual resort after fatigue, and is the sovereign remedy for nearly all their diseases. A round hovel or oven of mud is built, generally, over an excavation in the ground. An opening is left in the roof for the escape of the smoke, and one at the side, for entrance. As many persons as it can conveniently hold, enter, and make a fire close to the door on the inside. They continue to add fuel to the flame till they can no longer bear the intense heat, which throws them into a profuse perspiration. Thoroughly exhausted, they crawl forth from the hut, and plunge themselves headlong into the nearest stream. I have frequently seen the old men lying about on the floor of the oven apparently bereft of all their strength, whilst some of the younger persons enjoyed it, and sang and laughed under its influence. The women also frequently make use of these baths, repeating them till their diseases are cured.

A few weeks passed away, and we received intelligence of the arrival of the ship Harriet at Monterey. The captain had been arrested by order of General Echeandia, and was separated from his wife for having dared to break through the required formalities attached to the marrying of foreigners. They were to be thus separated until their arrival at the Mission of St. Gabriel, where the missionary president resided. Here, after complying with the requisitions of the church, they were to be remarried. It is uncertain whether the cause of so much trouble and annoyance to F— originated in the special care of the ecclesiastical functionary for the fair Californian, or was the consequence of the open violation of the law. Perhaps the parents may have been dissatisfied with the elopement, and for their better satisfaction had solicited the interference of the constituted authorities.

Rumors had been circulated for some days past that the soldiers and convicts meditated a revolt, in order to rob and murder the foreign residents.—A plan was devised by some Mazatlan troops, who came to guard the convicts.—Base cut-throats and villains! they would have carried it into execution had they supposed themselves sufficiently strong. —Hardly a day transpired without seeing them returning from the beach at evening, with their black silk handkerchiefs as banners! emblematical of the blackness of their intentions.—On one occasion, while celebrating the glorious 16th of September, the annual celebration of their independence, the principal demonstrations of joy were confined to the square of the Garrison.—The figure of a *"gachupin,"* or Spaniard, was hung in effigy, and as the valiant *"Mazatecas"* let off their rockets they cried "Death to the Spaniards and foreigners." The *"Comandante,"* though *particularly friendly* with two respectable old Spaniards (the only ones in Santa Barbara), and *extremely partial* to foreigners, yet was beheld in the midst of the crowd, as if foremost among the revellers.

The American residents were all well armed, and ready to unite on the first alarm. A large church bell, which had been suspended from one of the cross-beams of my store-room, was by agreement intended to announce the least appearance of treachery, for, as here lay the greatest temptation, undoubtedly here would have been the first point of attack.

The new Inspector, José Maria Padrés, pretending to take much interest in bettering the condition of the natives, soon commenced a work of destruction, under the name of reform. The act for the secularization of the Missions, passed by the Mexican Congress on the 13th of September, 1813, was now put in force, and, through the ready compliance of Echeandia, partially carried into effect. In some of the Missions the Indians abandoned their labor, and, when chastised, insulted the priests. These flourishing institutions, as they had been, were in danger of immediate subversion and ruin. Through the encouragement of Echeandia, vice of all kinds had become prevalent, and the poor misguided Indians saw in the terms *libre* and *independente* a sort of license for the indulgence of every passion. But, fortunately for the country, at this crisis the new General, Don Manuel Victoria, arrived at Santa Barbara, on the 10th of January, 1831, on his way to the seat of government, at Monterey.

Señor Victoria was a tall, lean, half Indian kind of person, with sufficient resolution and courage to constitute him, in his own opinion, a legion amongst this unsophisticated race of Californians. He came unattended, and required no ceremonoius reception. As soon as he received the command from Echeandia, his first step was to counteract the ruinous effects of the imprudence of his predecessor, and to restore the Missions to their former state. Echeandia retired to St. Diego; and Padrés to St. Francisco, where he remained some time, sowing seeds of discord and discontent among the inhabitants, till ordered to Santa Barbara, where he was put on board a vessel for St. Blas.

About this time we were much alarmed, in consequence of the burning of the woods upon the mountains. For several days the smoke had been seen to rise from the distant hills of St. Buenaventura, and gradually approach the town. At last it had reached the confines of the settlement, and endangered the fields of grain, and gardens. Soon it spread low upon the hills, and notwithstanding a strong westerly wind was blowing, the flames travelled swiftly to windward, consuming everything in their course. It was late at night when they reached the rear of the town, and as they furiously wreathed upwards, the sight was magnificent, but terrible. The wind blew directly upon the town, and the large cinders that fell in every direction seemed to threaten us with certain destruction. The air was too hot to breathe. The inhabitants fled from their homes to the beach, or sought the house of Señor Noriega, where prayers were offered and the saints supplicated. The vessels at anchor in the bay were also much endangered, for their decks were literally covered with burning cinders, and their crews incessantly employed in keeping them wet. During the entire night the ravages of the fire continued, and when daylight broke it had seized upon the vineyard belonging to the Mission. Here the green state of vegetation somewhat checked its progress, and it passed over to the mountains again, to pursue its course northward. On the uplands every thing was destroyed, and, for months afterwards, the bare and blackened hills marked the course of the devastating element.

The character of our new Governor soon began to reveal itself, in the execution of his determined spirit to do justice. Two Indians, who had been convicted of cattle stealing, were, by his orders, publicly shot in the Presidio of Monterey; thus effectually putting a stop to robberies of all kinds. But an act so rash and hasty was likely to destroy his popularity, and materially injure his career in California, although the result was so beneficial to the community. The act was unconstitutional, and served, among the discontented spirits of the country, to hasten the revolution, the germ of which Padrés had left behind him.

A few leagues from Santa Barbara is a hot spring, where the inhabitants resort in some cases of disease. I accompanied a few friends to the place, one of whom was desirous of proving its efficacy in curing rheumatism. We rode across the little settlement of Montecito, and soon came to a rough and narrow passage leading to the mountains, which we ascended till the path became so intricate that it was impossible to proceed further on horseback; so dismounting and securing our horses, we walked to the spring, where the waters were boiling up with much force. The place was very rocky, and the stream had washed away the earth, forming numerous cavities sufficiently large to contain one person. These were filled with water of different temperatures, varying according to the distance from the source of the spring, which in some places was so hot that I could not bear my hand in it. There are a few shanties on the spot for the accommodation of families, who frequently pass several days there during the summer months. After bathing, we returned home to the town, much enervated from the peculiar character of the waters.

A launch was to take place at St. Pedro, of the *second* vessel ever constructed in California. She was a schooner of about sixty tons, that had been entirely framed at St. Gabriel and fitted for subsequent completion at St. Pedro. Every piece of timber had been hewn and fitted thirty miles from the place, and brought down to the beach upon carts. She was called the "Guadaloupe," in honor of the patron saint of Mexico; and as the affair was considered quite an important era in the history of the country, many were invited from far and near to witness it. Her builder was a Yankee, named Chapman, who had served his apprenticeship with a Boston boat-builder. He was one of the crew on board the piratical cruiser that attacked Monterey, at which time he was taken prisoner, and had lived in the country ever since. From his long residence, he had acquired a mongrel language; English, Spanish, and Indian being so intermingled in his speech, that it was difficult to understand him. Although illiterate, his great ingenuity and honest deportment had acquired for him the esteem of the Californians, and a connection in marriage with one of the first families of the country. Father Sanchez, of St. Gabriel, used to say that Chapman could get more work out of the Indians in his unintelligible tongue than all the mayordomos put together. I was present on one occasion, when he wished to despatch an Indian to the beach, at St. Pedro, with his ox-wagon, charging him to return as soon as possible. His directions ran somewhat in this manner. *"Ventura! vamos! trae los bueyes* go down to the *Playa,* and come back as quick as you can *puede."*

I visited St. Diego about this time, stopping on the route at St. Pedro. My companion was Ferdinand Deppe, a fine gentlemanly fellow, a native of Germany, who was agent for a Mexican house, and was there conducting the business of the ship Harriet. It being late in the day when we started, he proposed taking a short cut across the hills, which brought us into the midst of a large tract covered with *choyas,* or prickly pears. They had wounded my horse's legs severely, and he commenced plunging and jumping, at every movement, adding to his own pains, and increasing my danger. After much trouble, we got clear of the abominable place, and I dismounted to overhaul and examine the extent of the damage. My horse had sticking to the inner side of his thighs and legs a multitude of the heads of the *choyas,* which, with a stick, I

64

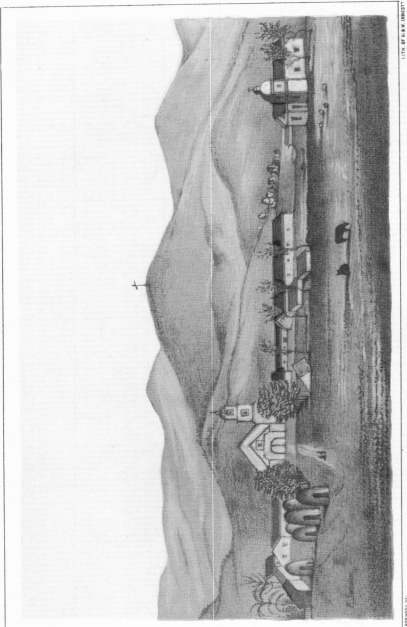

VIEW OF THE MISSION OF S.ᵗ BUENAVENTURA.

prepared to remove. At the very first effort I was rewarded by a presentation of both heels of the animal, which struck me just below the groin, and laid me prostrate on the ground. Deppe was amazed, and believed me killed, but a few moments convinced him of his mistake. I was considerably lamed, and having exchanged horses with him, we rode along slowly to the beach. The "Harriet" lay at anchor, and the new schooner "Guadaloupe" had just left the inner harbor for the usual place of anchorage. Several days elapsed ere I could walk, and I ever after looked upon the *choyas* with an evil eye.

No other incident worthy of notice occurred during my journey, and I returned to Santa Barbara, after a pleasant trip, in time to witness a bull and bear bait that was to take place at the Mission, the day following.

Old Bruin was first, however, to be caught, and about a dozen *vaqueros,* with their mayordomo, started off to entrap him. On such occasions, a bright moonlight night was always selected, and their usual mode of securing him was as follows. In some remote spot which the bears most frequented, a bullock was slain and his carcass left exposed. At an early hour the Indians repaired to some neighboring concealment where they watched the bear's approach, which was announced by the howling of wolves, and the noise of immense numbers of *coyotes*. He usually crept along suspiciously towards the bait, and while eagerly engaged in consuming it, the Indians suddenly pounced upon him from their ambush, and with their lassos thrown around his neck, tumbled him to the ground. Oftentimes at the approach of his pursuers he would rise on his hind legs, prepared for defence, when the lassos were either broken or forced from the rider. The expert *vaquero,* however, generally succeeded, and poor Bruin, foaming with rage, gagged, and secured with a dozen lassos, was drawn to the Mission; either upon a low, two-wheeled cart, or a large bullock's hide.

Success had attended them on this occasion, and at sunrise a large grey bear was secured to a tree in front of the Mission. It was past noon when I rode up and dismounted to look at the poor condemned brute, who, almost exhausted with heat and rage, seemed hardly competent to the trial that awaited him. Persons were standing around, thrusting pointed sticks into his sides, till the madness of the infuriated animal knew no bounds. A sailor, rather the worse for "aguardiente," reeled up to take part in the fun, and with his recklessness and wit added infinitely to the amusement. At length an unfortunate stagger brought him within reach of Bruin's paw, who seized him by the leg and drove his teeth quite through the calf. With extreme difficulty, they rescued him from his danger, and a skilful practitioner happening to be near, the wound was immediately sewed up.

The time arrived for the sport to commence, and every one repaired to a large square, formed by the junction of the long corridor with a temporary fence of poles. The bear, still encumbered with his fastenings, was first brought in, and then the bull came plunging into the enclosure, as if a match for a dozen such opponents. A lasso was fastened to the hind leg of the bear, leaving his fore paws at liberty for defence, and connecting with one of the bull's fore legs, so contrived as to give them a scope of about twenty feet for manœuvring. This being accomplished, the other fastenings were removed, and the two terrified creatures remained sole occupants of the square. The bull roared, pawed the earth, flung his head in the air, and at every movement of his opponent seemed inclined to escape, but the lasso checked his course, and brought them both with a sudden jerk to the ground. Bruin, careless of the scene around him, looked with indifference upon his enemy, seemingly too exhausted to bear the struggle, but the jerk of the lasso aroused him as if to a sense of danger, and he rose up on his hind legs, in the posture of defence. At this moment, the bull rushed upon him, and with his sharp horns seemed to have gored him through; but not so, for a mournful bellow told his situation. The bear had seized upon him by the nose, whilst his paws clung around his horns. A sudden exertion, however, liberated the bull from this embrace, and a second plunge drove his horns half way through his enemy's side, and tossed him high in the air, whence he fell powerless to the ground. One or two more successful attacks decided the fate of Bruin, and he was dragged from the arena, covered with numerous and ghastly wounds. The conflict in this case had been short, owing to the exhausted condition of the bear; but, on some occasions, it was continued even to the exhausting of a second bull; this was rare, however, and more frequently a strong bull was able to cope with two such adversaries.

On this occasion every body attended, as is customary in all their amusements, and men, women, and children took part in the discussions relative to the fight. Such exhibitions served for a topic of conversation amongst all classes for months afterwards, and the performance elicited as much applause as is usually bestowed on the triumph of some great actor in the theatres of our own country.

A slight misunderstanding in trade with one of the priests of San Francisco rendered it advisable that I should visit the north, and accordingly, having made all necessary arrangements, I was soon on my way for that quarter. Arriving at the Mission of San Luis Obispo on the second day of my journey, how great was my surprise, on riding up to the corridor, to be saluted by the Pádre in my own language. "How do you do, sir? Very good oysters, Mr. Fish! come in! May the devil skin you to make your mother a night-cap!" The most outrageous oaths rattled from his tongue with most amusing volubility. At last, tired of his display in English, he abandoned it for a language more harmonious in sound, and in which he was more competent to converse. The mystery was soon solved. An eccentric old Scotchman, named Mulliken, had resided with him a number of years during his administration of the Mission of Santa Cruz, and had amused himself in his leisure moments by adding to the old friar's limited stock of English; who, poor man! profoundly ignorant of the *real* meaning of his salutations, thought he had addressed me in the most *civil* and courteous manner! Father Luis had recently taken charge of this establishment, and Pádre Jimeno had gone to the Mission of St. Luis Rey. Everything was in fine order, and the hospitality of the new director equalled that ever bestowed by his predecessor. Horses were furnished me on the morning following, and I continued my journey to Monterey. Three days afterwards, late at night and suffering with cold, I rode into the town.

Soon after my arrival friend Deppe appeared as a visitor, and agreed to accompany me to the Missions of Santa Clara and St. José, for the annual feast of the latter was to be celebrated soon with considerable pomp, and he had much wished to witness a festival of the Indians.

I found a new resident at Monterey—David Douglas, Esq., a naturalist from Scotland, who had been indefatigable in his researches throughout the northern regions of America, and was adding to his treasure the peculiar productions of California. I was told he would frequently go

67

off, attended only by his little dog, and with rifle in hand search the wildest thicket in hopes of meeting a bear; yet the sight of a bullock grazing in an open field was to him more dreadful than all the terrors of the forest. He once told me that this was his only fear, little thinking what a fate was in reserve for him. He went afterwards from Monterey to the Sandwich Islands. One morning he was found at the bottom of a pit which had been prepared as a trap for wild bulls. It is supposed that from curiosity he had approached too near to get a sight of the furious animal that had been ensnared, and the earth giving way, precipitated him below. The merciless brute had gored him to death. His faithful little dog was found near the spot, watching a basket of his collections.

After two days' detention at Monterey I started off with Deppe on our way to St. Francisco. The commencement of the journey was along a sandy road, over numerous hills that gave us a fine view of the bay and shipping at anchor. Several scattered huts, grazing cattle, and now and then a deer enlivened the scene. A few leagues brought us to an extensive plain, which we crossed, and entered upon a narrow road leading, through a range of beautiful green hills, to the Mission of St. Juan Bautista. An *alameda*, or shaded walk, of some length, gave access to the establishment, on each side of which were gardens and cultivated fields.

This Mission was founded in the year 1797, and had in 1831 a population of about twelve hundred civilized Indians. It is conveniently located in the centre of a valley, with an abundance of rich land and large stocks of cattle. Pádre Felipe Arroyo was the missionary, whose infirm state of health kept him confined closely to his chamber. For amusement, when tired of study, he called in the children of the place and set them to dancing and playing their games. In his eccentric taste he had given them the names of all the renowned personages of antiquity, and Ciceros, Platos, and Alexanders were to be found in abundance. A particular regard for us procured from the old gentleman a sleeping apartment adjoining his own, not usually bestowed upon travellers. When we retired, however, we were surprised to find no sheets upon the bed, but in their stead, coarse blankets. Shut out from any means of access to the other parts of the building, except through the room of the Pádre, it was impossible to remedy the deficiency. Our light was extinguished, and soon Deppe's nasal organs announced how deep was his repose; but I lay restless and uneasy. I could not sleep; the blankets pricked my flesh, the room was warm, and at times it would seem as if a thousand needles penetrated my legs and sides. Can it be the blankets, thought I, or are they filled with fleas; and if so, how is it that Deppe sleeps so sound. The more I reasoned, the more horrible became my situation, and I feared I was to become a martyr to never-ending tortures. They were fleas indeed! and it appeared to me as if they came in armies to glut their appetites with human blood! It was terrifying! for I thought they would surely suck me dry before morning, and I jumped with horror from the bed to the floor. But it was like jumping "out of the frying-pan into the fire," for the floor was of tile, and the crevices their place of abode. I felt them jump upon my legs and feet, and reaching down my hand, I swept them off by the dozens. The bed was least exposed on this account, so back I got, when a sudden twitch of Deppe's frame, and an extra snore, or *snort,* revealed his similar fate. Rolling about from side to side, he could suffer no longer in silence, but cried out "Carramba! what de divil is in de bed?" "Fleas!" said I, "ha! ha! fleas! and they will devour us before morning!" Thus the whole tedious night was passed in scratching and complaining till morning broke, when, worn out with fatigue and loss of sleep, we finally closed our eyes and slept till roused to chocolate. As we passed the old friar, on our way to the breakfast-room, his friendly inquiries were incessant: "Buenos dias! como pasaron vmds. la noche?" To which I would have frankly replied, but politeness forbade, and a shrug of the shoulders brought forth the feeble and laconic answer, "Bien! gracias!"

The whole country is infested with fleas, and it is a rare thing to find a house without them, so that the natives have become accustomed to their bite, and think nothing of it. After this trial, I set myself down as fit to compete with any native, and really thought, since passing such a night, I could bear as much as the thickest-skinned among them.

By the time we got through with our chocolate the horses were at the door, and we hastened to take leave of Pádre Arroyo. The usual formalities of leave-taking having passed, we mounted and rode along with our vaquero on a pleasant gallop, till we had crossed the plain, when we came to a river, which had been concealed till now by the density of the trees. It was the River "Pajaro," which we were obliged to ford, and which, during the rainy season, becomes at times impassable. Having accomplished this, we crossed several hills, and stopped at the house of a Yankee carpenter, who had been several years in the country, and had married a Californian wife—a clever, good-natured mechanic, whose only fault (that of intemperance) had prevented his advancement in life, and kept him, as he ever will be, in an embarrassed situation. His ingenuity had given him a wooden house, a novelty in California, and the chairs and tables bore testimony to his industry. His wife gave us some milk, with bread and cheese, of which we partook, and continued on our route. From this place we rode through a flat, level country, of fifteen or twenty miles in extent, where, on each side, ranged high hills and mountains. These were covered with pines; and on the level below were thousands of scattered oaks. A flock of antelopes crossed our path as we rode along, and away they scampered for the mountains. These were the first I had seen in the country, as they are not numerous at the south. At length the highland on each side closed to a narrow passage, and we alighted at the farm-house of a Californian.

As we rode up to the entrance, a score of dogs came rushing out, as if to annihilate us, but a gentle reproof from the master, who appeared at the door, called them off, and we entered. This cottage was built of sticks, covered over with mud, and the roof with "brea." There were but two apartments, and these were occupied with several neat and comfortable beds. An elegance was displayed here which surprised me; but afterwards I learned that it was no uncommon thing to find laces and satins in the houses of the most needy. All their food was cooked outside of the house, and a few paces in front stood a garden, where vegetables were raised. A few of the tamest of the farmer's cattle were grazing around the house, and several young calves were shut up in a small enclosure. Dinner was prepared for us—horses were proffered to assist us on the journey, and, as usual among these hospitable people, no recompense was required.

It was growing late, and we started for the Mission of Santa Clara, which is about twenty leagues distant from St. Juan. A short ride brought us to the "Pueblo de San José," when we quickly passed up through the beautiful "Alameda," and stopped at the door of the Mission.

Being the festival eve, many of the Indians were starting off in numbers; and ere the sun had set, hundreds were upon the road for St. José.

Father Viader was to go in the morning, before breakfast, and, it being but a short ride, we concluded to remain and accompany him.

The morning presented the same lively scene of people going to the feast; and, at an early hour, the Pádre's carriage was brought to the door. It was a singular contrivance, invented by himself, and built by the Indian mechanics under his direction—a narrow body, of sufficient width for one person only, hung on a pair of low wheels; and the whole frame was covered with brown cotton. The seat, well stuffed with lambs' wool, served to compensate for the absence of springs; and the harness, which he had made from green hide, twisted into rope, though not very ornamental, was sufficiently *strong*, and answered every purpose.

All being in readiness, Pádre Viader got into his carriage. We mounted our horses, and off we started in grand equestrian order. The carriage was drawn by a fine black mule, astride of which sat a little Indian boy, who assisted in guiding the animal, in connection with a more experienced Indian, who, mounted on a fiery steed, led the mule with a "reata" fastened about his neck. On each side were two "vaqueros," with lassos fixed to the axletree, by which they facilitated the movement of the carriage over the road, and essentially aided the mule in ascending steep places. Three or four of the priest's pages attended him also; and in the rear followed a number of Alcaldes of the Mission. All were attired for the occasion, and from their hats were flowing red and blue ribbons, which, like pennons, fluttered in the wind.

A quick movement brought us to a view of the Mission from a neighboring rising ground, from whence we saw the gathering multitude; and as we approached nearer, the bells of the church rang a merry peal, in honor to the priest, which continued until the two missionary brothers were fast locked in an embrace; when the ringing ceased, and we retired within.

It is a prevailing custom at every town or mission in the country to give this demonstration of respect to the holy friar; and not unfrequently many of the inhabitants go out to meet him, and escort him to his quarters. This respectful observance to a priest rather provoked the jealousy of one of the Mexican governors, who, in a circular to this holy brotherhood, ordered that the bells should be rung whenever he approached their Missions. The order was complied with, and has been observed to his successors down to the present day.

Mass was soon commenced, and Pádre Viader at the usual period of the ceremony ascended the pulpit, and delivered an explanatory sermon relative to the celebration of the day. The music was well executed, for it had been practised daily for more than two months under the particular supervision of Father Narciso Duran. The number of the musicians was about thirty; the instruments performed upon were violins, flutes, trumpets, and drums; and so acute was the ear of the priest that he would detect a wrong note on the part of either instantly, and chide the erring performer. I have often seen the old gentleman, bareheaded, in the large square of the Mission beating time against one of the pillars of the corridor, whilst his music was in rehearsal.

After mass was concluded we passed out of the church to the priest's apartment through a shower of rockets, which were fired off incessantly in every direction. Dinner was served early to give us time to witness the performances of the Indians; and as there were many strangers at the Mission, a very lengthy table had been prepared, so as to accommodate all. An abundance of good things appeared and disappeared, till at length the cloth was removed; cigars were smoked, and the good old friars retired to enjoy their "siesta," whilst we repaired to the front corridor to behold the fun.

At a signal from their "Capitan," or chief, several Indians presented themselves at the corner of one of the streets of the "Rancheria" and gradually approached towards us. They were dressed with feathers, and painted with red and black paint: looking like so many demons. There were several women amongst them. Soon they formed a circle, and commenced what they called *dancing,* which was one of the most ludicrous specimens of grotesque performance I had ever seen. It did not appear to me that they had any change of figure whatever; but fixed to one spot, they beat time with their feet to the singing of half a dozen persons who were seated upon the ground. When these had performed their part, they retired to an encampment beyond the building and another party appeared, painted and adorned rather differently from the former, whose mode of dancing, also, was quite dissimilar. They retired after a while, and arrangements were made for a bear fight. Whilst

72

these amusements were going on, the Padres had risen, and we were called to chocolate; but the enthusiasm of the Indians hardly gave us time to finish, when we heard them crying "Aqui traen el oso!" He was soon ready, though almost dead from confinement, and the bull made but a few plunges, ere he laid him stiff upon the ground. This part of the amusement concluded, Deppe and I walked to the encampment, where the Indians were dancing in groups, as we had seen them at the Mission. Around the large space which they occupied were little booths, displaying a variety of ornaments, seeds, and fruit. All was hilarity and good feeling; for the prudence of Father Narciso had forbidden the sale of liquor. At sundown the bells were rung—rockets were let off—guns were fired; and long after supper, at a late hour of the night, we could hear from our beds the continued shouts of the multitude.

We returned safe to Santa Clara early on the following morning, where I was to adjust with Father Viader the misunderstanding which had called me to the north. This required but a short explanation, for his good and yielding disposition set every thing to rights; so I took leave of him and my friend Deppe, and departed for home.

Chapter VIII

ABOUT A MONTH AFTER MY ARRIVAL, A SHIP came into port and anchored. It was the Harriet; and soon friend Deppe and Captain F— made their appearance, coming up the street towards the house. As they drew near, F— held up a letter. Supposing it was merely a communication from some one residing in the country, I took no particular notice of it, until a closer glance revealed the well known writing of G—! "Give it to me! when did you get it? where is it from? How do you do?" I cried in a breath. Snatching it from his hand, I tore it open, and found that it was dated but two days back, and my old friend G— was at Monterey, with a new ship from Boston, called the California!

This was information so agreeable, that I was unable to sleep much during the night, and at an early hour I arose. Whilst packing up some goods, to go on board the Harriet, the door suddenly opened, and the large, glass eyes of "Cuatro Ojos" struck full upon me. If it had been the bowsprit of his new ship, I could not have been more surprised; however, we were soon seated together, and he explained the cause of his sudden appearance. The General had unceremoniously taken leave of Monterey, and was on his way down, to put a stop to some revolutionary movements that were in agitation at St. Diego. His abrupt departure prevented any satisfactory arrangement with G—, and this was the reason why he had come to Santa Barbara. He came passenger in a whale ship, whose captain politely landed him on his way down the coast. The General had been some days on the road, and he was looked for, hourly.

74

The following morning, I called upon the "Comandante" with G——, from whom we ascertained that letters had been received from Victoria, giving information of his proximity, and that he would soon be here. It was near noon, when he came riding slowly along the road to the Presidio. Twenty soldiers accompanied him, who were well armed and equipped for service. It was necessary to make application to him immediately, relative to business, so we repaired to his quarters, and had the good fortune to adjust every thing to our satisfaction.

The brig Plant had sailed from Boston in company with the "California," having been despatched by the owners to enable me to close up the interests of the Brooklyn voyage. By persuasion of G——, I accompanied him back, and left instructions for the master, on his arrival, to proceed to Monterey. The same morning that we commenced our journey north, Victoria proceeded to the south.

Upon our arrival at Monterey, immediate preparations were made for the examination of the C——s' cargo, and friend Cooper's house was selected as the most convenient location for deposite, as well as for security. The lighter portion of the cargo had been landed, and a few days more would have accomplished its entire inspection, when an extraordinary courier arrived with the intelligence of the defeat of General Victoria, by the rebellious party.

It seems that Victoria had placed implicit confidence in the faith of Don Pablo de Portilla, the "Comandante" at St. Diego, who had given him timely notice of the revolt, and had promised to co-operate with him in quelling the rebellion. For this reason, the General took with him but a few men; and, only in consequence of the repeated solicitations of Pecheco, who had no faith in Portilla, would he consent to his going also, with a detachment of ten or a dozen more.

On the 1st of December, 1831, a party of disaffected persons assembled together, and declared in favor of the late commander, General Echeandia. Don Pablo Portilla was appointed commander of the rebels. The charges of tyranny, and the unconstitutionality of Victoria's proceedings relative to the shooting of the Indians at Monterey, were sufficient to increase the rebel party in great numbers, as they marched to the "Pueblo de los Angeles," where they arrived and took possession of the town. The "Alcalde" was arrested, and with an additional force of more than one hundred men, making in all about two hundred, they advanced to meet Victoria, whose force was only thirty men.

The parties met, and the action commenced. Victoria, in advance of his troop, called upon Portilla to surrender. But no! treachery said, never! the poor General was deceived, but he was determined to be revenged, and, rushing sword in hand upon the rebels, he shouted his little troop forward. Pecheco was instantly killed from a cowardly shot in the back. Victoria, with savage fury, dealt his blows around, till, exultingly, he sheathed his sword in the body of one bold rebel, and stretched him on the plain. The others fled in every direction, and Victoria, triumphant, marched his little troop through the town to the mission of St. Gabriel, where, in consequence of loss of blood from wounds which he had received, he came to a halt. The *valorous* party whom Victoria had defeated, again rallied, followed him to the Mission, and demanded his surrender. The poor, weak, wounded soldier! they feared him even in his disabled state, and kept aloof, until he had sent them word that he was willing to resign the command, and return to Mexico. Faithfully, he kept his word; though numerous secret solicitations came from the north for his return. Arrangements had been made for his embarkation at St. Diego, should he yield; and every temptation was held out for him to join his faithful adherents at Monterey. But no! he had passed his word! and a retirement to the cloisters of Mexico was preferred to wreaking vengeance upon his enemies. He embarked for San Blas on board of the ship Pocahontas, in company with the Reverend Father Antonio Peyri, who, disgusted with the political changes in the country, had resigned his laborious duties as a missionary at the Mission of St. Luis Rey. I saw them both, only a few days previous to their departure, when the tear of regret coursed down the cheek of the good old friar, as he recalled to mind the once happy state of California. His great penetration of mind, led him to foresee the result of the new theory of liberty and equality, among a people where anarchy and confusion so generally prevailed, and who, at the time, were totally unprepared for, and incapable of self-government. He chose rather a retirement in poverty, than to witness the destruction and ravage that from this time ensued.

This state of things rendered it necessary for me to repair to Santa

76

Barbara, to look after our interests; for we knew not what would be the result of this unfortunate change. The Plant had not arrived, and we were fearful that she might have been lost in the heavy gales off Cape Horn. The victorious party, now firmly established at "los Angeles," proceeded to form a new government, and the "Excelentisima Diputacion," by virtue of an act of the Legislature, named its oldest Minister, Don Pio Pico, for Governor. Thus things were taking a pacific turn, when the news came, suddenly, of another "pronunciamiento" at the north, declaring a non-recognition of the "new Government" and its acts!

Now commenced the downfall of the Missions! Echeandia retreated to St. Juan Capistrano, where he sought the co-operation of the Indians. His promises of liberty and land were sufficient to entice all from their labors, and caused the subsequent abandonment of their former pursuits. Rapine, murder, and drunkenness were the result; and, in the midst, revelled the Mexican chieftain.

About this period, the latter part of January, 1832, a small brig entered the desolate Bay of St. Pedro, and anchored. On the succeeding morning, two passengers were landed on the barren strand, and there left with two bottles of water and one biscuit, with nothing to protect them from the inclemency of the season. Here, more than thirty miles from any habitation, save a small hut two leagues off, they passed a sleepless night. The casual stroll of an idle Indian in search of shells was the means of giving information to the Pádre at St. Gabriel, where, through his kindness and sympathy, they found a cordial welcome. They were Messrs. Bachelot and Short, two Catholic priests, who, in consequence of their unpopular religion, had been forced to leave the Sandwich Islands, notwithstanding their protestations against the arbitrary measure. All remonstrances were useless; they were insulted, driven on board, and the miserable craft was ordered to get "under way" without delay.

The ship California arrived from Monterey with G— on board, who gave us intelligence of the departure of troops, under command of Don Augustin Zamorano. They were on their way down the coast, to oppose the lower party, and would rendezvous at this town. Santa Barbara is the central position in California, and holds the balance of power between the north and south; so that whatever side she favored, was sure to succeed. Thus she generally remained neutral in political commotions, and acquired, in consequence, celebrity for her good and peaceable government. An old and experienced inhabitant, Señor N——, who had in earlier years filled the highest station in its political and military administration, still possessed a wonderful influence over his townsmen; for nearly all had served under his command. His superior knowledge and prudent management, ever kept them aloof from dangerous compromises; and on this important occasion they were to take no interest with the opposing parties.

The California had gone south; and as I sat writing one afternoon, my servant David passed through the room. I indulged for amusement, now and then, in a joke with him; so I told him "to repair to the beach, and inquire of our superintendent, how near the Plant was; for she had been seen that morning off Point Conception!" Elated with the *news* which I had jocosely given him, he started off in good-humor, and at an hour, when I had almost forgotten the circumstance, he came back with the answer, "the brig was close to the Castle Point, with a very light westerly wind." Dusk shut in, and the light of the moon revealed, shooting up above the western point of the bay, the white, light sails of a vessel. She came in and anchored; it was late, and no communication passed with her that night, but, to carry on the joke, I ordered David to take my horse down for the captain early in the morning. When I arose at sunrise, David had gone, and I saw through my window, a brig, indeed. Soon a horseman came galloping up the road and alighted at the door; it was the captain, and the brig was the Plant! This was joking in earnest, I thought, and too good a joke to be lost. She had been out over seven months from Boston, owing to stress of weather and the serious damage she had encountered off Cape Horn. The captain had put back to Rio de Janeiro for repairs, and this was the cause of her detention. Her arrival, however, was "better late than never," and we proceeded to Monterey to enter her cargo. A short passage of four days only brought us to her anchorage, and on the third after our arrival, owing to her cargo being small, the duties were speedily adjusted with the "Administrador" of the Customs, and we again weighed anchor for San Francisco. Here we were detained but a short time, and returned to Santa Barbara.

The army of Zamorano was here, and its close proximity to the party in "los Angeles" caused the greater portion of the latter to seek shelter farther south. This position of affairs determined Don Augustin to continue on and gain possession of "los Angeles," which he accomplished by sending a force under command of Don José Mª. Ybarra. The troops remained but a few days in the place, however, when they retreated to the Mission of San Fernando. The cause of which, was a secret compromise of Zamorano with the party below.

I proceeded at this crisis of the war to the Bay of St. Pedro, where, during my stay I received letters from Monterey announcing the arrival of the brig Newcastle, from Boston, via the Sandwich Islands, bringing news of the embarkation of troops for California; which news had been carried thither from San Blas by the brig Ivanhoe. This was the cause of much alarm to Echeandia and his party, who were draining St. Juan, and the splendid Mission of St. Luis of their richest possessions. Daily reports were received of robberies and murders, committed by the Indians at St. Diego, who were in a wretched state. At the Mission, below that place, which is called St. Miguel, they revolted and attempted to kill the priest, but he defended himself within his house, with the assistance of two soldiers, and finally drove them off. They subsequently united with Echeandia's party. Stabbings were frequent at St. Juan and St. Luis; and the drunken Indian, as he staggered along from his scene of debauch ejaculated, "Soylibre!" "I am free!"

Having a large quantity of hides and tallow deposited at St. Barbara when the Plant arrived, with the collections acquired up to this time, I had more than sufficient to load her for home. We proceeded, therefore, to carry into effect the necessary preliminaries, and soon the loading commenced.

One afternoon, standing on the beach in company with some friends witnessing the embarkation of the hides, all at once the cry of "Sail ho!" was given by the crew, and looking towards the point of land projecting from the fort, we saw a vessel under full sail, standing into the bay. The beautiful symmetry of her spars, sails, and rigging, added to the elegance of her hull, her trim appearance, her sky-sails and man-of-war semblance, called forth a variety of remarks from the bystanders. "My eyes!" says Jack to his shipmate, "isn't she a clipper?" "See! how she throws up the suds for'ard!" and as a gust of wind struck her sails, she lay over and displayed the smooth and bright appearance of her copper. "Look at her!" continued Jack; "*she's* got a driver, I know, or those flying kites wouldn't be there!" At that moment a white smoke issued from her bow; the kites disappeared, and the report of a cannon echoed up the vale; sky-sails, royals, and top-gallant studding sails, all were taken in together! and as the quick reducing of her canvas brought her to her top-sails, with jib and trysail, she slipped past the land like a duck upon the water! "She's a splendid-looking brig, isn't she?" says my friend R——: "who can she be for? Can she be a consort for the California?" "I don't know," I replied; "but we will see as soon as she comes to anchor, if you like; or, if you think proper, we will start now, and board her as she comes in." His assent to the proposition led us to the boat, which our boys immediately manned, and we started for the vessel. Ere we reached her, the swift movement, with which she came into port, had brought her to her place of anchorage, and as we passed up her side, a tall, gentlemanly fellow came to the gangway. "My name is R——," said I, "and yours is ——" "T——," said he, when a cordial conversation succeeded; during which my friend was introduced, and we passed down into the cabin. It was the brig Roxana, Captain F—— T——, of Boston, which had been sent out, by our merchants, to co-operate with the California. I took my letters, together with those for G——, and returned to the shore, that I might despatch intelligence of the brig's arrival. A man was procured immediately to proceed to "los Angeles," and before sundown he was on his way, with the news.

On the arrival of a new vessel from the United States, every man, woman, boy, and girl in the place took a proportionate share of interest as to the qualities of her cargo. If the first inquired for rice, sugar, and tobacco, the latter asked for prints, silks, and satins; and if the boy wanted a "Wilson's cook knife," the girl desired that there might be some satin ribbons. Thus, the whole population hailed with eagerness an arrival; and even the Indian, in his unsophisticated style, asked for "Paños colorados," and "Abalorios." "Red handkerchiefs" and "beads."

Chapter IX

FOUR DAYS AFTER THE COURIER'S DEPARTURE WITH the intelligence of the new arrival, G— had made his appearance at St. Barbara, and was on his way to Monterey, in the Roxana. The Plant was at anchor, still rolling to the swell, and as our crew slowly stowed on board, their daily quantity of hides, she gradually increased her draught of water. Three weeks passed away. The Roxana was here again, and the Plant ready for sea, bound to the United States, via the Sandwich Islands. My quarters were, consequently, transferred to the former, whose next place of destination was the port of San Pedro. Both vessels got under way; but, owing to the difference in their destinations, there was very soon a considerable space between them; so that ere many hours had elapsed, we beheld the last dip of the Plant's main royal in the distant horizon.

The succeeding morning found us safely anchored at a long distance from the landing, fearing the S.E. gales which prevail at this season of the year. Reports were circulated that a new vessel with a new cargo had arrived, which brought great numbers of persons to the brig, when the usual scene of confusion ensued. Several "Rancheros" were among our visitors, who had come from afar, to behold a "house upon the water." Whilst at dinner, we were particularly amused with their awkwardness, and when the pudding was served, it was looked at with astonishment. When the accompanying sauce was carried round, those who chose, added, with the assistance of the grater, a quantity of nutmeg. One of the "green ones," who had carefully watched this operation, in his turn seized the grater, and commenced rubbing with his *thumb nail* upon the indented surface; not succeeding by the application of his thumb, he paused; and from the general smile of the others, who were witnessing his perplexity, he began to think there was something wrong; so, looking towards me, he said, "Como es que yo no saco nada?" "How is it that I do not get anything?" I explained the matter to him, and told him to examine within, where he would find the source, whence the others had obtained the aromatic material. However, this is not quite so good a joke, as I learned took place afterwards, on board of another vessel, which I will insert here to compare with the story of the nutmeg. It was on a glorious fourth of July, and the day was observed with due festivity and rejoicing on board of the ——, from the Sandwich Islands. At dinner there was a great assemblage of guests from the neighboring farms of St. Francisco; when a large bowl was used for holding the pudding sauce, which, at the proper time, was introduced, and handed to the nearest one who had taken pudding. Liking its appearance, he took the bowl from the steward, returned his plate, and with his spoon, soon made a finish of the whole. This accomplished, smacking his lips, he said, "Que caldo tan bueno! Que lastima! que no lo trageron antes de la carne." "What good soup! What a pity that they did not bring it before the meat!" It is needless to say that the rest were obliged to eat their pudding without sauce.

Among our own countrymen, who had lived all their lives in the Western Prairies, till a taste for emigration had brought them here, we had occasional opportunities to witness a want of experience and cultivation, that in many cases did not fall far behind the ludicrous behavior of the rude Californians.

Whilst lying here, the small schooner U—— arrived; and, owing to her light draft of water, she was enabled to run into the creek, previously spoken of in the description of St. Pedro. Whilst at anchor there, she was visited by several Americans, detached followers of a hunting expedition. One of them had never before seen "salt water," and nothing nearer the semblance of a vessel, than a common Indian canoe. He embarked with great fear and distrust, and the smell of the sea, with the boat's motion, had probably made him sick. Stepping upon deck, he staggered against the main-mast. "Gory! how she totters!" said he: "if it hadn't been for that are post, I should have fell down."

The same person afterwards ventured to come on board the brig, by sitting himself down in the bottom of the boat, and holding with his hands upon each side of the gunwale. When he ascended to the deck, he required assistance, and the sailors were called to hoist him in, like a bag of tallow. However, not long after this, he had the courage to embark upon the "boisterous ocean" in a small, pine board canoe, to hunt the sea otter; and many a time, that would have made the stoutest seaman quail, he heeded not the storm. In like manner, probably, the Californian learned the use of nutmeg, and that pudding sauce was not soup.

While lying at anchor in San Pedro, we were frequently obliged to slip our chain and put to sea, to avoid S.E. gales; during one of which, a Mexican schooner was wrecked on the island of Catalina. She had been taken into one of the harbors, for the purpose of "heaving out." When the gale commenced, she was unprepared to get under way, and soon a heavy swell rolled in, which drove her on the rocks.

Leaving St. Pedro, we returned to Santa Barbara, when, the day previous to the one which I had appointed for sailing, a southeast wind set in, with rain, which lasted ten days. The brig was obliged to get under way, immediately, and was driven to leeward so far, that she was not seen again at her place of anchorage for two weeks.

Oftentimes, at this season, I have known it to rain unceasingly for a week, and sometimes, so furiously as to wash down the mud houses. Near the suburbs of the town is a ravine, leading from the mountains to the beach, which I have seen filled to its margin, carrying down large trees by the force of the current.

During my detention here, the wedding of D. Manuel Jimeno with Doña Maria de las Angustius de la Guerra, daughter of Sr. Don José Antonio de la Guerra y Noriega, took place. On this occasion the bridegroom neither had an opportunity of appropriating the services of an expereinced steward, nor had he a vessel to which he could repair, and make use of her choicest stores, as has been facetiously stated, in a popular work, to have been done by a foreigner who subsequently married a sister of the bride; but he had a brother, the director of the mission, who was determined to outdo all that had ever been known in California. On the marriage eve, the bride went with her father to the mission, dressed in her usual church costume, which was deep black; where the joining of hands took place towards morning, and, at a later hour, the church ceremonies were performed. Breakfast was served with considerable taste, a task to which the worthy friar was fully competent. At its conclusion the bride and bridegroom were escorted to the house of her father. Pádre Antonio had made his Indians happy by distributing presents among them; and many of the younger ones, well attired for the occasion, joined in the procession. They approached the town without any regular order, until arriving almost within its precincts; when, under the direction of the friar, they formed and marched in the following manner. First came the military band, consisting of about twenty performers, who were dressed in a new uniform of red jackets trimmed with yellow cord, white pantaloons made after the Turkish fashion, and red caps of the Polish order. Then followed the bride and bridegroom, in an open English barouche, accompanied by the sister of the former. After these, in a close carriage, came Don José and Father Antonio; in another, the *Madrina* and cousin; and lastly, numbers of men and women on horseback. Guns were fired, alternately, at the mission and in the Presidio, until their arrival at the house, to the "fiesta de Boda." At one o'clock a large number of invited guests sat down at a long table, to partake of an excellent dinner. The married couple were seated at the head with the father spiritual on the right, and the father temporal on the left. Dinner being over, part of the company retired to their homes, whilst some of the younger adjourned to a booth, which was prepared in the courtyard, sufficiently large to contain several hundred people. Here they danced a while, and then retired. Early in the evening, people, invited and uninvited, began to fill up the booth, and soon dancing commenced. The music consisted of two violins and a guitar, on which were performed many beautiful waltzes and contra dances, together with a great number of local melodies. During the evening all took active part in the amusement, and as the poorer classes exhibited their graceful performances, the two fathers, from an elevated position, threw at their feet, silver dollars and doubloons. The "Fandango," which

84

has been fully explained in a previous chapter, lasted until the morning light appeared, accompanied with all the variety customary on such occasions.

On the next day, Father Antonio, as a further compliment to the bride, had dinner prepared in the corridor of the Mission—the table reaching from one end to the other, and the place being adorned with flags. Here all the town was invited to participate, when old and young, rich and poor, lame and blind, black and white, joined in the feast. For several succeeding nights the "Fandango" was repeated at the booth, and they had enough of feasting and dancing intermingled with the amusements of the "Carnes tolendas" to last them for some time.

The usual season for "Carnes tolendas" is during the three days previous to Ash Wednesday, but here they commence two weeks earlier. Whilst these amusements last, it is dangerous for one to go into a house where he is acquainted, for he is liable to be well drenched with Cologne or scented water. This is accomplished by the following preparatory process. As many eggs as may be required, are emptied of their contents by perforating a hole at each end, through which they are blown by the mouth. The shells are afterwards immersed in a large basin of prepared essences, with which they are partly filled, and the holes then sealed with wax. Thus made ready, they are broken upon the heads of individuals; but it must be understood, that this is only done where great intimacy exists between the parties. Oftentimes invitations are given for a select company to assemble at a specified place, when all attend at the time appointed "armed and equipped" for a battle with the eggs. On such occasions, as the excitement grows warm, and their ammunition becomes nearly exhausted, they resort to wet napkins, which they slap at each other. From these they have recourse to tumblers of water; from these to pitchers, and from pitchers to buckets, until, tired and exhausted by the exercise, they desist.

During the continuance of the marriage festival spoken of, one of these frolics was held at the house of the bride. Among the persons invited were the Pádres Antonio and Menendez; at the close of the evening, when *buckets* were in constant requisition, the two friars became heated, and attacked each other with floods of water. Menendez, the weaker of the two, retreated to an adjoining dormitory and closed the door. Pádre Antonio, urgent to follow up the attack, pursued him; when Menendez, seeing no means of escape, seized from beneath the bed an article, oftener used than mentioned, and let it fly, contents and all, full into the face of Pádre Antonio, who had just appeared at the door. The consequences were, the loss of two of the poor friar's front teeth, and a conclusion of the *fun*.

Immediately after the Roxana's return, I embarked, and we sailed for the port of St. Francisco. As is usual, after a S.E. gale subsides, a strong S.W. wind set in. Twenty-one days afterwards, when in the latitude of Port Bodega, whither we had been carried by adverse winds, we were obliged to heave to, and lay more than forty-eight hours drifting directly upon the land. Had the wind continued twenty-four hours longer, we should have been driven on the coast; but it hauled to the west, and Captain T— ordered sail to be made, and the vessel was kept away for the *Farallones*. Five hours brought us to these islands; a short distance from them and the main, the sea was covered with white foam, tumbling and breaking in every direction. It was fearful to look at; and the captain, somewhat doubtful as to the propriety of attempting a passage through, turned to where I stood gazing upon the scene, and said, "What do you say, squire, shall we go it?" "As you please, sir," I replied. In a moment the brig's bow became enveloped in foam; a heavy comer came inboard, rushing over spars and bulwarks, and furiously passed her sides. On we sailed. Another and another sea came rolling behind us, seemingly disposed to sweep our decks. The orders of the captain as he cried "Steady!" to the man at the helm, with the exception of the noise of the agitated billows, were all the sounds that met my ear. At length a heavier roller struck her stern; but its force was spent, ere it reached us, and it harmlessly washed upon the deck. I jumped to the rigging, and there I remained firmly fixed, until our approach to smoother seas. We passed safely through the danger, and arrived at our place of anchorage; but had the vessel unfortunately broached to, when in the worst part of the passage, we must have been seriously injured. The cause of so much sea was, the length of time that the wind had blown so heavily from the southward and westward. This is not often the case, but when it does happen, the sea is soon calmed by the counter operations of the northerly winds.

The inclement season of the year caused us considerable detention, it being difficult to procure our hides from the missions, for the roads were almost impassable. We were at length, however, enabled to proceed to Monterey, where to our surprise we found a new order of things in governmental affairs. The new General had arrived. "Sr. General de Brigada D. José Figueroa, Comandante general y Gefe politico de la Alta California!!" He embarked at Acapulco, in the Mexican brig Catalina, accompanied by his officers and soldiers, and on his way touched at St. Blas to take eleven missionaries, who were from the College of Zacatecas. While at Mazatlan, where he had stopped for some military stores, the brig was struck with lightning, which passed along her main-mast into the hold, and set fire to some articles which were stowed near the powder. The fire was fortunately extinguished. While stopping at Cape St. Lucas, the troops revolted, and declared for St. Anna, who was then in arms against the government. They took possession of the vessel, and, leaving the general and friars at St. Lucas, obliged the captain to proceed to St. Blas, where they remained. On the passage, the military chests were broken open, and the money distributed amongst the soldiers and crew. The captain, after recruiting his vessel returned to St. Lucas, where the general, with the few faithful officers and soldiers, who remained with him, together with the friars, re-embarked, and arrived at their destination in January, 1833.

He assumed his authority at a period when anarchy and confusion spread throughout the country. The supreme government of Mexico had entirely disapproved of the conduct of Echeandia and Padrés, and ordered Figueroa, in case he should find that the scheme of secularization had been carried into effect, to suspend the operation, and restore the Missions to their former state.

A new "Administrador" of the Customs had also arrived, and was already put in possession of his office. His name was Don Raphael Gonsalez, alias "el Pintito;" as well calculated to discharge his duties, as he was to navigate a steamboat through the Straits of Magellan! A vessel with a small cargo had lately arrived, and the invoice was handed to "Pintito" for inspection, in which, where a repetition of either cases or bales occurred, the word iden was substituted, signifying ditto. After puzzling his brains for a considerable time, he inquired of the supercargo the character of the goods called *"iden."* This example must be sufficient to convince any one of his incapacity.

His wife was taken, as a specimen of Mexican beauty, to figure in the wild woods of California; but, how great must have been the surprise of both husband and wife, to find that she was by no means the fairest of the fair! A daughter had blessed their happy union, a lively, dark-eyed girl, who had married a youth, more for his comely features than for his manly virtues. This was Don José Maria Castañares, the acting secretary to his respected father-in-law. The new "Administrador" was a plain-looking man, rather spare, with Indian features, but possessing very polite and affable manners.

Accomplishing our business in two days, I took leave of the new comers and my friends, and proceeded down to St. Barbara. At the time of my first embarkation in the Roxana, my friend G— sailed in the ship California to St. Diego, where he was to superintend the stowage of hides, for she was to load for home, and to return afterwards to St. Barbara, to take on board a few more which we had collected there. Sufficient time had elapsed for this, and I looked daily for her arrival.

Whilst lying at St. Barbara, waiting, we heard of a circular which had been issued by Figueroa, granting pardon to all those who took part in the revolution against Sr. Victoria. Echeandia had retired to San Diego, to prepare for his return to Mexico. What a scourge he had been to California! What an instigator of vice! "Hombre de vicio," as he was called. The seeds of dishonor sown by him will never be extirpated so long as there remains a Mission to rob, or a treasury to plunder! If Mexico, in her zeal for the welfare of her territories, had been more circumspect in the choice of officers for California, she would not have experienced the humiliation that she has borne, nor incurred the expense of so many expeditions to reconquer it. Her own people have been in all cases the fomenters; and here, as has been frequently done in Mexico, they have aimed at the removal of certain governmental officers, not so much for the desire of reform, as for the division of the spoils! This is the pretended patriotism of all Mexicans who have taken active part in revolutionizing their own country, and which has been disseminated by them amongst the Californians, till, like themselves, they have become "Patriotas de bosla!" The cause of such ungovernable desires may be traced to their

88

education, and to the indolent manner in which they have been reared. Thus we may trace its origin to the time when Spain held sway over the American republics! to the old Spaniards, who, whilst rolling in wealth, indulged in excessive indolence. This trait of character still exists among their descendants, and you might as well expect a sloth to leave a tree, that has one inch of bark left upon its trunk, as to expect a Californian to labor, whilst a *real* glistens in his pocket!

But I will leave these reflections and continue my narration, from St. Barbara. We proceeded to St. Pedro. When nearly opposite St. Buenaventura, a sail was observed between the small islands which have been previously described, and the point of land which makes out below the Mission. As we neared each other I saw it was a ship, and at last, distinctly discerned her to be the California. We kept away to speak her. Both vessels were hove to, with their maintopsails to the mast, G— came on board with Captain C—, and after arranging certain business matters, which he had deemed necessary for my guidance, they took leave and returned to their ship. The sails were filled, a good breeze favored us, so that the California was soon out of sight, and we rapidly approached our place of destination. The wind freshened, and hauling to the N.E. from the land, gave us greater speed, so that during the night we had reached the western extremity of the Bay of St. Pedro. A thick atmosphere rendered nearer approach to the land unsafe, and Captain T— concluded to "hang on" till morning, between the island of Catalina and the projecting point of the bay. Vessels, when not enabled to enter the bay at night, are obliged to keep under sail, beating to windward, for should they heave to, they would be swept to leeward by the strength of the current. This is what is called "hanging on."

At daylight, when the Roxana's course was shaped for the place of anchorage, another sail appeared in company, the barque C—, of Boston, which was standing in also; but Captain T—, unwilling to permit that she should come to, before his vessel did, hurriedly dropped anchor near the point: not so the barque; her more experienced captain, distrusting the appearance of the sky, ran by us, deep into the bay, hauled on a wind, and stood out again to sea. Her after sails were hardly braced round when a sudden gust of wind came rushing from the mountains. In a moment her topgallant sails were lowered, her courses rose, and the

89

splashing waters, as they broke against her bows, told how swiftly she was borne on by the violence of the wind. Our situation was by no means comfortable, for, ere the topsails had been furled, a foaming sea gave notice of the approaching gust. Captain T— saw at once the danger, regretted his imprudence, and the men were ordered to "bear a hand" with the sails. "Come down," said he, "come down from the yards!" "Man the windlass, Mr. L.;" "jump forward there, men!" But another idea had struck him, which was put into execution in the "twinkling of an eye." The brig lay tailing in (within a stone's throw) towards the beach. The swell increased, and as she plunged heavily into it, it broke in over her bows and came rolling towards her stern. Our sails were still hanging from the yardarms, and their opposition to the wind, with the force of the swell, seemed urging us to the shore. "Avast heaving!" "Hold on, Mr. L.!" "Clap a buoy on the chain!" "Quick now!" "Move yourselves!" "Bear a hand, boys!" "Stand by the jib!" "Unshackle the chain!" "Let go!" "Hoist up the jib!" and running to the helm he shifted it to the other side, for his quick eye had observed her sternway. The brig fell off finely. The topsails were sheeted home, and as our good little craft leaped over the seas, we shaved the land close, and sailed from the dangerous spot.

This was only the commencement of trouble. We returned and anchored, but repeated storms obliged us frequently to get under way, till at last, having embarked all that we could recover at this time from our "Pueblanos," we weighed anchor and proceeded back to St. Barbara.

Preparations had been made for my return to the United States in the California; a state-room had been fitted up, and Captain C. and I had often talked over the good times we should have on the voyage. The idea, however, was disagreeable to friend G—. He did not like to remain alone in California, and proposed, in a letter which I received at the Pueblo, to write home for the ship's immediate return, and that I should abandon the idea for the present; so, during the passage from St. Pedro, I had an opportunity to think it over, as the Spaniards say, "despacio."

Our passage was pleasant, and two days after the brig's departure from St. Pedro, we beheld the green hills and low-roofed houses of St. Barbara. A light air kept our sails flapping till mid-day, when the sea breeze set in, and a half hour's sailing brought us to the anchorage. We anchored close along side of the California. G— came immediately to the brig, and we started for the shore. His first inquiry was relative to my decision. A short conversation on the subject ensued, when I acquiesced in his proposition—therefore, my return to the United States was postponed, and although five years had elapsed since I took leave of Boston, by this decision I debarred myself of the pleasure, for three years longer, of seeing my relatives. Friend G— was satisfied, and I partially reconciled to the detention. In a few days our business was completed, so that the California was enabled to sail.

About the first of April, 1833, the ship started for the United States. Her chain-plates dragged through the water, from the weight of her cargo, and yet she moved along with as much life and speed, as did the generality of vessels in ballast trim. The breeze was fresh, and I watched her from the door of my house, till, like a small speck, she was seen indistinctly with the naked eye, when I caught at a telescope, and looked, and looked—till the speck was gone! and thus vanished my ideas of return to Boston!

Having in store part of a cargo for the Roxana, I thought it advisable to make a trip with her to windward, and then after procuring a few more hides at the south, to load her up and send her home. To carry this into effect, G— embarked in the brig for St. Francisco, and I started to perform the journey by land. Arriving some time before G—, I was enabled to have everything ready for the brig when she came into port; so there was but little detention this time at St. Francisco, and we sailed for Monterey. We got under way with a light S.E. wind, which lasted during the day and night, and were drifted by the current within a very small distance of the largest island of the "Farallones." The weather became calm and pleasant, and the recollection of former scenes that passed through the mind of G—, as he leaned over the rail, gazing at the rocks, determined him to visit his old sealing ground. The boat was prepared—G— took a club to knock down a seal, should we see any, and I took my gun. Although many years had passed away, he had not forgotten the little cove where he used to land, towards which we pulled and landed upon the beach. The rocks were covered with thousands of birds; many of the young were taken by the sailors, and carried to the boat, whilst G— and I ascended to the place where his dwelling for-

91

merly stood; but, it had been invaded by the Russian sailors, who had used it for a turnip garden! There remained, yet, some coarse buildings, which, a few years since, the Russians inhabited. At last we arrived at a place where G— came to a halt; grounded his long club as if it were a musket, and, like an old soldier on some battle-field pointing out the movements of an army as they occurred in some memorable engagement, he told of encounters and victories. "There," said he, "you see that high rock leading from one end of the island to the other?" "Yes." "Well, many a time I have crossed that place, with as many skins upon my back as I could wag under! Here," continued he, "here, where this infernal turnip is growing, I had my trap to catch the small ground rats that infested the place. It was a half barrel sunk upright in the ground, so that one end was on a level with its surface—the head had a square hole cut in its centre, which was fitted with a trap-door, that would cant inwards from the slightest touch. Well," continued he, "I have known it to be nearly filled in one night! There, I have attacked more than twenty seals and killed them all but two! and here," (as he took me to a little cove between two high cliffs,) "here I have knocked down hundreds! But wait," said he, "there are two large fellows asleep. Now I will show you how I managed." I wanted to fire, but he said "No!" and carefully prepared to descend, so as to cut them off from the water; but in the attempt his courage failed, and the seals escaped. He was not *then*, what he was when monarch of the isle! A short walk over the premises succeeded, and we returned on board to continue our voyage to Monterey.

The wind set in from the N.W.—soon a stiff breeze followed, and before morning we were close under point Año Nuevo. Here the brig lay to, for daylight, when we ran into the bay and anchored. The General having gone south with his troops, the place appeared deserted; many had gone to their farms, and the streets were still as death. From Monterey, we went down the coast, landed our collections at Santa Barbara, and continued our course for St. Pedro and St. Juan. We anchored at the latter place during the month of June, at a time when no danger is to be apprehended from the S.E. gales, and just to the southward of a high projecting point of land, where, at low water, several large rocks were seen close under the brig's stern. Landing on the beach was usually very dangerous, and at this time it needed all the skill of the helmsman to keep us from a drenched skin. There are two points for embarking cargo: one is where the hides are taken directly to the beach, and the other, where they are thrown down upon it from a high cliff. Leaving St. Juan, we returned to Santa Barbara, loaded the brig, and despatched her to the United States.

About this time, the schooner L——, from the Sandwich Islands, was seized at St. Francisco, and notwithstanding she had passed the "Aduana" at Monterey, all her cargo was taken on shore, together with her sails, and detained for a long time. The vessel was afterwards given up, but her cargo had sustained much damage, and there was a great deficiency in her stores.

Time passed away rapidly. The year was nearly at a close. The season for rain had set in, but as yet none had fallen. The hills and fields were parched by the heat of the sun, and all vegetation seemed partially destroyed. Every one cried for rain! One wished it for his corn, another for his beans, another for his wheat, and all for their pasturage, the scarcity of which was likely to cause trouble among their cattle. At this important crisis, the holy father of the mission was besought, that the "Virgin de nuestra Señora del Rosario" might be carried in procession through the town, whilst prayers and supplications should be offered for her intercession with the Almighty in behalf of their distress. This was complied with, as was customary on such occasions, and conducted in the following manner. First, came the priest in his church robes, who, with a fine clear voice, led the Rosary. On each side of him were two pages, and the music followed; then, four females, who supported on their shoulders a kind of litter, on which rested a square box containing the figure of the Holy Virgin. Lastly, came a long train of men, women and children, who united in the recital of the sacred mysteries. The figure was ornamented for the occasion with great finery, and every one who pleased, had contributed some rich ornament of jewelry or dress, for its display. In this manner, they proceeded from the church, through the town, to the beach; chaunting verses between the mysteries, accompanied by violins and flutes. From the beach, they returned to the church in the same order, when the prayers were concluded.

After this performance, all looked for rain with as much faith as our countrymen look for the steamer from Liverpool on the thirteenth or fourteenth day after her time of departure! Should their expectations, however, not be realized, the procession would be repeated until they were!

Chapter X

ABOUT THIS PERIOD OF MY NARRATION THE jurisdiction of the missions was divided; and one half of them were delivered over to the "Pádres" from Zacatecas. Their division would either comprise all the establishments at the northward of St. Miguel, or all those south of St. Antonio. To determine which, Father Narciso Duran, the President, proposed that the decision should rest upon his brother missionaries and be determined by ballot. In this way the rich and fertile missions at the north fell to the management of the new friars.

With sorrowful hearts they were given up; and their former directors were located at other parts of the territory. Father Narciso settled at St. Barbara, where he has since remained an active distributer to the temporal, as well as spiritual wants of his people.

Whilst G— and myself remained as temporary residents on shore, no particular occurrence transpired, excepting an occasional robbery, or murder, at the south; for still the missions in that quarter were unsettled, and hardly a day passed without some new act of violence occurring.

A white man was stabbed by a black fellow; but this being considered only an ordinary occurrence, no notice was taken of it. A sergeant of artillery who had cut the throat of his comrade, was put on board the barque Leonor, bound to St. Blas. There being no constituted tribunal here to take cognizance of the deed, the villain was sent to Mexico, where, the probability is, he was promoted, and will be ordered back to commit more murders! This has been too often the case, and the assassin, emboldened in consequence, hesitates not to kill, when he feels it indispensable to his purpose. What is most astonishing is, why the Indian does not take example from his Mexican brethren, and like them, kill and plunder. Thanks to the worthy missionaries, who have taught him and made him superior to those of higher pretensions to civilization!

To pass away the time, we frequently went out into the neighboring woods, or along the creeks in quest of game; of which we always succeeded in obtaining large quantities, so that our larder was ever well stocked with ducks, geese, rabbits, quail, and sometimes a fat deer. A large pond, called "las salinas," situated at the base of thick wooded hill, was our favorite retreat, where, under cover of the trees, we waited the coming of the ducks.

On one of these excursions, we rode to the entrance of the wood, and leaving our carriage, walked through the narrow pathway leading over the hill, to the further extremity of the pond. Having remained later than usual, G— was anxious to return, and proposed our leaving; but I wished to have one more shot, and told him if he would go slowly along, I would overtake him by a short cut over the hill. He started, therefore, taking his course along the pond's margin. After he had been absent some time, I followed, as I had promised. Arriving at the carriage, I saw nothing of G—, and supposing he must have continued his way to the house, jumped in and drove off. The road was along a hard, sandy beach, over which the horse trotted well. Not overtaking him, and seeing nothing of him ahead, I began to fear I had left him behind; yet, I had remained a long while at the pond, and certainly he had had more than sufficient time to reach the carriage. Thus I reasoned, as I looked behind me, and then whipped up the horse to urge him forward. On I drove, faster and faster, until reaching the house, where Daniel was standing, as usual, at the door. I enquired if G— had returned. The answer was, "No! he had not been seen." The fact was now revealed— he was behind! I would have returned to meet him, but knew not which route he would take, there being two or three that led to the town; and, while resolving what to do, I saw him with his hunting-coat over one arm, and hat in hand, coming towards the house. As he entered he threw them down, upon the floor, and waited patiently for explanation;

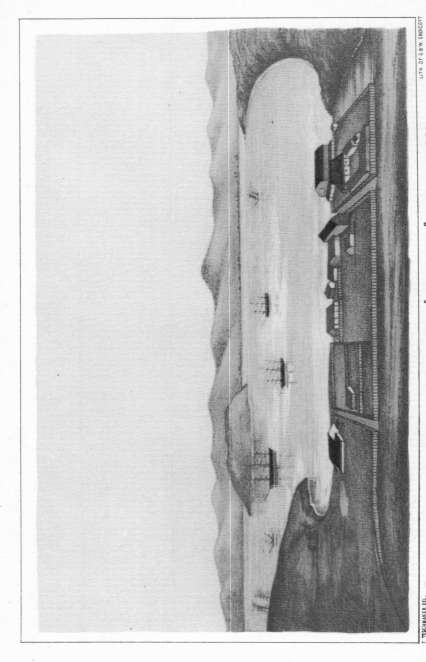

VIEW OF THE PLACE OF ANCHORAGE AT "YERBA BUENA" IN S^T FRANCISCO.

F. TESCHMAKER DEL.

LITH OF G & W. ENDICOTT

and the perspiration rolled down his face in streams whilst listening to my story, which he would not credit. He insisted that it was done intentionally, for he saw me look behind several times, and the more he waved his handkerchief, the faster I drove. He never believed otherwise, nor could be convinced but that I intended it as a joke!

Some time after this, whilst the ship L——, of Boston, was lying at anchor here, I saw a sail one morning in the passage way, between the island of Santa Cruz and another smaller island east. Calling to G——, I said, "Here comes the California! It must be she, for there is no vessel, that I am aware of, at any port south." The glass was brought to bear immediately upon the stranger, when we were both well satisfied of her being a ship, at least. She kept standing in towards the anchorage, and at noon, we made her out an American vessel. As the wind increased, she approached faster, until at length we saw distinctly the house on deck, and her painted ports. Towards sundown, she stood close into the kelp that floats near the beach, and then tacked ship to the south, off shore; being much below the place of anchorage. As she filled away on the other tack, the sun struck brilliantly on her broad painted waist, when G—— exclaimed, "It is a sloop of war!" She stood off thus a while, then made another stretch in, and as there was a probability of her soon reaching the anchorage, I accompanied Mr. S——, of the L——, to the beach. He had just returned from a visit to the Mission, and kindly invited me to his ship, to see the stranger. When we arrived on board, our new comer was standing in, with a very light breeze, which, from its scantiness, compelled her to pass some distance off, and anchor astern. Captain B——, of the L——, went, in his boat, alongside and returned; but I could obtain no satisfactory information respecting her from him, for he, ever full of fun, proclaimed her "A New York ship, with the yellow fever on board—put in, in distress." Shortly, a boat shoved off from the vessel, came alongside, and Captain A——, of the California, was soon on deck, squeezing my hand; and I hastened to take leave of our friends of the L——, that G—— might be convinced of his mistake; for the new comer was not the "sloop of war" he took her to be! Her prompt return from Boston was gratifying to both G—— and myself, and we joyfully went to work preparing her cargo. To enter into all the particulars of the voyage would be but to repeat, in a great meas-

97

ure, that which has already been described; for this reason, I shall confine myself to other more important events.

As before with other vessels, we repaired to Monterey, entered the ship, and regulated the duties on her cargo with our friend *"El Pintito."* One afternoon, whilst at his office arranging our papers, some necessary formality rendered it important that one of the papers should have the signature of the *"Sub Comisaria."* I took it to go to the office, but G— said to me, "No! you remain here, and I will go with the paper." He had been absent but a short time, when a messenger came running in, with the intelligence that G— had been bitten terribly in the leg, by a large dog that was chained at the door. The necessary remedies were immediately applied, but it was a long time before he could walk.

The bay presented a lively scene at this time, being filled with a kind of small fish called "Sardinas," thousands of which, in endeavoring to escape from the pursuit of larger fish, were cast upon the beach. These attract a multitude of birds that devour them, on shore and in the water. Numerous whales feed upon them also, and constantly play about the ship. At times these enormous creatures will raise themselves almost entirely out of the water, and fall into it again with great force. While preying upon this food, they are not unfrequently attacked by the sword fish and killer, when, like the sardinas, they are driven upon the beach to die. The Indians, during this yearly visitation, may be daily seen up to their knees in the surf, with their nets, which are easily filled, and thus the inhabitants are supplied with provision, and at night bears come from the woods, heralded by the howling of wolves, and the barking of coyotes. It is a merry sight, to behold, on a bright sunny day, the joy of the Indians, at the landing-place, as they scoop with their nets— the leaping of the silvery fish that are thrown upon the rocks—the darting of the birds, and the splashing of the water as they pounce upon their prey—the jumping porpoise—the spouting whale, all of which attract hundreds of spectators to the beach, and keep them there for hours beholders of the scene.

98   Departing from this place we proceeded to San Francisco, thence south as far as St. Diego, and back to Monterey. During the trip there were but few occurrences of note, and soon after its accomplishment the ship sailed for the United States.

About the latter part of May, 1834, an important movement was made on the part of the Government, when the whole armed force of Monterey, under command of D. Nicolas Gutierez, was brought into active service, to quell a revolution, said to have been projected by two distinguished individuals at the south. The facts are these: Don José Noriega of Santa Barbara, for some time back had contemplated purchasing a large tract of land called *"Simi,"* which was then in the possession of a dissolute person, named Rafael Pico. On a certain day, by agreement, the parties, interested, met at the Mission of St. Gabriel, to draw up the necessary documents. For this purpose, several persons were required as witnesses. There was also in process, at the same time, an examination of the archives of the Mission, by Pádre President Narciso, who was assisted by Noriega in the work, which required several days for its accomplishment. A poor, ignorant fellow, a soldier, attached to the Mission guard, having been witness to nearly the whole operation, suspected that some secret plan of conspiracy was forming against the government, and hastened to the town of Angels with the information, which he privately imparted to the *Alcalde*. At this time a *brother-in-law* of Noriega filled this all-important station; and another brother was there from Santa Barbara on a visit. No sooner had they received the intelligence, than all haste was adopted for the purpose of conveying the same to the Governor at Monterey. The brothers had long possessed vindictive feelings towards Noriega, in consequence of his opposition to the plan of secularization; and now an opportunity offered to gratify those feelings, and secure his banishment, together with that of the good old Father Narciso. The brother from Santa Barbara hastened his departure, and on his route home, communicated the secret, in confidence, to Pádre Blas; who, in the general change in the locations of the priests, had been ordered, by Father Narciso, to the Mission of St. Buenaventura. This friar had been censured by his Prelate, for unbecoming conduct, and he, therefore, rejoiced at the information; rubbing his hands with ecstasy, he offered to assist in getting the intelligence to Figueroa. Horses were furnished, and a *son* of the *affectionate brother* was despatched post-haste to the capital. In the meantime, our old President and Señor Noriega returned to Santa Barbara. Several days had elapsed, when, early one morning, a friend tapped at the window

99

of D. José, and asked admittance. He was the bearer of important intelligence, and announced the arrival of Gutierez with troops, who had come to take Noriega and Father Narciso prisoners, as being charged with revolutionary designs against the Government. The affair being examined into, they were honorably acquitted; and subsequently, Figueroa made ample amends to the accused.

For several years past a few evil-minded persons had sought the ruin of the Missions in California, by dividing their possessions among the Indians. Various decrees had passed the Mexican Congress relative to their secularization, which were afterwards made null by counter resolutions. Here, in the territorial department, as I have before observed, the same eagerness was also manifested for their entire destruction; and rumors were afloat that the determined spirit of Sr. Padrés, and the love of enterprise in Sr. Bandini, the representative of California to the Mexican Congress, had formed another more effective scheme, for the ruin of these rich and flourishing establishments. The administration of Gomez Farias, as President of the Republic, was favorable to the plan; and the powerful influence of Padrés procured from his Excellency his sanction to an act of the Mexican Congress, passed on the 17th of August, 1833, entitled, "An Act, for the secularization of the Missions of the Californias; for the colonization of both territories; for the appointment of Sr. Don José Maria de Hijar 'Gefe politico' de la Alta California, y Director de la Colonizacion." This movement would have been politics as well as advantageous, had it not been for other views, which time disclosed. The Government, actuated by motives of interest for the progress and welfare of California, had taken the grand enterprise under its protection; and "Padrés," delighted to see the realization of his favorite scheme so near its fulfilment, procured for himself the appointment of "Sub Director!"

This intelligence, together with the instructions to Governor Hijar relative to colonization, &c., had been published in "El Diario del Govierno," and circulated throughout the Missions. It was sufficient to rouse the spirit of the holy missionaries, who had labored the greater part of their lives in fostering the interests of the Indians, and they determined to defeat, if possible, the scheme. If the property were to be destroyed they resolved that the *natives of the country* should reap its benefits as long as it lasted, and from this time the work of destruction went on.

At many of the establishments, orders were given for the immediate slaughter of their cattle; contracts were made, with individuals, to kill them and divide their proceeds with the Missions. At St. Gabriel, the ruin was more perceptible than at other places, owing to the superiority of its possessions. Thousands of cattle were slain, for their hides only, whilst their carcasses remained to decompose upon the plains. In this way, a vast amount of tallow and beef was entirely lost. The rascally contractors, who were enriching themselves so easily, were not inclined to avail themselves of this opportunity of so doing, to the fullest extent; but, as it was, they secretly appropriated *two* hides for their portion, to one on account of the Mission. A wanton spirit of destruction seemed to possess them, co-equal with their desire for plunder, and they continued to ravage and lay waste. In like manner, other interests of the establishments were neglected by the missionaries, and gradually fell to decay. His Excellency, the Governor, was soon officially apprized of the appointment of Señor Hijar to the civil command in California, and that a multitude of persons, of both sexes, were to accompany him as colonists, to whom the pay of half a dollar a day was assigned till their arrival, with a free passage, and maintenance during the voyage.

Figueroa immediately proceeded to appropriate a suitable spot for colonization, and departed for the Russian establishment at Ross. He explored the adjoining country, where he made choice of a pleasant location, and placed there a small detachment of troops for the defence of the colonists. While returning to the capital, and before his arrival, he received an "ecstraordinario" from the supreme government, which had come all the way from Mexico by land. The tenor and purport of the communication was an order, from the Secretary of State, to the General, not to deliver up the civil command to Señor Hijar, but to continue the fulfilment of his duties as political governor—that Santa Ana had assumed the government, having displaced Gomez Farias. By the same conveyance he received the first information of the arrival of Hijar at the port of St. Diego, in the brig Natalia, where he had disembarked on the 1st of September, 1834, with a portion of the colonists. On the 25th of the same month, the Mexican sloop-of-war "Morelos" arrived at Monterey, with Señor Padrés, several new officers, and the remainder of the colonists.

On account of the distance between Monterey and St. Diego, Señor Hijar did not arrive at the seat of government till the 14th day of October. Figueroa received him with public demonstrations of friendship and respect, and after the usual compliments and civilities had passed, he informed him of the recent communication from Mexico. Deprived of the political command, Hijar's position as director of the colony was unimportant, unless aided by the possession of the missionary institutions. To this investment of power Figueroa was opposed, which produced much altercation between them, and a lengthy correspondence.

The discussion caused considerable dissatisfaction among the colonists, who, in the ardour of their conversation, made public many matters which, for their own honor, they ought to have withheld, for thus they revealed the plans of the "Compania Cosmopolitana," as they styled themselves. They possessed no capital to act upon, but the interests of the missions, which had been granted to them by government— that is, Gomez Farias authorized the appropriation of fourteen thousand dollars, payable in tallow, from the missions in California, for the purchase of the brig "Natalia." An unjust project indeed! for no possible benefit could result from it to the Indians. They told also, with the same publicity, that this "Compania" were to monopolize the whole commerce of the country; placing at each mission and town, a house of deposit, and the necessary number of vessels, on the coast, for the importation of foreign and domestic goods, and for the exportation of the produce of the country. This was the object of the colonial expedition that had cost the country so many sacrifices! This was the aim of Señor Padrés, who had lavished all his strength to accomplish it, and which was deserving of great merit; evincing, as it did, a proof of his *eminent patriotism!*

The Natalia was driven on the beach while lying at Monterey, and dashed into thousands of pieces, and in a short time not a vestige of the wreck remained. Thus perished the commencement of their speculations, and they were left to the formation of other schemes. The Natalia was the vessel, on board of which Napoleon made his escape from the island of Elba.

The colonists were finally located at St. Francisco Solano, on the northern side of the port of St. Francisco; where the spirit of anarchy and disorder paved the way for a revolution, to separate the political command from Figueroa, and place it in the person of Señor Hijar; but the plan was discovered and, fortunately, frustrated. An individual of the colony, who had been selected for a Commissioner, from Señor Hijar to the Mexican government, proceeded, in company with a friend, to the Pueblo de los Angeles, under pretence of embarking for Mexico; but the following official announcement of the "Ylustre Ayuntamiento" to the Governor, will show how false was the pretext.

"Secretary of the Ylustre Ayuntamiento of the Pueblo de los Angeles." "An unorganized body of about fifty persons from Sonora, seduced by the promises and lies of Don Francisco Torres, and Don Antonio Apalategui, have pronounced this morning in favor of a plan, which I have the honor to transmit to your Excellency; the purport of which, is for their own personal benefit. They remained under arms until three o'clock in the afternoon, when Don Juan Gallado, their agent, presented himself at the 'Juzgado,' and delivered over to the authorities, the persons of Torres and Apalategui, who were immediately imprisoned." Now for the plan.

"A multitude of citizens having assembled on the seventh day of March, 1835, to take into consideration the most convenient method to save the territory of Alta California from the evils which it had suffered, and was still suffering, under the administration of General Don José Figueroa, the following was considered: first, that this chief has not complied with divers orders of the Supreme Government of the Union, for the improvement of the inhabitants of this country; that abusing their forbearance, he has exceeded the power given him by the laws, improperly assuming the political and military power, contrary to the Federal system, and contrary to the express laws which prohibit this union of powers; that by the law of secularization of the Missions he has made a scandalous monopoly, reducing their productions to an exclusive commerce; suppressing the good faith of the "Excelentisima Diputacion," and causing them to regulate to his caprice a general law; that infringing on the privileges of "Comisarias," he disposes of the soldiers' pay at his own will, without the knowledge of the "Gefe de hacienda,"

103

and without the formalities of the law, and regulations required in such cases. Secondly—that the territorial "Diputacion" had no power to regulate or add a general law, as it had done with the secularization of the Missions. Thirdly—that, they have reached by gigantic strides a state of ruin, by the unauthorized measures which have been taken for the seclusion of the Indians, and the distribution of their interests; and fourthly—that some Commissioners, either from their entire ignorance of the management of this class of negotiations, or by their malicious conduct, have endeavored to forward their own private interests, ruining, in this manner, those of the Missions, to the notable injury of the Indians, who have acquired them by their own personal industry; and they have agreed to the following. Article 1st. Gen. Don José Figueroa is declared unworthy of the confidence of the public; therefore, the "Alcalde primero Constitucional" of the capital will take provisional charge of the political government of the territory, and Captain D. Pablo de la Portilla, as the senior officer, and next highest in rank, is called to the military. 2d. The measures taken by the territorial "diputacion" respecting the regulating of the missions are declared null and void. 3d. The Reverend Missionary Fathers will take exclusive charge of the temporal affairs of their respective missions, as they have done heretofore, and the Commissioners will deliver to this religious order, their relative documents of administration. 4th. By the anterior article no obstacle will be made to the measures of the Director de la Colonizacion, that he may fulfil the instructions given to him by the Supreme Government. 5th. The present plan will be subject to the approbation of the General Government. 6th. The forces, which have pronounced for the plan will not leave their arms until they have seen realized the above articles, and they are constituted the defenders of the administration of justice, and its respective authorities."

Although this revolution commenced and ended on the same day, in the "Pueblo de los Angeles," yet, in other places it continued to exist, fostered by the principal aspirants for power. Under the pretext of establishing the colony, they endeavored to organize a force to support their pretensions. For this purpose they brought with them from Mexico, a quantity of arms and ammunition, which they concealed, but which were discovered in time to prevent mischief.

A country like California, requires robust and enterprising men—men accustomed to labor in the field, and to a life of simplicity and economy. The colony, under management of Hijar and Padrés, was composed of persons of every class, except that which would have been useful. Not one agriculturalist was to be found among them. They were artists and mechanics, who had been allured by the accounts of those who were to reap the harvest of this speculation, and made to believe that they could soon enrich themselves, in idleness, in this rich and fertile country. There were to be seen goldsmiths, blacksmiths, carpenters, shoemakers, tailors, painters, printers, and musicians; all of whom could have gained an honest livelihood in their own country. Their disappointment led them into many difficulties, and they were accused of revolutionary designs. Unsuccessful attempts were made at different places, which finally resulted in the banishment of them and their leaders to Mexico. They were embarked at St. Francisco on board of the Italian ship "Rosa," and subsequently transhipped at St. Diego on board of the American schooner "Loriot," bound to St. Blas.

Although this scheme of Padrés had been foiled, a desire for the accomplishment of the Mexican decree relative to secularization, was frankly acknowledged by many Californians. The "diputacion" *"approximated to the law"* (as was observed by a member of that illustrous body), and administrators were appointed by them to look after the temporal affairs of the missions. Thus, many of those most interested, received appointments, and were enabled to enrich themselves with the spoils. Many that were poor soon became wealthy, and possessors of farms, which they stocked with cattle. In this way the "Excelentisima Diputacion" placed in the hands of Señor Figueroa these valuable institutions.

The General did not long enjoy the resources thus given him. Harassed and tormented continually, by repeated attacks of the missionaries and representations of the Indians, and perplexed by the disordered state of the country, his mind and body became diseased; till at length, after a few months' sickness, he was brought to the grave. His death was unfortunate for the country; for his mildness of character, added to a knowledge of the art of pleasing as well as governing, made him a proper representative to guide the Californians. At the time this solemn event transpired, the "Excelentisima Diputacion" was in session at Monterey; when the following preamble and resolutions were offered by one of that august assembly.

PREAMBLE

"To perpetuate the memory of the departed Señor General de Brigada D. José Figueroa, Comandante General, y Gefe politico de la Alta California. Most excellent Sir,—Our chief is dead! The protector of the Territory—the father of our California—our friend—our adviser, General D. José Figueroa. The people hover around his funeral couch, and with their eyes fixed upon his inanimate corpse, become dumb, and weep for the hero that death has laid low. The mournful, the unhappy intelligence flies abroad; all are afflicted, and plunged in one general sorrow.

"The bell's doleful sound, and the loud report of artillery, bring forth tears from the heart. All is bitterness—all is grief! The Californians weep for a beneficent father, who has given an incalculable impulse to their prosperity, and with unexampled diligence, with constant and unparalleled exertions, contributed largely to the public weal. For him, who extinguished the flame of discord, and prevented this virgin land from being sprinkled with the blood of its children;—for him who planted the olive of peace, and cultivated beneath its shade, those virtues which emanate from the loyal bosoms of these inhabitants;—for him who gave security and extension to agriculture, and protection to our commerce;—for him who knew how to check anarchy, when daringly it approached our peaceful shores;—for him who consoled the widow, shielded the orphan, succored the soldier;—for him who protected merit and encouraged honor;—in one word, they weep for him who labored to regulate our social order. Our foreign friends testify, by their grief, their friendship and the exalted sense which they had of his superior tact to govern. The savage Indian, the child of the desert, shows in rustic manner that he also feels the loss. The name of General Figueroa is repeated everywhere; his merits are spoken of, his political prudence; his zeal for the public good; and the gift which he possessed to captivate the will; his honor, his probity were acknowledged by the people, who proclaimed him an eminent patriot, and 'de hijo benemerito de la patria.' All praise and acknowledge the excellence of General Figueroa; and shall not the 'Excelentisima Diputacion' express how much it participates in this sorrow? I see in the worthy members of which it is composed, unequivocal proof of the pain caused by the premature death of our beloved chief. This sorrow is just; yes, it is just, it is laudable. Know all the world, and see, that in 'Alta California,' true merit is appreciated. And now, that we have at the foot of the altar, whilst adoring the inscrutable dispensations of the Almighty, implored his divine clemency for the man of whom his omnipotency has deprived us; and now that we have contributed all the political and military funeral honors due to his rank, let us give ('benemeritos Diputados') a public and eternal testimony of our gratitude and love for General Figueroa; let us perpetuate his memory, and let us give to his obsequies all respect and honor. Let us immortalize his glory and our gratitude, and encircle his brow with a crown of 'siempre viva.' Yes,—most excellent sir, listen, and please approve of the following propositions, or resolutions.

"1st. The portrait of General D. José Figueroa shall be collocated in the Hall of Sessions of this 'Excelentisima Diputacion,' in proof of the esteem they bear for his distinguished merit.

"2d. To perpetuate his memory, and the gratitude of this Corporation, a durable monument shall be erected, with an appropriate inscription, in one of the most public unoccupied sites in the capital; and to fulfil which, the 'Ilustre Ayuntamiento' shall be authorized to have its sole direction and care.

"3d. Three copies of these proceedings shall be drawn. One shall be delivered to the executors of our beloved deceased General and Chief, another copy transmitted to his widow and children, and the third shall be passed to the printer, that it may be annexed to the 'manifesto' of said General, which is now in course of publication. Monterey, 9th of October, 1835.

"Juan B. Alvarado."

These resolutions were adopted, and were followed by two others, offered by the Secretary.

"1st. That the three resolutions of Señor Alvarado shall be put into execution immediately.

"2d. That at the bottom of the portrait of Señor General D. José Figueroa, shall be affixed the title of 'Bienhechor del territorio de la Alta California.' Monterey, Oct. 14, 1935.

"Manuel Jimeno."

The foregoing document was placed before the "Ilustre Ayuntamiento," who contemplated placing upon the monument the following inscription:

THE PROVINCIAL DEPUTATION
AND THE "AYUNTAMIENTO" OF MONTEREY,
AT PUBLIC COST,
IN PROOF OF GRATITUDE,
DEDICATE THIS MONUMENT
TO THE ETERNAL MEMORY OF

GENERAL D. JOSE FIGUEROA,

MILITARY AND POLITICAL CHIEF
OF ALTA CALIFORNIA;
THE FATHER OF THE COUNTRY,
WHO DIED IN THIS CAPITAL,
THE 29TH OF SEPTEMBER, A.D. 1835,
AGED 43 YEARS.

Days! months!! years!!! have rolled away, and yet naught has been done to perpetuate the memory of the exalted man! the country's loss! This serves to show a want of sincerity in those *who most deeply deplored his death*, and the instability of their character.

The remains of his Excellency were finally embarked in the American brig "Avon," and carried to St. Barbara, where they were deposited in the vaults under the Mission church. During their conveyance from the vessel to the shore minute guns were fired, and a large procession followed to their interment.

By testament of Figueroa, Don Nicolas Gutierez succeeded to the command, soon after his arrival from St. Gabriel, where he had been charged with the temporal care of that mission. But it was for a short period. A few months afterwards a vessel arrived at Santa Barbara with a new Governor named "Chico," who disembarked immediately, and proceeded by land to the capital.

Prejudiced against many of the Californians, and violently incensed at the foreign residents, Chico commenced a tyranny that soon brought him into disgrace; and finally ended in his expulsion from the territory. Gutierez assumed the command once more, and things went on quietly till a disturbance broke out between him and the officers of the Custom-House Department.

The "Administrador" of the Customs at this period was D. Angel Ramirez, a Mexican, who had formerly held a similar post at Mata-moras, and was originally a *friar of the Zacatecas Order*. The next in authority was D. Juan Bautista Alvarado, a native of California, who had figured for several years as Secretary to the "Diputacion," and had been considered one of the bright luminaries of this lovely hemisphere. His early education commenced (as did that of most of the young men in California) under the patronage and tuition of one of the holy Missionaries. Possessed of good natural talents, he was quick to learn; so that from frequent intercourse with the foreign residents of the country, he had acquired considerable of the English language. This gave him access to their amusements and convivialities, and prepared for him that support which he subsequently received. It was with D. Juan that Gutierez quarreled, in consequence of some necessary etiquette that should have passed between them relative to the placing of guards at the landing-places. A violent dispute took place, with some high-sounding threats, which ended in an order from Gutierez for his arrest. But escaping from the town, he flew to the protection of his friends.

There were many Englishmen and Americans living in the suburbs of Monterey; and on the route to St. Francisco, at a place called "Natividad," there dwelt a bold Tennessean, whose name was Graham. He had pioneered his way across the Rocky Mountains, in company with several others, who, like him, preferred the hunter's fare to a life of ease and comfort in their own country. Finding in Upper California a climate suited to his taste, he had located himself there, and erected a rude dwelling, where he followed the distilling of spirit from grain. Here, at this rude hut, our hero, D. Juan, stopped and told his story; explained his plan of revenge, and begged the influence and aid of the

109

Tennessean. His pleadings were not in vain. "Go you," said Graham, "go you, and gather together your friends in the north, and I will call around me here, a force that will make the old devil of a Mexican tremble." In a few days a force of fifty riflemen, headed by *Captain* Graham, and one hundred Californians under command of *Don José Castro,* were encamped near a wood in the rear of the capital. Here a consultation was held by the officers, and an agreement entered into between Graham and Alvarado, that in case of success against the Mexican governor, and obtaining possession of the country, it should be declared independent of Mexico.

The combined forces entered the capital under cover of night, and took possession of its fort without firing a single shot. Gutierez was shut up in the *Presidio,* with his soldiers, who numbered double those of his enemies. When morning came, parleying commenced, and continued some time, without any advantageous result to either party, till, at length, a brass four-pounder levelled at the house of Gutierez, sent a ball through its roof, which brought him to immediate terms. The Mexican troops laid down their arms; then, Alvarado and Castro, at the head of their valiant party, marched triumphantly to the "Plaza."

Señor Alvarado, by unanimous consent, was placed at the head of the government, and Señor Guadaloupe Vallejo was called upon to take the military command. On the 7th of November, 1836, the following resolutions were proclaimed to the inhabitants of Monterey. 1st. "Upper California is declared to be independent of Mexico, during the non-re-establishment of the Federal system, which was adopted in the year 1824. 2d. The said California shall be erected into a free and governing state; establishing a Congress, which shall dictate all the particular laws of the country, and elect the other supreme powers necessary; declaring the actual 'Most Excellent Deputation' constituent. 3d. The Religion shall be the Roman Catholic Apostolic, without admitting the exercise of any other; but the government will not molest any persons for their particular religious opinions. 4th. A constitution shall regulate all branches of the administration, 'provisionally,' in conformity, as much as possible, with the expressed declaration. 5th. Until what is contained in the foregoing articles shall be put in execution, 'Señor Don Mariano Guadaloupe Vallejo' shall be called upon to act as Commandant-General. 6th. The President of the 'Most Excellent Deputation' shall pass the necessary communications to the municipalities of the territory."

The expulsion of Gutierez, his officers and troops, together with other Mexicans, followed these proceedings. Undoubtedly the principal actors, in the formation of this new constitution, were the ex-Friar Don Angel Ramirez and Don Cosme Peña, a Mexican lawyer. It was reported, at the time, that a flag had been prepared for the *new Republic*, and deposited in the house of the former. It was the Texian—the Lone Star! They never made use of it, however, but continued to administer their government under the Mexican banner.

Several Mexican vessels lying at anchor, in the harbor of Monterey, were taken possession of, by the Californians, but were subsequently released, and permitted to depart. One of them proceeded, immediately, to St. Blas with the important intelligence, which was communicated, forthwith, to the Mexican government. Furious proclamations against these daring rebels were issued, and an appeal was made to the citizens, for their patriotic assistance, to crush, with one mighty blow, such audacious presumption. A formidable expedition was to proceed to California, but, after a while, the excitement subsided, and the Californians were permitted to govern themselves. This being (in the opinion of the Mexicans) the best method of chastisement.

However, as yet, Alvarado was uninformed of the views entertained by his countrymen at the south; and, consequently ignorant of the effect produced by his proclamation. He accordingly despatched José Castro to St. Barbara, whom he empowered to treat with its inhabitants. The fifty riflemen, with the Tennessean at their head, accompanied the Plenipotentiary, and they were quite sufficient to pioneer the way for Alvarado, who soon followed, and took up his quarters at the Mission.

Chapter XI

LIKE THEIR ILLUSTRIOUS PREDECESSORS, THE Californians seemed to think that the Missions were their own, to make use of as necessity required. So, like true professors of *Echeandia's policy,* they plundered, and permitted plunder. Such a depraved system was not likely to succeed long; enemies were created from envy, and soon began to appear. In the "Pueblo de los Angeles" a party was formed which avowed adherence to Mexico. This was followed by an express from Mexico, with documents, constituting and appointing D. Carlos Carrillo, "Governador de la Alta California."

Don Carlos, incited by a few friends, declared war against his nephew Alvarado, which was unsuccessful. He, and his advisers, were taken prisoners. The latter were sent to the Presidio of Sonoma, on the north side of St. Francisco; while the former was confined in his house at St. Barbara.

Our hero, Alvarado, having so unceremoniously disposed of his uncle, Carrillo, prepared an account of his proceedings, for the Mexican government. A messenger was despatched to St. Blas, who promptly returned, with their entire approval of Alvarado's conduct. But it was necessary to appease the vanquished party, and Carrillo was presented with the island of St. Rosa, as a testimonial of the government's high regard. The central government was now recognised; Castro was appointed Prefect of the northern district, and Cosme Peña of the southern. Thus, Upper California formed two districts, each representing a state government, subject to the jurisdiction of the supreme power at Monterey. A new "Diputado" to the Mexican Congress was elected, and matters went on quietly, whilst the "Presidios," at the different places, were suffered to fall to ruin. At St. Diego, the officer in command was permitted to unroof the houses and the church, and dispose of the tiles to meet demands, which he had against the government. The forts were neglected, and Alvarado cared little for the safety of any other place but the one where he was located.

Thus, firmly established in power, the governor felt more sensibly the dignity of his situation, and wished to put an end to the freedom with which his rude foreign friends were wont to treat him. He became more reserved; he was ever "not at home" to their calls, and avoided them at all times. Such ingratitude was not to be borne by the Tennessean! No! He boldly told him to his teeth, that to *him* he owed his elevation. Every day his disgust increased for "los malditos estrangeros," and an opportunity to rid himself of their importunities and threats, soon offered.

Graham had a fine horse, which he had trained for the turf, and had challenged the whole country to the course. At length, a countryman of his, residing in the "Pueblo de los Angeles," made arrangements to run the noble gelding, with a high-mettled racer from St. Diego. A document was drawn up on the occasion, which was intended, solely, to bind more strictly the parties interested. This document was construed into a plan for overturning the government—a plan to plunder, and destroy, what was left of the Missions—a plan to deprive the Californians of their lives and country. As ridiculous as this may appear to the reader, nevertheless, it is a fact, to which I can testify, from information I received on the spot, shortly after its occurrence. This intelligence was secretly conveyed to all the authorities throughout the country, with explicit orders from Governor Alvarado, to secure and imprison the foreigners. But to take the Tennessean, it was thought requisite to send an armed force, under the command of the renowned José Castro! The manner, in which they managed to get possession of his person, has been already stated in other publications. Suffice it to say, our countryman was asleep in his rude dwelling, when the report of a pistol awakened him, and he sprang quickly towards the door. Several villains discharged other pistols at him, so near as to fire his shirt in many places. He attempted to escape, but was seized, and dragged to prison.

113

As soon as practicable on the part of the government, a vessel was chartered, and the Americans and Englishmen who had been collected at the different points, were embarked in chains, and sent to St. Blas.

This achievement was followed by a public expression of thanks to the Omnipotent power, who thus saved California from destruction. Mass was performed, and at its conclusion the following bombastic proclamation was distributed.

JUAN BAUTISTA ALVARADO,
GOVERNADOR CONSTITUCIONAL
DEL DEPARTAMENTO DE LAS CALIFORNIAS,
TO ITS INHABITANTS

"Fellow-citizens! a sordid and mercenary faction, incited by some ungrateful foreigners, whom you had received to your hospitable land, purposed to deprive you of the richest of treasures, your lives and country; and sacrifice to their ungovernable desires the highest authorities. 'El Govierno Departamental,' with the assistance of its subalterns, and the honorable military garrison, was enabled to smother the conspiracy at its commencement. The necessary proceedings were taken, but for want of a competent tribunal, the villains were sent to the Supreme Government, together with the leaders of the faction, and a multitude of other foreigners, who were illegally introduced into the country, and who had no other object here but the increase of public disorder. They were deserters from merchant vessels, and vessels of war, who were secretly hidden in the 'ranchos' and woods, and against them we have proceeded, according to the powers conceded to the government by article 12th of the law of the 1st May, 1828.

"Fellow-citizens! I can assure you that the country has been saved from imminent danger; for which I ought to congratulate you, recommending to your generosity and friendship those who ought to be considered as Mexicans, and who reside in the country under the protection of its laws; manifesting by this, your natural inclination to order, and the hospitality with which you have always received strangers. And rest assured that the government will use every means in its power to insure the peace of this precious portion of the nation, relying upon your constant and pure patriotism, in which your fellow-citizen will ever join with you.

"Juan Bautista Alvarado."

This important event took place in April, 1840. Had the Californians been wise enough to have examined into the charges, and chastised where chastisement was due, the affair would have ended where it commenced; but, erring, as they always did, when meddling with foreign interests, they were sure to be on the wrong side.

What must have been their surprise, when one day, towards the last of June, a French ship of war entered their port, and anchored close to the beach, so as to bring her guns to bear directly upon the town! What must have been their terror when immediately afterwards came another ship, bearing at her peak the broad stripes of our country! "I come for vengeance," said the first, "why have you killed a Frenchman?" "I come for justice," said the other, "what have you been doing with my countrymen?" Alvarado was now fallen indeed! His valiant Castro had gone to Mexico with the prisoners, and Vallejo was more than two hundred miles off. Resistance was impossible, and retreat to a neighboring mission, by feigning a disturbance amongst the Indians there, was hit upon as being the most plausible method of getting out of an awkward dilemma. So, one morning early, he very unceremoniously departed. This was the *satisfaction* given to our captain of the St. Louis!

After the ships of war had sailed, the Governor came back, when I called upon him to arrange some affairs of my own; for I had just returned to California after an absence of two years. We had some conversation respecting the expulsion of the foreigners, their reported conspiracy, the arrival of the St. Louis, and also, respecting the officer who had been left on shore by her commander, to look after the interests of the American residents.

Señor Alvarado firmly believed in the intention of Graham to revolutionize the country, although possessed of no facts to prove it. "I was insulted," he said, "at every turn, by the drunken followers of Graham; and when walking in the garden they would come to its wall, and call upon me in terms of the greatest familiarity: 'Ho! Bautista, come here, I want to speak to you.'—'Bautista, here.'—'Bautista, there'—and Bautista every where." No doubt the Governor had reason to be dissatisfied; but I really believe that there were others more to be blamed than Alvarado, for the outrage committed upon our countrymen. "Mexico was responsible for his conduct," he said, "and if he had erred—why, *Mexico* must suffer the consequences!" He observed, that he could not receive the officer, who had been landed from the St. Louis, as a diplomatic character, but would give him all the protection and hospitality due to a worthy citizen of the United States.

Affairs continued under the control of *Juan Bautista*, without any important occurrence, excepting a breach which occurred between him and Vallejo, who had retired to his place of residence at Sonoma.

At this period of events, I embarked on board of the ship Alert, and again visited St. Diego. Here everything was prostrated—the Presidio ruined—the Mission depopulated—the town almost deserted, and its few inhabitants miserably poor. It had changed! From being once the life of, and most important place in California, it had now become the gloomiest and most desolate. With great difficulty I succeeded in procuring horses to return north, by land, and in doing which the person with whom I contracted compelled me to pay an enormous compensation. For a distance which I had often performed, during the flourishing state of the missionary establishments, at an expense of five or six dollars, I had now to pay forty! So much for secularization! so much for the Californian Government! I started in company with friend M——. We arrived at the Mission of St. Luis Rey early, and partook of the hospitality of Don José Antonio Estudillo, who had been recently appointed Administrador of the Institution. His daughters had grown up to be young ladies, and were said to be engaged to two European Spaniards. After passing the night with Don José Antonio, we continued on, next morning, passing St. Juan in our route, and, at an advanced hour of the day, halted for refreshment. Whilst doing so, a guide who had accompanied us through the journey, cautioned us to be careful of our horses, but the warning had scarcely escaped his lips when off they started, in different directions, at a rapid rate. Fortunately, one stopped, upon which he (the guide) mounted in pursuit. Night came on, and four hours elapsed ere he returned, bringing with him one of the extra horses, and the one on which I had performed the journey. His own horse, to which was affixed our portmaneau, with two others, were missing. It being then eight o'clock at night, we resumed our journey, upon the worn-out animals, trotted over an extensive plain, where, at times, the wind came in gusts from the mountains, and reached "El Rancho de Santa Ana" almost dead from fatigue. As we alighted at the house, a dolt of a fellow accosted us, and said we could not be admitted, for "Alli estan las mugeres,"—"The women are there," so we were obliged to put up with a coarse kind of bed, outside the house, in the corridor. Tired, we soon fell asleep, and did not awake till late next morning. Continuing our journey for the Pueblo, we stopped at the house of Tomas Yorba; again, at "El Rancho Nietos," and arrived early at the town.

We took up our quarters with Mr. A. S—, who came from Mexico in 1829 with Señor Noriega, and was now a merchant, doing an extensive business with the "Pueblanos." Having failed in his project of colonization, he had resorted to this mode of obtaining a livelihood, and, in so doing, had amassed a handsome property. His house, the handsomest in the town, was a place of resort for the Americans who occasionally visited "los Angeles"; which, in consequence of its dimensions, was called by the natives "el Palacio de Don Abel." Being a warm politician, something of a surveyor, and a physician, they looked upon him as *the* man of the village; seeking for him to officiate in either capacity, as occasion required. He had been elected to the honorable dignity of "Syndico" to the "Ylustre Ayuntamiento," and had been lauded for the zeal with which he discharged the duties of his office; but no higher public occupation, I believe, had ever fallen to his lot.

Leaving the Pueblo, we proceeded towards St. Pedro, where we embarked, and sailed for Monterey. While sojourning here, in July, 1842, the Mexican schooner Columbine came into port from St. Blas, and anchored. The Custom-House barge put off, to pay the usual visit. Rumors were circulated that her deck was crammed with men. Some thought they were Mexican troops. Some said they were "presidarios,"— and some, (jokingly) that they were Graham's party. In the meantime the boat returned, and the truth was ascertained. Graham and his party *had* returned. The indefatigable Tennessean had achieved an honorable conveyance back, and was enabled to face again the author of his disgrace. What were the feelings of Alvarado? He would have prevented their landing, but dared not interfere with a determination of the supreme power, when backed, or rather enforced, by English and American influence. They came on shore, dressed neatly, armed with rifles and swords, and looking in infinitely better condition than when they departed; thanks to the energetic measures of the British consul! His prompt interference and authoritative manner procured their immediate release in Tepic, and the imprisonment of their Californian guard; thus turning the tables completely upon the Californians. The Mexican government was obliged to maintain them, during their detention in Mexico, and finally chartered a vessel to carry them back. Castro's conduct underwent a strict investigation, and it is said that it would have gone hard with him, if he had not managed to escape through the connivance of his government. The foreigners, thus restored to their former residences, were permitted to resume their various occupations.

My friends H— and S— had dissolved their business connexion; and whilst the latter continued in the same line of employment, with the additional responsibility of "Alcalde Constitucional" of the place; the former had retired to one of the loveliest of spots, called "El Alisal," to educate young men for a business or professional life.

I had an opportunity one day to witness the wisdom of S—'s judicial proceedings. A "Ranchero" who had visited one of the American trading ships, saw among many things that were to be seen in the trade-room, a trunk, to which he took an extraordinary fancy. Its price was asked of the supercargo, and a bargain was struck between the two. The trunk could not, however, be delivered, till emptied of its contents; and the "ranchero" consented to await the ship's return from San Francisco, ere he received it. The vessel sailed, and in a few weeks returned to Monterey. Among the first who went on board was the "ranchero," demanding his trunk. It was shown to him, but he denied its being the one for which he bargained; he must either have *that* one or the money, which (without the knowledge of the supercargo) he had given to a *friend* who was on board at the time he made the bargain, and who had requested that the trunk might be charged in his account. A violent dispute ensued, till, at length, the supercargo, worn out and irritated beyond measure, requested a boat from the first officer, and then told the "ranchero" if he did not walk into it quickly he would have to *swim*, for the mate would throw him overboard. This induced him to retreat; but he went off uttering threats and curses against the "maldito Ingles." Arriving on shore, he repaired immediately to the "Juzgado," and laid his complaint before the "Alcalde." On the following morning the super-cargo was summoned to appear forthwith, to answer to a charge of fraud. Repairing to the place of justice, he listened to the story of his accuser, and then explained to the "Alcalde" the circumstances as they occurred. The cause was argued by the parties interested, as is invariably the case in California, and it rested upon the "Alcalde's" decision, which was a delicate point; the defendant being a foreigner, like himself, and the accuser a Californian. If he should decide in favor of the supercargo, it would be partiality; if in favor of the *ranchero,* injustice. Therefore, the following judicious decision was passed. The supercargo was com-pelled to take an order upon the person who received the money, to col-lect the same, if possible, and remit it to the "Ilustre Ayuntamiento" on account of the individual interested. The Californian appeared well sat-isfied in his own mind that he had gained his point; and the supercargo had no objection, on the other hand, to oblige his friend the "Alcalde."

During this visit to Monterey, I accompanied H— to his "Alisal," which is a romantic spot, in a valley, between large hills covered with trees. In the centre, a fine stream winds its way towards an extensive plain, and supplies the "Lagunas," where the cattle resort to drink. There are fine gardens, and plenty of good ground for cultivation. The soil, on the highlands, has the appearance of possessing mineral quali-ties, and, a short distance from the house, may be seen an excavation, from which considerable quantities of silver ore had been obtained. It was the *first* mine discovered in California. Others were subsequently found at different points in the country, and at one time the mania for mining was so great, that every old woman had her specimens of what she called ore. Finally, a rich mine of "placer" gold was, by chance, dis-covered, near the Mission of San Fernando. It extends for several leagues through a valley. Some of its gold has already found its way to the United States, and quantities have been carried to Mexico.

While passing the night at "El Alisal," I was suddenly awakened by a sound, resembling the report of heavy artillery, accompanied by the jarring of the house. Women screamed, children cried, and, as I groped through the dark, towards the door, I heard the cry, "Temblor!" Some were for throwing themselves from the windows, others leaped down the stairway; and for a few minutes we had one of the most confused scenes imaginable. The fright subsiding, H— stopped at my room, in his search for damage, and said the walls beneath were badly rent; that this was the twenty-fifth shock they had experienced within the last two months. One day, they had five successive shocks, which made the whole building tremble violently. Frequent as these occurrences are, they are confined to this spot alone; their cause, I presume, may be attributed to the existence of mineral formations in the earth.

A "rodeo" was held on the following day, when all the neighboring "rancheros," as usual, were invited to attend. It was for the purpose of branding and marking the cattle belonging to H—, who, for his family's amusement, had erected a platform near the scene of action, that they might better witness the proceedings. This operation is performed once every year, by all holders of cattle, and is conducted as follows. After collecting the animals from the different points of the farm, into one body, a portion of them are driven into a "coral," where they are branded with the mark of the owner, and the operation of castration is performed on the calves. This being completed, they are let out and driven off, others taking their places; and thus, the process continues until all have passed the inspection of the operators. This sometimes occupies several days, and, while it continues, the young men have an excellent opportunity of displaying their skill in horsemanship.

Returning to Monterey, I took passage on board of a Mexican vessel, and proceeded to Santa Barbara. Here I received intelligence of the arrival of Castro, from Mexico, and of his having been suddenly taken ill on the road, which undoubtedly proceeded from the excitement, caused by intelligence having been given to him, that Graham and his followers had preceded him, and were actually in the country. Being enabled, however, in a few days to resume his journey, the "Coronel," as he was now styled, made his grand entrance into the town. No guns were fired on the occasion, nor was there any martial display of troops; but a few of his dearest friends went forth to meet him. The "Comandante" of the place, was one who had worn himself grey in service, and had served under royal authority, before Castro was born; yet, because he was a "gachupin," he was obliged to be contented with the rank of Captain, whilst others, who were once boys under his tuition, were denominated "Coronels" and Generals. Rumor had preceded Castro, of his having escaped from the authorities of Mexico; to ascertain the truth of which, the "Comandante" sent an officer to demand his passport. The requisition was contested in a message full of insult. This, the old veteran could not brook, but sat himself down, and wrote a communication to the "valiant Coronel," which soon brought him to his presence. He had no passport with him. He said "it had been carelessly left in his trunk, supposing that no one would demand it; however, as soon as the trunk came to hand, he would send him the document for inspection." This was satisfactory, and he departed.

Business called me to the *"Rancho del Refugio,"* where the ship A— had been despatched to be laden with hides and tallow; and, having witnessed almost their entire embarkation, I returned. On the morning of the following day, which was Sunday, the ship was in sight, but at a long distance from the shore. I went to church, and on my return homeward, she having approached nearer, I observed her colors were hoisted at half-mast. My first conjecture was, that some one had been lost overboard, or had been drowned in embarking the hides at the "Refugio." The ship came to, however, and the colors were run up to their proper place. Presuming the position of the flag was accidental, I thought no more of it, until Captain P— came on shore, and informed me of the melancholy loss of one of the boys. The poor fellow had gone in to bathe, and after wading up to his middle, had thrown himself forward to swim; not being aware of the powerful under-current, he was speedily taken outside the surf, beyond his depth, and drowned. The captain was employed all the afternoon in searching for his body; but not succeeding in finding it, he offered a reward to several natives who had arrived at the beach, to continue the search, and if they found it, to take it to the town. About mid-day a person came to the house of the "Comandante," with the body rolled up in blankets and mats, and thrown across a cargo mule. From thence it was taken on board the ship. The carpenter prepared a coffin, and the next day was appointed for the funeral.

At 10 o'clock a gun was fired from the ship, the colors were all hoisted at half-mast, and the coffin was gently lowered into one of the boats,

121

which was manned by young lads, who pulled for the shore. Another boat followed with the greater portion of the crew. Arriving at the beach, the coffin, shrouded by the American ensign, was transferred to a bier, and borne along slowly by the boys towards the grave. The men followed in the rear, as also the captain and supercargo, with many of the foreign residents.

Thus we slowly proceeded through the centre of the town, till we reached the place of burial, which was a short distance in the rear, and adjoining an enclosure where were deposited the remains of Mr. Hardy Pierce, of Massachusetts. The usual funeral prayers were read by the captain, and at their conclusion poor Lowell was committed to his narrow bed—the grave—in a foreign land, and thousands of miles from his mother, brothers and sisters. As the earth fell upon his remains, we, one by one, retired from the scene, deeply impressed with the importance of being fully prepared, ourselves, for a like sudden dispensation of the Almighty.

For a great length of time the Californians had been in anxious expectation of the coming of a bishop, who had been appointed for their diocese by his holiness, the Pope. At length a courier arrived from St. Diego, on the 16th of December, 1841, announcing the fact of his having disembarked at that place. He came passenger on board of an English brig from San Blas, accompanied by several priests, two schoolmasters, three schoolmistresses, and four novitiates. The news was received with the most enthusiastic expressions of joy by the inhabitants of Santa Barbara; guns were fired, and sky-rockets let off in every direction. At the Mission the bells rang a merry peal, and the music of the band was heard at intervals, as its harmonious sounds floated through the air.

Several days subsequent to this demonstration of joy, we had an exhibition of the "Pastores," by the *Indians* of the Mission. They had been practising for some time, under the direction of Pádre Antonio Jimeno, and a great triumph was therefore anticipated over the performances of the *"gente de razon."** This exhibition took place on Sunday afternoon, in the courtyard of Señor Noriega, where four or five hundred persons were collected, to enjoy the amusement. Their performances were pronounced excellent, and I think they far surpassed

122

*The white people.

those of the whites, which I had witnessed some years previous, at St. Diego. At the conclusion of the "Pastores," a celebrated juggler came forward, and amused us a half hour longer, with some expert, and wonderful tricks of legerdemain.

The schooner Leonidas arrived, from St. Diego, with intelligence of the Bishops' intended embarkation at that place, in the barque Guipuzcoana. Her owner, Don José Antonio Aguirre, had lately married there, the daughter of Señor Estudillo, and designed bringing his wife to Santa Barbara, where he had been preparing for some time previous, a suitable residence. The venerable Bishop, and his retinue, had been invited to accompany the bridal party, and it was too good an opportunity for him to accomplish the remainder of his journey, to admit of a refusal. Great preparations were made, upon hearing this news, and all were anxious for the Bishop's arrival; for he was a functionary that but very few in California had ever beheld.

The vessel was in sight on the morning of the 11th of January, 1842, but lay becalmed and rolling to the ocean's swell. A boat put off from her side, and approached the landing-place. One of the attendants of his Excellency, who came in it, repaired to the Mission, to communicate with the Father President. All was bustle; men, women, and children hastening to the beach, banners flying, drums beating, and soldiers marching. The whole population of the place turned out, to pay homage to this first Bishop of California. At eleven o'clock the vessel anchored. He came on shore, and was welcomed by the kneeling multitude. All received his benediction—all kissed the pontifical ring. The troops, and civic authorities, then escorted him to the house of Don José Antonio, where he dined. A carriage had been prepared for his Excellency, which was accompanied by several others, occupied by the President and his friends. The females had formed, with ornamented canes, beautiful arches, through which the procession passed; and as it marched along, the heavy artillery of the "Presidio" continued to thunder forth its noisy welcome. At the time he left the barque she was enveloped in smoke, and the distant report of her guns, was heard echoing among the hills in our rear.

The bride, with her mother and her sisters, remained on board till afternoon, when they, also, repaired to the festive scene.

123

At four o'clock, the Bishop was escorted to the Mission, and when a short distance from the town, the enthusiastic inhabitants took the horses from his carriage, and dragged it themselves. Halting at a small bower, on the road, he alighted, went into it, and put on his pontifical robes; then resuming his place in the carriage, he continued on, amidst the sound of music and the firing of guns, till he arrived at the church, where he addressed the multitude that followed him.

The Reverend Bishop Francisco Garcia Diego, is a Mexican, and a Friar of the Franciscan order. He had been a teacher of theology in Mexico, and afterwards, in 1833, was "Comisario Prefecto" of the Missions of Upper California. Having passed several years in the country, he knew well how to work upon the minds of the Californians, in order to win their esteem, and to make himself popular. Santa Barbara was selected to be the "Episcopal See"; and plans were drawn up for the erection of his Palace, a Cathedral, a Monastery, and a Theological School. The inhabitants were called upon to unite in forwarding these plans, and the Bishop trusted for resources to the "Fonda Piadosa de California," "Pious fund of California," in Mexico, for their accomplishment. Large piles of stones were heaped up, in several places, for laying the foundations of the above-named edifices; but, as the Mexican government have seen proper to appropriate this fund to less pious purposes, there they will undoubtedly remain, for some years, as monuments of the frailty of human speculations.

About this time, on the arrival of the Hudson Bay Company's barque "Cowlitz," we were visited by Sir George S——, Governor McL——, and others, who were passengers on board. They came to California for the purpose of obtaining information relative to the character of the country, and making arrangements for the transportation of horned cattle to Oregon. An agent had been left at San Francisco, where they had previously touched, to accomplish the scheme, and at Monterey they had arranged with Alvarado for the delivery of the cattle at the northern missions. Thus large quantities of sheep and bullocks were driven to the Columbia. This served to establish the fact of the facility of communication between the two countries. The agency has been continued at San Francisco, and at one time it was said that the company intended to monopolize the trade on the coast, and put an end to all competition,

124

as it had done at the north. Their establishing a commercial dépôt at this particular point, San Francisco, might suggest to the minds of some persons that it was intended for an introduction to further acquisitions. However, that is no business of mine. The country would prosper under their jurisdiction, as it undoubtedly must, if it should ever come under our own. Whatever may be its fate, it can never be in worse hands than the present.

Chapter XII

WHILE PREPARING FOR A TRIP TO SAN DIEGO, and about to leave, I received an invitation to participate in a "merienda," which was to be given by Doña Maria Antonio N—. As strangers who visit Santa Barbara are often entertained in this way, a description of this may be interesting.

Early on the day appointed, I found all busily employed in preparing for the entertainment, and that several ox-carts laden with children, and servant girls were about to start off. The company were to assemble at the house of Don Anastasio C—, a brother of Doña Maria Antonia. All having arrived there, and the necessary arrangements being concluded, at the word of command our Gañanes or drivers stuck the points of their long poles into the sides of the oxen, and the procession started for the "Laguna blanca," the place selected for the scene of our diversion.

The cart of Doña Maria Antonia took the lead, drawn by two stout oxen. It contained, besides herself, her daughter, daughter-in-law, grand-daughter, and Doña Concepcion, her sister; leaving just sufficient room for me to squeeze in between the latter and Doña Maria Antonia, with my legs dangling out behind. The cart was well made, arched over, and covered with bleached cotton, like many of our wagons at home. The next, in succession, was a cart containing the children with their respective Indian attendants to guard them from accident. This was lined inside with hides, which made a secure, as well as comfortable conveyance. After this followed another, filled with the families of Joaquin and Raymundo Carrillo, and still another, the fourth, the wheels of which squeaked under the immense weight of roast turkeys, chickens, beef, mutton, *tamales, dulces,* etc. The rear was closed by about fifteen or twenty persons on horseback.

After a slow but pleasant ride of one hour we arrived at the spot selected for our encampment, "la Laguna blanca," a spacious amphitheatre, and one of the most lovely places that could have been chosen for the occasion. The surrounding hills were plentifully covered with small oak trees, and the grass around was beautifully enriched with flowers. In the centre of the area was a circular pond, bearing the name already stated, which had been increased by recent rains to a circumference unusual, excepting at this season of the year. During the preparations for dinner I took my rifle and strolled into the woods in quest of game; succeeding in killing some quails, I returned just in time to take part in the feast.

A large white table-cloth was spread on the grass, upon which were tastefully arranged our different dishes of meats, pastry, fruits, and sweetmeats; and around these we accommodated ourselves, some reclining, others seated upon the ground. At the conclusion of the dinner the boys amused us with a "toro" or bull, which they had brought from a neighboring farm; but he soon managed to escape, and made his way to the centre of the pond, where he remained quite secure from their torments. Being foiled in this amusement they commenced racing their horses, and gave us a good specimen of their superior skill in riding. While they continued these diversions, others of the party were scattered about in little groups, where the music of the guitar and singing seemed more attractive.

At evening we returned to the Presidio, in the same order in which we left it; each one well satisfied with the day's amusement.

Leaving Santa Barbara I sailed to one of the southern ports. Several new farms are established in the interior of the country, upon grounds which were formerly a part of the possessions of St. Gabriel. These I had long desired to see. They are located in the neighborhood of the river Santa Anna, and between the mission and the large establishmnt at San Bernadino. So, having made arrangements for horses, I started in company with my friend M——, and we shaped our course for the "rancho" of Don Tomas Yorba. On our way we stopped at the farm-house of Juan B. Leandry, who was alone, his family being absent at a wedding feast at the Pueblo. Leandry had been but two years a "ranch-ero," and now possessed a stock of about six thousand bullocks, besides horses, sheep, and all the necessary appendages to constitute a farm of first rate character. A vineyard occupies a large space on the left of the house, from which he anticipated the pleasure of one day remitting a cargo of wines to the United States. Should he continue his inde-fatigable labors, he will have one of the richest "haciendas" in the country. He gave us dinner, after which we resumed our saddles, and soon reached Santa Anna. Not finding Don Tomas at home, we con-tinued through a pass in the mountains, along the banks of a river; and at sunset entered upon the plains of the "Rancho de San Juan del Rio," the dwelling place of Señor Bandini. We found our friend Yorba here, and the first expression of Bandini, as he took us by the hand, was "Cuanto hay de bueno por aqui!" "How much good we have here!" Soon after supper we retired to rest, and fell into a deep slumber which lasted till seven o'clock next morning, when a gentle tap was heard at the door, and in popped our agreeable friend Bandini. Having asked how we had passed the night, he quaintly told us that our horses were missing, and that we should have to remain and pass the day in "San Juan del Rio!"

After partaking of a hospitable breakfast, we went to a "rodeo" at the farm of one of the largest cattle holders in the country. Having rode a short distance, we saw large clouds of dust rising in that direction, and soon afterwards, cattle were distinctly perceived, gathered in a large body of between five and six thousand. The proprietor, Don Antonio Maria Lugo, now possessing from twelve to fourteen thousand bullocks, was once a common soldier in the army. At the time of his retirement from the service, he was presented, by a friend, with two or three cows, which by carful management have made him the richest farmer in California. With all his wealth, he lives miserably poor, depriving him-

A. ROBINSON DEL.

LITH OF G. & W. ENDICOTT

A VIEW OF THE MISSION OF SANTA BARBARA .

self of the comforts of life, yet he thinks nothing of squandering thousands upon others. Although advanced in years, he has lately married a young and pretty girl, who takes pleasure in entertaining the visitors of her husband.

As we returned, we visited the planting grounds of Bandini, which were beautifully laid out, on the side of the river.

On our route back to the Pueblo, we passed through a long valley, which was the scene of destruction during the slaughter of the Mission cattle in 1835. Its devastation was still visible, for skulls and bones were lying about in every direction.

At the farmhouse of Isaac W— we stopped awhile to rest our horses. It is the most spacious building of the kind in the country and possesses all desirable conveniences. Soon after leaving this delightful spot, we reached the dwelling of our friend Don Abel, at "los Angeles."

An arrival at St. Pedro, from Mazatlan, brought intelligence of the coming of a new General to California, with six hundred men. This was a movement of Santa Anna, who began to fear an innovation of the foreigners on the northern confines of San Francisco. Many Americans had already made their appearance along the margin of the Sacramento, where a Swiss gentleman, named Sutter, had commenced the formation of a colony; and day after day notices were to be seen in the American papers, that parties had left, or were leaving our Western States for California.

This alone was sufficient inducement to prompt the Mexican Government to an act so important; but it had also another reason. The political Governor of California had solicited the appointment of a new General, with an additional force of one hundred men, and *Vallejo*, the General, had also requested the displacing of *Alvarado*, and the appointing of another in his place.

Now was the time for the Mexican power to seek to re-establish its authority, while disaffection lasted; and an expedition was accordingly equipped for the purpose. One day, towards the last of August, 1842, I sailed from St. Pedro, and proceeded along down the coast towards St. Diego. On the following morning, when approaching Point Loma, a small vessel was perceptibly making sail from her anchorage in the outer bay. When we entered the harbor, where she had preceded us, she had dropped anchor again, and the men were busy furling her sails. They had communicated with the shore, and as we were curious to ascertain who were on board, we immediately repaired in our boat to "Hide Park." It was a small brig, bringing the new Mexican General and his officers. This was news indeed! This was an event worthy of particular respect, and we hastened back to prepare our guns for a salute. As his Excellency landed on the beach, he received a *yankee* welcome, and that alone; for the "Dieginos" were without powder, and the guns of the fort were dismounted.

Soon afterwards I visited the town, and called upon the General. The conversation between us resulted in my learning that he was "Don Manuel Micheltorena, Comandante General y Gefe politico de la Alta California." He had been in the celebrated campaign with Santa Anna against the Texians, and was now despatched by his government to fulfil the arduous duties, which had for nearly six years so much perplexed the Californians. Three vessels were daily expected with troops, and ammunition. They had left Mazatlan in company, and might be looked for every moment.

Five days afterwards, the brig "Chato" arrived, with ninety soldiers and their families. I saw them land, and to me they presented a state of wretchedness and misery unequalled. Not one individual among them possessed a jacket or pantaloons; but naked, and like the savage Indians, they concealed their nudity with dirty, miserable blankets. The females were not much better off; for the scantiness of their mean apparel was too apparent for modest observers. They appeared like convicts; and, indeed, the greater portion of them had been charged with the crime either of murder or theft. And these were the *soldiers* sent to subdue this happy country! These were the valiant followers of a heroic General, who had fought on the battle field, where he had gained laurels for himself and country! These were to be the enforcers of justice and good government! Alas! poor California! when such are to be thy ministers, thou art indeed fallen! The remainder of the "convict army" arrived in course of time, and I had an opportunity of seeing them all, afterwards, at the Pueblo, when on their route towards Monterey, the seat of government. They mustered about three hundred and fifty men, and their General had given them, since their arrival, a neat uniform of white linen. Here, their stay was protracted, in order to drill, and prepare for service, in case of opposition from Señor Alvarado. Day after day, the place resounded with the noise of the trumpet and the drums; and a level spot, on the river's margin, was the scene of military manœuvres. At night, the gardens and vineyards were plundered, and the neighboring farms suffered greatly, from the frequency of the soldiers' visits.

During these acts of the military, and the detention of Micheltorena in "los Angeles," grand preparations were making at Santa Barbara for his reception there. A liberal subscription was raised by some of the principal inhabitants, and measures were taken accordingly.

A large enclosure was made for the exhibition of bull-fighting, and a profusion of good things was provided for a dinner and "Fandango." The day appointed, at length, came, but no General was there to participate in the festivities. The foreigners, who had contributed to the preparations, were not to be cheated out of their amusement, and some of them proposed carrying into immediate effect, the object of their subscription. They were readily joined by the Californians, and the following day was selected for the entertainment.

A bull-fight in California is far different from the brutal exhibitions of Spain and Mexico. Here, the bull is not killed, or lacerated; the object of the amusement being merely the exhibition of equestrian performances. All the young bachelors are expected to be present, which generally secures a full attendance of ladies, who stand on stages and platforms erected around the enclosure, ready to bestow their smiles and approbation on those of their choice; hence the waving of handkerchiefs and shawls is incessant.

When a bull enters, (it being customary to admit only one at a time) he usually rushes in as if ready to attack anything before him, till the shouts of the multitude, and the confused fluttering of scarfs, shawls and ribbons, disconcert the animal, and he retires to the least occupied part of the square, where he remains pawing up the earth. Presently, a horseman comes forth, with a scarlet cloak, or gaudy "serape," which he waves toward the bull; the animal rushes at the object, and the skill of the rider consists in avoiding a collision. Sometimes a dozen riders are thus in the area at once, and in the confusion, it not unfrequently happens that a horse is gored, or a rider thrown. The more valiant appear on foot; and as they nimbly escape danger, or boldly throw themselves into it, the interest is exceedingly increased. When one bull is worn out with fatigue, another is let in to take his place; and occasionally a rocket or squib is thrown to excite his fury. The boys, on horseback, await to receive the harassed creature as he is let out, to drive him off outside the town; and in his retreat he is sure to be overturned by them at least half a dozen times.

The "Fandango" followed the bull-fight; and the company showed, by their hilarity, that no regret was felt for the non-arrival of Micheltorena.

Several days afterwards, while the Mexican forces occupied the mission of San Fernando, orders, from the General, were received by the civil authorities, of Santa Barbara, directing them to prepare quarters for his officers and soldiers, who were on the eve of marching for that place. Other intelligence immediately followed this important notice of Micheltorena, which not only excited the Californians, and terrified the Mexicans, but astonished the world! This was the capture of Monterey by the American squadron, under command of Commodore Jones!

As I lay slumbering on my bed at the house of Señor Noriega, at midnight, on the 24th of October, 1842, I was suddenly aroused and alarmed, by the abrupt entrance of a person into my host's apartment, adjoining my own. It was his son, who in quick succession rattled forth the following—"Los Americanos han tomado a Monterey! Una Escuadra Americana está fondeada en el Puerto! Guerra con Mexico!" etc. "The Americans have taken Monterey! A squadron is at anchor in the port! War with Mexico!" "Wheugh! here's a go!" said I. "What is the matter? What is all this you are talking about?" "Talking about," said he, "why, we are going to cut the throats of all you Yankees!" "Look here!" he continued, (as he entered my room and handed me a copy of the proceedings drawn up at the Capital, with the Proclamation of the Commodore), "read this!" I did so, and saw the reason for such a movement. Mexico had declared an unjust war. Monterey had capitulated on the twentieth, when the Americans took possession, and hoisted the "stars and stripes."

The news soon spread abroad, and at daylight, groups were assembled at different places, discussing the affair. The Americans were elated, and some of the most wealthy of the Californians seemed not displeased that they were to have a government more stable than that under which they had been living. "Will they meddle with our farms?" "Will they interfere with our religion?" "Will they trouble us in any way?" These were the questions asked, and replied to in the negative. The large guns in the Presidio were dismounted and buried, the garrison sought the protection of Micheltorena, and the place was promptly abandoned to the Americans!

What was our surprise, when, on the day following, a courier brought the intelligence "that the war was a *mistake!*" that the town of Monterey had been restored to the Mexican authorities, and friendly salutes had passed between the fort and the shipping!

Alvarado, who was still Governor and in command at Monterey, observed at the time of capitulation, that he preferred a surrender to the Americans, to the degrading necessity of submission to the newly-arrived Mexican General, who had been sent by the Mexican government to supersede him.

Micheltorena was at a "rancho," about nine leagues to the north of the mission of San Fernando, when he received the first information of the war, and he retreated precipitately to the Pueblo. The valiant forces of this couragous Mexican General never *travelled faster!*

They halted not till sheltered in the midst of "los Angeles." This, I presume, was the *"forced march,"* which Micheltorena took to repel the invasion of Monterey! and which he afterwards mentioned in his statement of the affair to his Government.

The war being over, every thing was restored to its former quiet state. Micheltorena finally reached Monterey, and continued his administration of the Government without opposition, till the Californians were emboldened, a third time, to make a stand for independence.

Sometime during the month of November, 1844, the disaffected people of the north, headed by Vallejo, Castro and Alvarado, took possession of the mission of San Juan; where the *wisdom* of Micheltorena had induced him to place his ammunition stores, to prevent their falling into the hands of the Yankees, in the event of another invasion by sea.

A proclamation was issued by the Governor allowing eight days for the rebels to lay down their arms. Micheltorena went forth to meet them; parleying commenced, and ended in a treaty, favorable to both parties. After the expiration of a few days, each party produced a treaty that was denied by the other, and the Californians again assembled, and prepared to invade the town of Monterey. On the 6th of January, 1845, the General, with his soldiers, left the place, and was joined by Captain Sutter, and one hundred foreigners, most of them settlers on the river Sacramento; besides about seventy Indians, who had been taught the use of firearms. The whole proceeded in pursuit of Castro, who had fled to the town of "los Angeles," which is situated four hundred miles to the southward. Owing to the protracted movements of Micheltorena, who made on some days but three or four miles progress, it was forty days ere he arrived in the vicinity of the town, and consequently, the foreigners had become discouraged, and nearly all left him. This gave time for Castro to increase his numbers; which having done he returned, and met the government forces. On the 21st of February the parties came in sight, when a few shots were interchanged, which fell harmless on both sides. The day following, the cannonading again commenced, and resulted in the surrender of the Mexican General.

It was reported that four persons were killed, several wounded, and some horses shot. Castro had, with his party, about fifty foreigners from the south. At the commencement of the action, the foreigners on both sides, by agreement, retired from their several parties, and left them to fight the battle alone, which accounts for the small number killed, and the speedy victory.

Señor Pio Pico, being the oldest member of the state "Diputacion," was declared Governor, and Don José Castro was appointed "Comandante General."

Micheltorena, his officers, and soldiers, with the exception of a few, who had married in the country, were put on board of the American barque Don Quixote, and taken to San Blas.

The last accounts from Monterey were up to June 18th, 1845. Pio Pico still continued Governor of the country. It was said that another General had been appointed, who was expected from Mazatlan, with eighteen hundred men. Funds, to the amount of seventy thousand dollars, had been deposited for him with a merchant in that place; and two wealthy persons in Tepic, had bound themselves to make good the payment of the officers and troops. This may, or may not, be true. It cost the treasury more than seventy thousand dollars to place Micheltorena in St. Diego, and it will cost, at this rate, over two hundred thousand to send such a force as is now in preparation.

Since closing this work for publication, I have received further information from California, by letters, dated October 1st, 1845. A friend writes thus: "The country never was in a more disorderly, miserable condition, than at the present moment. We have no government. Pio Pico, who was nominally Governor, has been arrested and imprisoned. The people at the north, as usual, are opposed to those of the south, and will be satisfied with none other than Alvarado, for chief magistrate. Two commissioners have arrived from Mexico, to ascertain why the Mexicans were expelled. The soldiers from Mazatlan, have not arrived; but we understand that one thousand men and four vessels are preparing for the expedition."

Conclusion

THE WRITER, IN THE PRECEDING CHAPTERS, HAS given a correct and impartial account of the peculiar character of California and its inhabitants. A portion of the country, however, most interesting in its natural features, has been, perhaps, but too little dwelt upon; it is that, embracing the extensive Bay of St. Francisco, into which flow the waters from the Sacramento, San Joaquin, Jesus Maria, and other lesser streams. The surrounding country, diversified by hills and plains, is very beautiful; the soil is rich and heavily timbered; and the high mountains which rise around are thickly adorned with cedar trees. There are extensive prairies also; and large tracts of excellent tillage ground on the banks of the rivers. It is the grand region for colonization; and if peopled by our industrious backwoodsmen, who are gradually emigrating from the Western States, it must hold, in a very few years, a conspicuous station among the nations of the earth. Its locations are well adapted to purposes of agriculture, and such is its mildness of climate, that all the tropical fruits might be raised there, if cultivated. The large rivers are navigable for steamboats, for more than one hundred miles, and are well stocked with salmon and other fish. The cold, blustering winds, and disagreeable temperature of the climate, alluded to by other writers, are solely confined to the lands adjacent to the seacoast; for, a very few leagues beyond the limits of "Yerba Buena," we find a totally different atmosphere.

As the traveller proceeds south from St. Francisco, he passes through a similar description of country till beyond Monterey; when the plains become more contracted, and less fertile, till he is forced at last upon a hard sandy beach. Riding through little openings among the hills, he enters again upon wider strips of land, as the mountains retreat from the sea. In this way he may continue towards St. Diego, day after day, the face of the country varying, until it becomes barren, and cheerless.

There is a vast extent of land, however, beyond the mountains, which is but imperfectly known to the Californians. This has been repeatedly visited by foreigners, who have said much in its favor. It is unoccupied, and is the only part of California, with the exception of land north and east of San Francisco, that is attainable, for the purpose of colonization. All that portion that is within twenty or thirty miles of the seacoast, is, at present, either occupied by cattle farms, or by the much restricted possessions of the missions.

Now, that Upper California remains in its unsettled state, it opens a field for immigration, and the unfriendly feelings of its inhabitants towards Mexico, will, undoubtedly, lead them to favor other nations. *St. Francisco, then, is the point,* as also the lands around the bay, the banks of the Sacramento, and Jesus Maria. These are the best lands, and are well calculated for the raising of wheat and other grains, and for the rearing of cattle. These immense tracts of land, and the facility of water intercourse between them and the bay, by rivers and creeks, render their situation highly important.

The white population of Alta California, may be estimated at about eight thousand, and the Indian, which in 1829 amounted to over thirty thousand, will now scarcely number ten—while the former has increased, the latter has rapidly diminished. This may be owing to various causes: —The abject state to which the missionary establishments have become reduced,—the consequent partial abandonment of them,—the introduction of vice and disease,—and the Indian likewise being left to provide for his own necessities. Dependent, as he had been for years, on the care of his spiritual Father, he took no thought of the morrow, but lived on, in a state of recklessness which unfitted him for any other condition. This indifference of character led him into every kind of immorality, and he has plunged headlong into the destruction which so naturally followed.

137

Until recently, the Government has held out no encouragement whatever to immigrants. The lands on the seacoast, having been princcipally occupied by the missions, gave no room for the introduction of foreign settlers, so that but very few have obtained a footing, in California, except at places remote from the ports and harbors. To secure lands for farming purposes, it was in former years, necessary to get the written consent of the missionary under whose control they were, ere the government could give legitimate possession, therefore their acquisition depended entirely upon the good will of the Friar. It may be justly supposed, that by this restriction, the advancement of California was *rather retarded*. So it was! for the immigrant was placed at the mercy of a prejudiced missionary who might be averse to any thing like secular improvement; for although these religionists were generally possessed of generous feelings, still, many of them were extremely jealous of an infringement upon the interests of their institutions. In fact, the abundance with which the missions were stored, and the bountiful distribution of their yearly productions by the missionaries, rendered any exertion on the part of the Californian unnecessary for his support, and but few persons cared for the means of independence, preferring idleness to industry and improvement. No officer in the Spanish service could marry without special license from his Catholic Majesty; thus, the increase of colonization was easily regulated, which accounts for the limited number of colonists in the country.

After the Mexicans had adopted the republican form of government, orders were received for the liberation of the Indians, and the missionaries were directed to apportion to each on, a certain quantity of land, for their maintenance. From this time, the white inhabitant began to turn his attention, more particularly, to agriculture, and the immense tracts of land that were occupied by the missions, were mostly divided into numerous farms. At first, the change was considered disastrous to the prosperity of California, and the wanton destruction of property which followed, seemed to warrant the conclusion; but the result, however, proved quite the contrary. Individual enterprise, which succeeded, has placed the country in a more flourishing condition, and the wealth, instead of being confined to the monastic institutions, as before, has been distributed among the people.

138

The liberality of the Californians, since their first opposition to Mexico, has induced many foreigners to settle in the country, and several hundreds of Americans may be already found located at different points. Their industrious habits have procured for them many very promising settlements, where the lands, under judicious management, produce abundance, and contribute greatly to the beauty of the surrounding country.

Agriculture, as may be supposed, has not much improved since its first introduction by the Spanish friars; for the same modes of cultivation are still adhered to, which they introduced at the commencement of their labors in California.

The grains principally cultivated are wheat, barley, maize, and several kinds of beans or *frijoles,* as they are called, by the natives. Oats are not raised for any purpose whatever, but they grow spontaneously on the prairies, and upon the hills, where they are left to dry and rot with the yearly pasturage. The sowing of grain commences in November, when the rains set in; and the harvest is in the months of July and August. Owing to inattention, perhaps, in procuring good seed, their wheat is not so fine as it might be; for in no part of the world, can be found a soil and climate, better adapted to its production.

Most kinds of vegetables are raised in gardens, and there is hardly a house in the country that has not its small patch of ground devoted to that purpose.

Both flax and hemp have been raised in California, and also cotton, to considerable advantage. The vine is thrifty, and is cultivated every where; from which is made very excellent wine and brandy.

Notwithstanding the immense number of domestic animals in the country, it is rather surprising that the Californians give so little attention to the dairy. Butter and cheese are extremely scarce, and but seldom used; and I have known instances, in which a proprietor of three or four thousand cows, has been obliged to send all over the village, where he resided, to obtain milk for his family. From this circumstance, it may be supposed that they are totally ignorant of its value:—not so; for since the introduction of foreign settlers, they have been well instructed in the art of making both butter and cheese; and it is only from sheer indolence, that these articles are not more plentiful.

In the intercourse between California and the Sandwich Islands, which has considerably increased in latter years, large quantities of wheat, beans, flour, cheese, and soap, have been annually exported from the former; the proceeds of which have usually returned in a variety of goods from the English and American markets.

The trade with California is, however, confined principally to American ships, direct from the United States; for they have but two or three small vessels of their own, and not more than twenty or thirty on the whole extent of the Mexican coast!

The Californians have made several attempts to rid themselves of the Mexicans, as has been related in the preceding chapters; and they were left for several years without interference on the part of the Mexican Government; so that not until this interference was sought by them, did it again attempt any control over their country. The distance between California and Mexico renders it easy to effect a separation, provided there could be found sufficient unity among the Californians; for a very small number could successfully resist any attacks made by such a power as Mexico. "The shores of the Mexican Republic," says A. Forbes, Esq., "on the Pacific are ill calculated for maintaining any maritime force; it has none at present; and from its unhealthy situation, scarcity of materials and want of sailors or maritime enterprise, it is not likely ever to have on the Pacific any formidable navy." These remarks compared with the following, relative to the situation of California, serve to prove its advantages. "California," he says, "is calculated, in an eminent degree, to become a maritime power; its coasts are healthy; its harbors excellent; and its capacity to produce materials for ship-building and marine stores is almost without limits. If, therefore, there should ever exist a sufficient population to maintain a separate sovereignty, or the occupiers of the country be of a quality and character capable of taking advantage of those resources, Mexico, instead of being able to reduce California, would be obliged to succumb."

The natural resources of California may have drawn the attention of the British Government to its importance, and fears were entertained by them, at one time, that the Russians, who were settled upon its northern frontier, would either encroach upon, or take entire possession of it. These fears, however, proved groundless, for the Russians have, for the last three or four years, abandoned the settlement. In commenting upon this, Mr. Forbes says, "The danger does not lie there—there is another restless and enterprising neighbor, from whom they will most probably soon have to defend themselves, or rather to submit to; for although the frontiers of North America are much more distant than the Russians, yet to such men as the back settlers, distance is of little moment, and they are already well acquainted with the route. The northern American tide of population must roll on southward, and overwhelm, not only California, but other more important states. This latter event, however, is in the womb of time; but the invasion of California by American settlers is daily talked of; and if Santa Anna had prevailed against Texas, a portion of the inhabitants of that country, sufficient to overrun California, would now have been its masters."

That the British Government have had interested views in relation to California, is also intimated by Mr. Forbes, who says, "There have been some thoughts of proposing to the Mexican Government that it should endeavor to cancel the English debt, which now exceeds fifty millions of dollars, by a transfer of California to the creditors. This would be a wise measure on the part of Mexico, if the government could be brought to lay aside the vanity of retaining large possessions. The cession of such a disjointed part of the republic as California would be an advantage. In no case can it ever be profitable to the Mexican republic, nor can it possibly remain united to it for any length of time, if it should even be induced to rejoin this state, from which at present it is, to all intents and purposes, separated. Therefore, by giving up this territory for the debt, would be getting rid of this last for nothing. But would the English creditors accept of it? I think they might, and I think they ought. They have lately displayed an inclination to treat and receive lands as a part of the debt where no lands exist belonging to Mexico. In the settlement made with Lizardi and Co. as agents for the Mexican Government in London, lands are stipulated to be delivered at a certain price per acre, in Texas, in which Mexico does not possess an acre, in the state of New Mexico, which is many hundred leagues inland in Sonora, and God knows where. To the good fortune, however, of the English creditors this contract has been disapproved of by the Mexican Government, and it is hoped that some more rational scheme will be hit upon to give the creditors some sort of tangible security for at least a part of what they have been so scandalously fleeced out of. If California was ceded for the English debt, the creditors might be formed into a company, with the difference that they should have a sort of sovereignty over the territory, somewhat in the manner of the East India Company. This, in my opinion, would certainly bring a revenue in time, which might be equal to the interest of the debt, and, under good management, and with an English population, would most certainly realize all that has been predicted of this fine country."

Gold and silver mines have been found in Upper California, from which, considerable quantities of ore have been obtained: skilful miners are only required, to make them profitable. It is said that coal has recently been discovered; which, if true, will greatly facilitate the introduction of steam navigation in the Pacific, and be the means of making California one of the most important commercial positions on the west coast of America; particularly, if ever a communication should be opened by means of a canal across the Isthmus of Panama. That such an event may transpire, is not improbable; the day is not far distant, perhaps, when it will be realized, and one may visit this fertile and interesting country, and return to the United States, in one half of the time now required for the long and tedious outward navigation.

The resources of California, its magnificent harbors, climate, and abundance of naval stores, would make it the rendezvous for all the steamers engaged in the trade, between Europe and the East Indies, as well as those from the United States; and the facilities for emigration would be such, that soon the whole western coast of North America would be settled by emigrants, both from this country and Europe.

During the anarchy which existed in past years, throughout this fertile country, there were many of the native Californians who would have been thankful for the protection of either England or America; and, indeed, a great many desired it, in preference to the detested administration of Mexico. Perhaps, there are many who still feel as they did then: and in this age of "Annexation," why not extend the "area of freedom" by the annexation of California? Why not plant the banner of liberty there, in the fortress, at the entrance of the noble, the spacious bay of San Francisco? It requires not the far-reaching eye of the statesman, nor the wisdom of a contemplative mind, to know what would be the result. Soon its immense sheet of water would become enlivened with thousands of vessels, and steamboats would ply between the towns, which, as a matter of course, would spring up on its shores. While on other locations, along the banks of the rivers, would be seen manufactories and saw-mills. The whole country would be changed, and instead of one's being deemed wealthy by possessing such extensive tracts as are now held by the farming class, he would be rich with one quarter part. Every thing would improve; population would increase; consumption would be greater, and industry would follow.

All this may come to pass; and indeed, it must come to pass, for the march of emigration is to the West, and naught will arrest its advance but the mighty ocean.

Identification Key

This key was compiled by the author, Don Alfred Robinson, for the first edition of 1846 and was copied by Elena Robinson Godwin.

Index

145

146

Part II

Chinigchinich

Chinigchinich

A HISTORICAL ACCOUNT OF THE
ORIGIN, CUSTOMS, AND TRADITIONS OF
THE INDIANS AT
THE MISSIONARY ESTABLISHMENT OF
ST. JUAN CAPISTRANO,
ALTA-CALIFORNIA

BY THE REVEREND FATHER
FRIAR GERONIMO BOSCANA, *1776–1831*

BIOBOOKS · OAKLAND, CALIFORNIA
1947

Translator's Introduction

IN THE TRANSLATION OF THIS MANUSCRIPT, I HAVE endeavored to retain the original style of the Spanish writer, and have adhered, as closely as practicable, to a literal version of the same.

It is apparent that Father Boscana intended to confine his description of the Indians to those who were made converts at the Point called St. Juan Capistrano; but I presume the same will correspond with the character of the natives generally, of Upper California. The mission of St. Juan was first founded in 1776, and, like those which preceded it, was conducted under the administration of two Friars of the St. Franciscan Order. Its domains were large, and distributed into numerous farms, for the purpose of domesticating cattle. A guard of three or four soldiers, and a sergeant, enforced the will of the missionaries, and kept in check such unfriendly Indians, as were not inclined to avail themselves of the advantages of civilization. Under this kind of administration, the natives were taught many trades; and became, not only useful to themselves, but also to the community. Hardly any attention was paid to the improvement of their minds, beyond the forms and rules of their religious belief; so that scarcely any of them could read, and none could write. They have been careful to preserve the traditions and customs of their ancestors, and are permitted to indulge in the observance of them, on their feast days, which occur several times during the year. Thus, I have had frequent opportunities to witness many of the absurdities, and extravagances, described by Father Boscana.

The manuscript ends rather abruptly; and it is uncertain if the holy Father ever intended it for publication. After his death, in 1831, it was found among his effects, with other writings, which came into the possession of the Syndic of the Missions, who kindly presented it to me. The reader will decide as to its merits.

A. R.

vi

Introduction

THE MOTIVES WHICH HAVE INDUCED ME TO WRITE
the present history, have been, principally, to fulfil my obligations as
Apostolical Missionary; to have before me the means of presenting to
these poor Indians an account of the errors entertained by them during
their state of heathenism, and to contrast the same with the light they
now enjoy as Christians. Also, to leave to my successors such instruction,
as will relieve them from the trouble and labor that I experienced, in
procuring a knowledge of the belief, usages, and customs, *i.e.*, the Religion, which these natives possessed in their heathen state; persuaded
as I am, that being ignorant of this, it will be difficult to remove their
erroneous belief, and give them an understanding of the true Religion.
It is difficult, I confess, if unacquainted with their language, to penetrate their secrets, as they do not *all* understand the signification of their
usages and customs; this knowledge being confined to the chiefs of their
tribes, and the old men who officiate as priests; and when they reveal
any thing, to their children, it is only to such as they intend to rear for
their successors, and these, are enjoined to keep fast the secrets, and not
communicate them to any one, under pain of severe chastisement. A
veil is cast over all their religious observances, and the mystery with
which they are performed, seems to perpetuate respect for them, and
preserve an ascendancy over the people. This is the reason that the
ceremonies of the dances, in their grand feasts, (which are properly

exercises of religion,) cannot be understood. They have never had the use of writings, letters, or characters of any description. All their knowledge is from tradition, which they preserve in songs for their dances, and these are introduced, by the chief, at their festivities, in a language distinct from that, in common use. Others unite with them, but without understanding the meaning of what they do, or articulate; perhaps, the songs thus introduced, are in the primitive language.

Perchance, some one may enquire, how I have obtained so much information, relative to the secrets or religion of these natives, when, up to the present time, no other Father has written on the subject.

We are to suppose it a truth, that there are many things hidden, not only, in the Divine Prophecies, but in human events, also, which cannot be comprehended, or known but by the Divine Will; and as God, almost always, makes use of the most humble instruments for his purpose, to me, he assigned three aged Indians, the youngest of whom was over seventy years of age. They knew all the secrets, for two of them were *Capitans,* and the other a *Pul,* who were well instructed in the mysteries. By gifts, endearments, and kindness, I elicited from them their secrets, with their explanations; and, by witnessing the ceremonies which they performed, I learned, by degrees, their mysteries. Thus, by devoting a portion of the nights to profound meditation, and comparing their actions with their disclosures, I was enabled, after a long time, to acquire a knowledge of their religion. There are yet, many things, which I do not understand, because they have not been disclosed to me, with that clearness that I could wish, but, always so confusedly, that I was unable to penetrate their meaning.

Chapter I

Of What Race of People Are These Indians?

TO COMMENCE THIS RELATION, IT MAY BE PROPER, in the first place, to search after the origin, or lineage of these Indians of New California. But it is impossible to find any account of where they originated; as those of this mission, (St. Juan Capistrano) and indeed those of all the missions in the province, have no tradition, and are entirely ignorant of their descent. Without examining into the opinion of others, as to their being descendants of the Jews, Carthagenians or Phœnicians, I shall confine myself to the class that came to populate the Mexican Territory, and from these have doubtless descended the natives of California.

The tribes that populated the Mexican Territory at different epochs, according to the writings of Father Torquemada in his "Monarquia Indiana," were four; and as follows: "Tulticas," "Chichimecas," "Aculnas," and "Mexicanos." Of these distinct tribes, my opinion is, that the race of California proceeded from the Chichimecas, because, from the Tulticas they could not have originated, as is manifest from their characters, and inclinations; for "Tultica" signifies Art, and these Indians do not manifest the least industry or ingenuity. They are, in every respect, like the Chichimecas, according to the description given of them by Father Torquemada. "Near the northern boundary of Mexico there was a province, the principal city of which was called Amaqueme; its inhabitants, Chichimecas, were people entirely naked, fierce in appear-

1

ance, and great warriors. Their arms the bow and arrows; their ordinary sustenance game and wild fruits, and their habitations were caves, or huts made of straw. As it was their manner of life habitually to roam about among the mountains, in search of game, they paid but little or no attention to the art of building." This is the picture given by Father Torquemada of the Chichimecas, and comparing them with the natives of California, they are found the same in every respect.

Although the habitations of the said Chichimecas formed a kind of village, still they had no police, nor acknowledged any higher power than that of "Capitan" or chief, and toward him was observed but little respect; indeed, hardly sufficient to designate him from the rest. They did not live permanently in one place, but roamed about, from spot to spot, as the scarcity of game compelled them. Of medicine they had no knowledge; consequently, no means of curing the sick, and the bodies of their dead were immediately burnt. Idolatry prevailed among them, but not a belief in a plurality of gods; neither did they sacrifice, as was was the custom among the Mexican Indians.

Having thus described the Chichimecas, we see precisely the character of the Californians, with the exception, that the last mentioned lived in villages, and were governed by a chief, whom they entitled "Not," signifying lord, or master; he possessed but little influence over his subjects, and they in return entertained no respect for his authority, as we shall see hereafter. The name, *Chichimeca,* signifies a "sucker." Their principal sustenance was the flesh of animals taken in hunting excursions, and which was generally consumed in a raw state, after sucking all the blood; and from this, arose the term Chichimeca.

The Californian, often made his repast from the uncooked animal, and at the present day, flesh, very slightly cooked, is quite common among them. They also extract the blood in like manner, and I have seen many instances of their taking a rabbit, and sucking its blood with eagerness, previous to consuming the flesh in a crude state. The diversities of language, and other pecularities, render it extremely difficult to ascertain to a certainty, if all the inhabitants of Alta California descended from the Chichimecas. Those between Monterey and the extreme northern boundary of the Mexican domain, shave their heads close; while those to the south, between Santa Barbara and towards St.

2

Lucas, wear their hair long, and take pride in cultivating its length as a mark of beauty. Those between Santa Barbara and Monterey, differ considerably from these, as regards their habits; being much more industrious, and appear an entirely distinct race. They formed, from shells, a kind of money, which passed current among them, and they constructed, out of logs, very swift and excellent canoes for fishing. Their dead, they interred in places appropriated to that purpose. The diversity of language is so great, in California, that almost every 15 or 20 leagues, you find a distinct dialect; so different, that in no way does one resemble the other. It is natural to suppose, that the Chichimeca nation, would have had but one language, notwithstanding, it might have varied a little, from one place to another, as is seen in other parts of the world, where are to be met with certain provincialisms, which are not to be found in the original tongue. But here, it is not so; for the natives of St. Diego cannot understand a word of the language used in this mission, and in like manner, those in the neighborhood of St. Barbara, and farther north. If it should be suggested, that people thus separated, could have corrupted the original language, in all its phraseology, and manner of pronunciation, I would reply, that such *might* be the case; but still, there would be some connection, or similarity, so that they could understand each other. This has placed me somewhat in perplexity; and I am without means of discovering the cause of such dissimilarity in a spot, confined like California; and I shall leave the subject to some of my brother missionaries, or to those who may peruse these writings, to explain.

Chapter II
On the Creation of the Universe

ALTHOUGH THIS CHAPTER HAS FOR ITS title, the *creation of the world,* the reader must not suppose it has any relation to the account given by Moses in the first chapter of Genesis. I do not intend any such thing; but merely to make known the belief of these Indians in their heathen state. We must not be surprised, if there be found many contradictions and extravagances; for these rude Indians were ignorant of the true God, without faith, without law, or king, and governed by their own natural ideas, or by tradition; we should, therefore, not wonder at their inconsistencies, and want of discernment to discriminate the truth from falsehood; for, deprived of the light of the Gospel, they ever walked in heathen darkness. Before I commence with their ideas of the world's origin, I must premise, that the Indians of this particular location (the mission of St. Juan Capistrano) account for the creation of the world in one way, and those of the interior (about 3 or 4 leagues distant) in another. In substance the same. One, as fabulous as the other. For this reason I will give both relations, and commence, in the first place, with the account of those in the interior.

Their belief is this: before this world was, there existed *one above,* and *another below.* These two were *brother and sister.* The one above, signified the *heavens,* and the one below, represented the *earth.* But the heaven and earth here mentioned, *were not as they appear now to us,* but of another nature, which they could not explain. We may, there-

4

fore, consider them as imaginary. All below was dark, without sun, moon, or stars. The brother came unto the sister, and brought the light, which is the sun, saying he would take her unto him to wife; she resisted, reminding him of their affinity, and desired that he would return and leave her in peace. But in time they were wedded, and the first-fruits of their union were earth and sand. After which, were produced rocks and stones of all kinds, particularly flints, for their arrows; then, trees and shrubbery; next, herbs and grass; and again, animals, principally the kind which they eat. Finally, was born one that they called *Ouiot*. This was an animated being. The father and mother of *Ouiot* were not mortals, as we said before, but were of a nature they could not explain. This said *Ouiot* had children, and was king, or grand captain of the first family; and, as I understand it, we are to suppose them, like their parent, a species of animal, distinct from any which now inhabit the earth; or, in other words, imaginary phantoms. Upon enquiring how this grand captain could have had children, and what was the name of his partner, they could not explain; but he had children, and many, both male and female.

As Captain *Ouiot's* descendants multiplied, the first born of his mother, (the earth,) increased in size, and extended itself to the south; (it will be well to state here, that it is the general belief of the Indians that they originated in the north) and as they increased the earth continued to augment. Captain Ouiot having become aged, his eldest vassals formed a conspiracy to destroy him; alleging as a reason for so doing, that his years prevented his attending to their wants; and, in fact, that he was too old to govern. A consultation was held, to resolve upon what method to carry into execution their designs, and it was decided that he should be poisoned. They mixed a poisonous ingredient in his beverage, and administered it to him. After drinking of this he immediately became sick, and left the mountains where he had lived, and resorted to the place which is now occupied by the beach, or sea shore; for it is supposed, that at this time, there was no sea. His mother, hearing of the danger of her son, mixed for him a remedy, which was prepared in a large shell, and placed it in the sun to ferment. The "Coyote," attracted to the spot by its fragrance, overturned it, and thus frustrated the intention of his mother. At length the captain died; and, although he told them that in a short time he should return, and live with them again, they never have seen him more. I must state, that, at this time, there was no kind of grain or flesh to eat, and their food was the earth, which, according to their description, I understand to have been a kind of white clay, often used upon their heads by way of ornament. After the death of "*Ouiot*," they remained, for some time, undecided, whether to inter his remains, or to burn them; however, it was determined by the elders, that they should do the latter. The fire was prepared, the body placed upon a pile erected for the occasion, and fearing that the "Coyote" would come, and eat him, they sent out and burnt his retreat; but he had made his escape, and soon presented himself at the place of sacrifice, declaring he would be burnt with his captain; and, suddenly leaping upon the pile, he tore off from his stomach a large piece of flesh, and ate it. The remainder of the body was afterwards consumed by the flames.

The name of the *Coyote* was *Eyacque*, which implies second captain; and from this time they changed his name to that of *Eno;* signifying a thief and cannibal, and thieves were generally termed *Eyoton*, derived from Eno and Ouiot.

After burning the body, a general council was called, to make provision for the collecting of grain and seeds; the acorns, &c., &c., and the flesh of animals; such as deer, rabbits, hares, squirrels, rats, and all kinds which they fed upon. While consulting together, they beheld for several days, and at distinct times, a spectre, unlike themselves, who appeared and disappeared; sometimes in one direction and sometimes in another. Alarmed at its appearance, they determined to speak to it. Having summoned it to their presence, inquiries were made if he were their Captain *Ouiot.* "I am not *Ouiot,*" said he, "but a captain of greater power; and my name is *Chinigchinich.* My habitation is above. On what matters are you debating, and why are you thus congregated?" he inquired. "Our captain is dead," said they "we have come to his interment, and were discussing in what manner to maintain ourselves upon the seeds of the fields, and the flesh of animals without being obliged to live upon the clay, or earth, as we have done."

Having listened to their answer, he spake unto them, and said, "I create all things; I will make you another people, and from this time, one of you shall be endowed with the power to cause it to rain, another to influence the dews, another to produce the acorn, another to create rabbits, another ducks, another geese, another deer." In fine, each one received his particular occupation, and power to create such food as they now eat. Even now, such as claim to be descendants of this people, pretend to be endowed with the same powers, and are frequently consulted as to their harvests, and receive in return for their advice, a gift of some kind, either in money or clothing, and, in fact, the result of their harvest depends entirely upon the maintenance given to these sorcerers, and the supplying all their necessities. To offend them, would be to destroy all their productions of flesh and grain.

Chinigchinich, after having conferred the power, as we have said, upon the descendants of Ouiot, about the time of "dixit et factum est," created man, forming him of clay found upon the borders of a lake. Both male and female he created, and the Indians of the present day are descendants of these. He then said unto them these words—"Him who obeyeth me not, or believeth not in my teachings, I will chastise—to him I will send bears to bite, serpents to sting, misfortunes, infirmities, and death." He taught them the laws they were to observe for the future, as well as their rites and ceremonies.

His first commandment was to build a temple, where they might pay to him adoration, offer up sacrifices, and have religious worship. The plan of this building was regulated by himself. From this time they looked upon Chinigchinich as God. The Indians say, he had neither father nor mother, and they are entirely ignorant of his origin. The name Chinigchinich signifies "all-powerful" or "almighty," and it is believed by the Indians, that he was ever present, and in all places: he saw every thing, although it might be in the darkest night, but no one could see him. He was a friend to the good, but the wicked he chastised.

Chinigchinich was known under three distinct names, as follows: *Saor, Quaguar,* and *Tobet.* Each one possessing its particular signification, denoting diversity or a difference of times. *Saor,* signifies or means, that period in which Chinigchinich could not dance; *Quaguar,* when enabled to dance; and *Tobet,* when he danced enrobed in a dress composed of feathers, with a crown of the same upon his head, and his face painted black and red. They say that once, while dancing in this cos-

7

tume, he was taken up into heaven, where are located the stars. His order was, that they should use this mode of dress in their grand feasts—an observance regarded to this day.

Let us now return to the children of *Ouiot,* to know what became of them, and their descendants. It is said by some, that the God Chinig-chinich, after he had formed the Indians out of the clay of the lake, transformed *them* into men like the others. To this opinion I am inclined, as being the most reasonable, for the power which they received from Chinigchinich, to create animals and grain, has been claimed, as has been seen, by those who pretend to be their descendants; and if he had not transformed them into Indians, no one would have remained with the power, for, the children of *Ouiot* were not Indians, or rational beings. It is affirmed by others, that when they saw the Indians that were created by Chinigchinich, they disappeared, and went off, no one knows where; and, consequently, that there are no descendants of *Ouiot* in existence. Nevertheless, they all consult alike relative to their harvests, and pay for the advice given to them. This is the belief that these Indians of the interior had respecting the creation of the world, and its origin.

Chapter III

Of the Creation of the World According to Those Residing on the Sea-Coast

IN THE PRECEDING CHAPTER, WE HAVE BEEN amused by the belief of the Indians, *Serranos*, relative to the creation of the world. Now, let us compare the same with that of the *Playanos* —that is, those who came to settle in the valley of St. Juan Capistrano. An invisible and all-powerful being called *Nocuma* made the world, the sea, and all that is therein contained, such as animals, trees, plants and fishes. In its form it was spherical, and rested upon his hands; but, being continually in motion, he resolved to secure the same by placing in its centre a black rock, called *Tosaut,* and it remained firm, and secure as at the present time. This black rock, the Indians say, is from a small island near the beach, and the fragments which they often collect, serve as trowels, with which they smooth their mud walls.

The sea, at that time, was no more than a small stream of water, running from the south to the north, encircling the world: so filled with fish, that they were literally piled one on top of another, in such a state of inconvenience, that they held a consultation, and some were for landing upon the earth; others were of opinion that it would be impossible, for they would perish when exposed to the air and the heat of the sun, and besides they had no legs and feet as other animals have. While conferring upon this matter, there came a large fish, bringing with him the rock *Tosaut,* which, having broken, they found in its centre a ball formed like a bladder, filled with gall. This they emptied into the water, and from its fresh state it was converted into a bitter condition. The water then immediately swelled, and overflowed upon the earth, covering the space which it does now, and the fishes were rejoiced to find themselves so amply supplied with room, and at the change effected in the taste.

Nocumo having created all the things contained in the world, and secured it with the rock *Tosaut,* as before remarked, created man, or the first Indian, out of the earth, and called him *Ejoni.* Afterwards he created woman, and gave her the name of *Aé.* It is not known of what she was made, but the supposition is that she was created from the earth, like the man. Many years after the creation of *Ejoni* and *Aé,* one of their descendants, called *Sirout,* (which signifies a handful of tobacco) and his wife called *Ycaiut,* (which signifies above) had a son, and they gave him the name of *Ouiot.* This name, according to the explanation given by the Indians, signifies something which has taken root, denoting that in like manner, he would, in course of time, extend his power and dominion over the earth, as the largest trees spread their roots in every direction. I have not been enabled to ascertain if the name *Ouiot,* properly implying dominator, was given to him at the time of his birth, or at the time of his celebrity as the great Captain. Be it as it may, let us examine his history, or life.

Out of the confines of a Rancheria, called *Pubuna,* distant from St. Juan Capistrano N.E. about eight leagues, came the monster *Ouiot,* and the Indians, at the present time, preserve the account in their annals. At that time, all the inhabitants were at peace, and quietly following their domestic pursuits; but *Ouiot,* being of a fierce disposition, a warrior, ambitious, and haughty, soon managed to gain a supremacy over many of the towns adjoining that where he originated. During the commencement of his reign, he was pacific, kind and generous to such a degree, that every one appeared happy, and contented with their chief; but after the lapse of a few years, he gradually exposed his ferocity, and persecuted many of his vassals; cruelly treating them, and some he put to death. In fact, he soon became the detestation of all his subjects.

Having suffered so much from *Ouiot,* they determined to rid themselves of the tyrant, and release themselves from the oppression in which they had lived for so long a period. A consultation was held by the elders, and it was decided that he should receive his death by means of poison. The rock *Tosaut* was procured, and whilst in the act of pulverizing the ingredient, they were perceived by one called *Cucumel,* who immediately gave information to *Ouiot,* that they wished to destroy him by poison. Said *Cucumel* was a small animal inhabiting holes in the ground, from which, in the daytime, he issued to obtain his sustenance. The said *Ouiot,* believing he was hated and despised, and fearful of the death revealed to him by *Cucumel,* despatched messengers in every direction to ascertain the truth; threatening, at the same time, those who might have been concerned in the conspiracy; but, obtaining no information, he rather looked upon it as a jest. In the meantime, his enemies had secretly prepared the mixture, and were consulting how to administer the same, saying that it was so active and effective, that the mere application of it to the flesh, would cause almost instantaneous death. One of them was entrusted with its execution, and at night, finding *Ouiot* asleep, he placed a small quantity upon his breast. On waking, he experienced a sickness and weakness in his limbs, and fearing very much that he should die, he immediately called in, all the intelligent from the different towns. But the more they administered for his relief, the worse he became, until, at length, he died.

After his death they sent off couriers to all the towns, and settlements, which *Ouiot* had governed, summoning the people to the interment of their Grand Captain; and in a few days, so great a collection had assembled, that the City or Town of Pubuna could not contain them, and they were obliged to encamp in the outskirts. They consulted together as to the propriety of burning or interring the body, and they decided upon the former. The funeral pile was made, the deceased placed upon it, the pile was fired, and during the time of its burning, they danced and sang songs of rejoicing.

These ceremonies concluded, and before the return of the people to their different places of abode, a council was called to regulate the collecting of grain or seeds of the fields, and flesh, to eat; for up to this time they had fed upon a kind of clay. While conferring upon this subject, there appeared to them one, called *"Attajen,"* which name implies man, or rational being; but they knew not from whence he came. To his enquiry, "Why they were thus congregated?" they answered "that their Grand Captain was dead, and that they had met together to assist at the funeral ceremonies; and now, previous to their retirement, the elders were consulting as to the manner they should subsist for the future, without the necessity of living upon clay as they had heretofore." *"Attajen"* was much pleased with the relation that he had heard, and said unto them, "Ye are not capable, nor can ye do what ye think, or wish to do. I am the only one that has power, and I will give it to ye, that ye may have an abundance to eat, in your habitations." And, accordingly, he selected from the multitude a few of the elders, and endowed them with the power to cause the rain to fall, to make grain, and others to make animals, such as rabbits, hares, deer, &c., &c. And it was understood that such power was to descend to their successors.

Many years, and perhaps ages, having expired since the death of *Ouiot,* there appeared in the same town of Pubuna, one called *Ouiamot,"* son of *Tacu* and *Auzar.* I imagine that this new character was not, or, at least, his parents were not inhabitants of the place, but had originated in some distant land. The said *Ouiamot* did not appear like *Ouiot,* as a warrior, but as a God. To him they were to offer presents. And this was the *God Chinigchinich,* so feared, venerated, and respected by the Indians, who taught first in the town of Pubuna, and afterwards in all the neighboring parts, explaining the laws, and establishing the rites and ceremonies necessary to the preservation of life.

The manner in which he commenced to dogmatise, manifesting his extravagances, was as follows. One day, at a very large congregation of the people, he danced before them, adorned in the robes which have been already described; his flesh painted black and red, and calling himself *Tobet.* He said that he had come from the stars to teach them those things of which they were ignorant. After dancing a considerable time, he separated the chiefs and elders from among them, and directed that they alone should wear the kind of dress which had adorned his person, and then taught them how to dance. To these Indians was given the name of *puplem,* who would know all things, and relieve the infirm and diseased. In other words, they would become the sorcerers or soothsayers, to whom the Indians might invariably apply for advice, and relief from their necessities. In the event of a scarcity of food, or any infirmity, they were told to appear, dressed like unto *Tobet;* that is, after the manner in which he appeared to them, dancing; to supplicate him, not in the name of *Ouiamot*, but of Chinigchinich, and their wants would be relieved. The sick would be cured, and the hungry receive food. In all cases they were to return thanks, and even now, to this day, whenever they chance to secure an animal of any kind, they say, "guic Chinig-chinich," that is, "thanks to Chinigchinich, who has given me this."

This Chinigchinich, as we shall style him hereafter, taught them how to build the *Vanquech*, which means temple, or church, and how they were to conduct themselves therein—forbidding any others than the chief and puplem entering its sanctuary. Here they were to teach only the laws and ceremonies, and those who entered, would be called *Tobet*, and the remainder of the people *Saorem*, which signifies, persons who do not know how to dance; that is, more properly, those who could not make use of the vestments of Chinigchinich. The name of *Quaguar*, was given to him when he died and ascended above, among the stars. This is the explanation of the three terms which is given in the preceding relation relative to Chinigchinich.

Chinigchinich having become seriously indisposed, and while instructing the elders how to rear the young, as well as in the rules they were to observe for the future, they enquired of him where, or to which one of his rancherias he wished to go when he died? He answered, "to neither, for they were inhabited by people, and he should go where he would be alone, and could see the inhabitants of all the pueblos and rancherias." They offered to bury him, placing him under the earth, but he said "no," that they they would walk upon him, and he would have to chastise them. "No!" said Chinigchinich, "when I die, I shall ascend above, to the stars, and from thence, I shall always see you; and to those who have kept my commandments, I shall give all they ask of me; but those who obey not my teachings, nor believe them, I shall punish severely. I will send unto them bears to bite, and serpents to sting them; they shall be without food, and have diseases that they may die." Chinigchinich, at length, died. His memory was so revered among the Indians, that they ever besought him in all their undertakings, and regarded him with fear and respect.

We have thus seen the belief of these Indians, respecting the creation of the world, and their God, and from its narration, we comprehend their religion, usages and customs. I do not understand why it is, that in

13

neither of the two narrations, is there any mention made of the heavens, and that all their ideas of things appear to be confined to the earth, with the exception of the stars. What I should like to know, is, from whence they received such accounts? for, notwithstanding their imperfect, as well as fabulous description, they have some allusion to the truth. We have the six productions of the mother of *Ouiot,* corresponding to the six days of the creation of the world—The Indian formed of the earth or clay, like our first parent—and *Ouiot,* analogous to Nimrod of the Holy Scripture. I do not know to whom we may compare *Ouiamot,* unless it be to Simon Magus, as his teachings were idolatrous.

Chapter IV
Description of the Vanquech or Temple

LTHOUGH GOD NEEDS NOT A MATERIAL temple, to be adored, praised and venerated, to fill all the world with his essence, presence, and power: nevertheless, he has always desired that there should be sacrifices, and prayers offered unto him, to obtain his mercy and forgiveness, in places determined upon by him; as may be seen in Deuteronomy in the Holy Scriptures. He ordered the patriarch, Abraham, to sacrifice on a mount of his own selection. Moses was ordered to build a tabernacle, and 440 years afterwards, Solomon, was commanded to build the magnificent temple of Jerusalem.

Satan, jealous of the honor due to the true God, wishes that man should also adore him, and offer up sacrifices in temples, by him ordained, thus endeavoring to draw him from the knowledge of the true God, one in essence, and three in person. He has taught man a diversity of Gods, and a variety of forms for his temples. I will therefore explain, in this chapter, the location and form of the temple, called Vanquech. The name of temple, or church, we know is derived from *contemplatione*, a place dedicated to prayer. If the Vanquech of these Indians can be thus termed, the reader will best decide.

The temples erected by command of the God Chinigchinich, or the celebrated idolater Ouiamot, were invariably erected in the centre of their towns, and contiguous to the dwelling-place of the captain, or chief; notwithstanding their houses were scattered about without any particular regard to order, still, they managed to have the location of his house as near the middle as possible. They formed an enclosure of about four or five yards in circumference, not exactly round, but inclining to an oval. This they divided, by drawing a line through the centre, and built another, consisting of the branches of trees, and mats to the height of about six feet, outside of which, in the other division, they formed another, of small stakes of wood driven into the ground. This was called the gate, or entrance, to the Vanquech. Inside of this, and close to the larger stakes, was placed a figure of their God Chinigchinich, elevated upon a kind of hurdle. This is the edifice of the Vanquech.

Not being acquainted with the art of drawing, I cannot give a true picture of the figure adored by them, but will explain the same as well as I am able. In the first place, of the skin of a *coyote*, or *gato montes*, which was taken off with great care, including the head and feet, they formed a species of sack. This they dressed quite smooth, like deer skin, but without taking off the hair. Inside of this, were placed the feathers of particular kinds of birds, horns of deer, lions' claws, beaks and talons of the hawk and crow, and other things of this class; particularly the beak and talons of a species of hawk, called *pame,* that we shall describe hereafter, from the feathers of which they formed a kind of petticoat, to dress their Chinigchinich, such as was used by the captain and chiefs, and called *paelt*. Inside of this sack, they placed some arrows, and upon the outside, a few more, with a bow. It resembled in appearance, a live animal, and projecting from its mouth might be seen the feathers of the arrows.

When the Captain sent out orders by the crier of the general council, for the Indians to go out in search of game, or seeds, one of the *puplem,* (signifying one who knows all things) sketched upon the ground in front of Chinigchinich, a very ridiculous figure, and the crier called upon all to go and worship it. Having congregated together, according to their custom on such occasions, (male and female) the men armed with their bows and arrows, and well painted—the chief and the puplem dressed in their appropriate costumes, resembling devils more than human beings—they went in succession, running one behind the other, led by their captain, until they arrived opposite Chinigchinich, and the figure upon the earth. The leader then gave a jump, springing

16

AN INDIAN DRESSED IN THE "TOBET"

very high from the ground, accompanied by a loud yell, and with his bow and arrow, prepared as if to shoot at something in the air. Each one in his turn performed the same evolution.

The ceremony being concluded on the part of the men, the females followed, headed by their *Capitana* in like manner as the men, differing only in this respect, that instead of running, they moved along in slow procession, and when in front of the Vanquech, they inclined the head, presenting at the same time their *bateas,* or instruments collected for the occasion. This ceremony concluded, they all dispersed to the mountains. The object of this performance, was to implore protection from all danger and sickness while in their pursuit of game.

Very great was their veneration for the Vanquech, or temple, and they were extremely careful not to commit the most trivial act of irreverence within. No one was permitted to enter it on their feast days, but the chief, the Puplem, and elders. The remainder of the people remained outside of the stakes. The younger class did not dare to approach even the entrance. Profound silence was observed generally throughout the assembly, interrupted occasionally by a whisper. Of those inside, sometimes the chief, or one of the Puplem, danced, making all kinds of grotesque figures; after which they partook of an entertainment, when all ate from the same vessel.

It has always appeared to me extremely ridiculous that his Satanic Majesty, desirous of the honors and veneration due to God alone, should have adopted so ludicrous a form of worship, as that which was observed toward Chinigchinich. When in his presence, the Indians were entirely naked, and remained for hours in a posture equally awkward and fatiguing—a sort of squat; resting their heads, generally, upon their right hands, without moving during the ceremony of adoration.

Extraordinary as was the veneration observed for their Vanquech, no less so were the privileges allowed to those who sought its protection. Whatever criminal, guilty of the highest misdemeanor—of homicide, adultery, or theft, escaping from justice, should be enabled to reach its sanctuary, unknown to his accusers, from that moment he would become free, and at liberty to go abroad without any fear of molestation, on the part of those aggrieved. No mention would be made of the crime of which he might be guilty, yet, it might be said, in derision of

17

his having sought refuge in the Vanquech, "you went to the protection of Chinigchinich, if you had not, we should have killed you; but, nevertheless, he will chastise you for your wickedness."

They believed, that, as their God was friendly to the good, and punished the wicked, he also would not permit any one to be molested, who sought his protection; thus, the criminal escaped punishment at the time. Yet it must be understood, that although the delinquent went free, the crime did not remain exempt from punishment; for vengeance was wrought upon the children, grandchildren, or some near relative, whenever opportunity to the aggrieved offered; and the tradition was handed down, from father, to son, until the same was accomplished. In like manner, the captain could preserve his life when charged with squandering the grain, which was deposited with him. If he, by good luck, achieved a refuge in the *Vanquech,* no one could harm him, nor enter therein, particularly if he were adorned in the robes of the "*Capitanejas.*" Should any one enter in defiance of this custom, he would be immediately despatched by his companions, for death was the penalty. The captain would be deposed, however, but they would suffer him to go at large, deprived of his title and supremacy, and the puplem would elect as his successor, one of his children; charging him to hold in recollection, the fate of his father; to be faithful, or the same punishment would attend him.

Chapter V

Obedience and Subjection to Their Captain

THEIR FORM OF GOVERNMENT WAS MONARCHICAL, acknowledging but one head, and the *Puplem,* or general council. This body served as a kind of check to the will of the captain, and without its sanction he could do nothing of importance. Before treating upon the obedience observed towards their ruler, and his advisers, I will first explain the forms and ceremonies adopted in their elevation to office. In the event of the decease of their captain, or his inability to govern, from extreme age,—or of his desire to elevate a son to the command, a general feast was prepared, and all the neighboring chiefs and friends were invited to attend. (I must note here, that each town or Rancheria, had its chief, or captain.) Upon their arrival, after all were collected together, the object of the invitation was made known to them, and the cause of the old chief's relinquishing the command to his son, was explained. If this were satisfactory, their consent was given, and a day specified for the event, which was generally the succeeding one. A crier was despatched to give notice of the election to the inhabitants, and they were invited to take part in the feast of the new captain.

Every thing being prepared, they placed the crown upon his head, and he was enrobed with the imperial vestments. Anciently, the diadem of kings and emperors consisted of a kind of bandage, wound around the head, as we may infer from the account of Alexander Magnus, who upon beholding a valiant soldier, wounded, took from his head the

19

diadem, to bind up the wound of his vassal. Of *this* class was the diadem used by the captain. His hair was tied close to the neck, plaited, or rather twisted, and instead of a bandage, he wore a species of cord made from the hair, which was passed three or four times around his head. A thin piece of wood, about half a yard in length, sometimes, of a shape similar to the blade of a sword, and often rounded like a wire, they secured to the cord, which they adorned with feathers of the hawk, the crow, and other birds. Lastly, they put upon him a kind of petticoat, formed also from the feathers of birds, reaching down almost to the knees, while the remainder of his body was painted black. This was called the dress of the *"Capitaneja,"* and was the *Tobet,* so termed by Chinigchinich.

His toilet being concluded, as above described, he went into the Vanquech to dance before Chinigchinich, and the instruments, used upon such occasions, were not very musical, nor of any great variety; being composed mostly of the shells of turtles, with small stones inside, which they rattled continually, as an accompaniment to their voices. After dancing until he felt somewhat fatigued, the other captains entered, dressed with their several insignia, and placed him in their centre. After dancing around him a short time, the ceremony was concluded, and he was acknowledged as their captain.

The feast, generally, lasted three or four days and nights, and the old captain procured for the occasion, an abundance of their choicest kinds of food, which he presented to the guests, and to all the inhabitants of his dominion.

The new captain did not assume the reins of government, until his father died or resigned them to him, and then, the only ceremony necessary in taking the command, was, to make known the fact to the neighboring chiefs. In the right of succession to the command, having no male descendant, the females also participated; and were permitted to marry with whomsoever they pleased, even one not descended from the true line of captains. In such a case, the husband was not acknowledged as chief, nor was the wife allowed to govern; but always the nearest male relation assumed the power. The first male child, as soon as born, they proclaimed captain, and from that time he was known as such, although the relative governed during his minority. On the day of transferring the government, all the neighboring chiefs were invited, and a grand feast given on the occasion. It was the custom among these Indians, in all their feasts, to carry presents to the person who gave the invitation, and he in return, was obliged when invited, to give one of equal value.

As it regards obedience and subjection to their captains, what I have been enabled to ascertain, is, that the conduct of the people was in no wise influenced by their authority, but that they lived a life of insubordination, without laws or government. The malefactor went unpunished, and the meritorious unrewarded. In fact, each one lived as he pleased, and no one interfered, do what he would. Notwithstanding this, the Indians say, that in the days of their gentilism, they had but very few quarrels and disturbances. The reason of this, I presume, was, the fact of their being nearly all related to each other, and the frequent exhortation of the fathers to their children, to be good. When one committed a fault against another, if the aggrieved could avenge himself, he did so; death, generally, was the result, and no one interfered or spoke of it.

Although the Captains did not exercise any power, whatever, in the administration of justice, or in any other way, still the people possessed great respect and veneration for their persons, particularly the youthful part of the community, who were early instructed to look upon them, as well as upon the Puplem and elders, with fear and trembling. This was, as before stated, their daily instruction, and on this account no one dared to treat them with disrespect, or to injure them by word or action, for death would have been the consequence, and its execution carried into effect as follows:—The case having been declared in the council, an elder was appointed to make public the crime, which he did by crying most bitterly throughout the rancheria, saying, that "so and so, has said or done this or that, to our captain,"—that "Chinigchinich is very angry, and wishes to chastise us, by sending upon us a plague, of which we may all die. Arm yourselves, then, both old and young, to kill the offender, so that by presenting him dead to Chinigchinich, he may be appeased, and not kill us." This was repeated several times throughout the town. As the Indians were easily influenced, they immediately went out, armed, in search of the delinquent, and when they fell in with him, they despatched him, and, together with the arrows with which they killed him, he was borne to the presence of Chinigchinich. The parents of the deceased were permitted afterwards to take possession of the body, and perform the accustomed ceremony of burning it.

The captain was authorized to decide upon all differences, occurring between his rancheria and the neighboring towns, to declare war, to make peace, and to appoint the days on which they were to celebrate their feasts, as well as those for the hunting of game, and the collecting of grain. This was about the extent of his authority. In case of a declaration of war, he convoked the Puplem, and explained his intentions; a consultation was held, to decide whether they alone, could carry on the warfare, without the assistance of the neighboring tribes; but no reflection was made as to the justice or injustice of their intentions. Immediately a crier was sent forth, to order the preparation of arms and men. The women were compelled to make an abundance of *pinole,* and to get ready the provisions necessary; and on the day determined upon for their march, the crier called them together, and they set forward, headed by the captain, who acted as general-in-chief, every one strictly obeying his orders.

They had a *pul,* (a kind of astrologer), who knew by the moon's appearance, the time to celebrate the feasts, and from his information, the captain made them public; and this was generally done by sending round a crier, on the evenings previous to their celebration. In the same manner, was made known the time to collect grain, and to hunt: but he, who advised the captain, was the one originally endowed with the power of providing their game, herbs, &c., &c. On such occasions, all turned out in quest of food, both men and women, boys and girls; and on returning to their rancheria, the greater part was deposited with the captain, who took care of the same for the feast. In their ordinary excursions for game, &c., the captain was obliged to hunt for his own subsistence, and although he frequently received a portion, still it was not considered obligatory on the part of the giver.

Some of them had two or more wives, that they might be more plentifully supplied with seeds, and vegetables, and thus have it in their power to make provision for the poor and feeble.

Chapter VI
The Instructions Given to Their Children

ONE OF THE DIFFICULTIES MOST PERPLEXING to the Indians, was, the rearing and educating their children. They were unacquainted with the arts, excepting those most necessary for their maintenance, and ignorant of all useful knowledge to keep them from idleness; so that their only education consisted in the construction of the bow and arrow, with their peculiar uses, in procuring game and defending themselves from their enemies.

Although, ignorant as they were of the knowledge of the true God, the moral instruction given by parents to their children, was contained in the precepts of Chinigchinich, which were strongly impressed upon their minds, that they might become good, and avoid the fate of the evil. The perverse child, invariably, was destroyed, and the parents of such remained dishonored. At the age of six, or seven years, they gave them a kind of god, as protector; an animal, in whom they were to place entire confidence, who would defend them from all dangers, particularly those in war against their enemies. They, however, were not to consider this animal as the *real* God, for he was invisible, and inhabited the mountains and bowels of the earth; and if he did appear to them at any time, it was in the shape of an animal of the most terrific description. This was not Chinigchinich, but another called *Touch,* signifying a *Devil.* That they might know the class of animal, which the God, Chinigchinich, had selected for their particular veneration, a kind of drink was administered to them, made from a plant called *Pibat,* which was reduced to a powder, and mixed with other intoxicating ingredients. Soon after taking this preparation, they became insensible, and for three days were deprived of any sustenance whatever. During this period they were attended by some old men or women, who were continually exhorting them to be on the alert, not to sleep for fear the *coyote,* the bear, the crow, or the rattlesnake might come; to observe if it were furious or gentle, and to inquire of the first that should come, what were its desires. The poor Indian thus intoxicated, without food or drink, suffering under delirium, beheld all kinds of visions; and when he made known that he had seen any particular being, who explained the observances required of him, then they gave him to eat and drink, and made a grand feast; at the same time advising him to be particular in obeying the commands of the mysterious apparition.

They did not *all* partake of the drink, and those who did not, were adorned with feathers, and were painted with a mixture of black and red. They were thus taken to the Vanquech in fantastical procession, and placed at the side of Chinigchinich. On the ground, and directly before them, the Puplem sketched a most uncouth and ridiculous figure, of an animal, and prohibited them from leaving the Vanquech during the time of penance, (generally three days) and in case of hunger or thirst, they were advised to suffer with patience. Should they partake of any thing, the figure before them would inform to that effect, and Chinigchinich would chastise them severely, by sending them sickness that would take away their lives. These and many other ludicrous stories were told to them, and the poor Indians placed the most implicit confidence in them.

The following circumstance was related to me, which transpired during the time of their heathenism. A young man, who had been taken to the Vanquech to perform the accustomed penance of fasting, the second day feeling somewhat afflicted with hunger and thirst, secretly retired from the temple, and entered a house that was near by, whose inhabitants were absent; and having found food, he ate and drank sufficiently, and returned without any one having seen him. After the accomplishment of the time, being one day in company with many of his friends, he related the circumstance, and gave out, as his opinion, that all that

24

was told them by the Puplem, regarding the figure upon the ground, *was a mere story,*—for he had eaten, and drank, and even injured with his foot a portion of the figure, and no bad result had happened to him; therefore they ought not to believe the Puplem. But his companions, instead of profiting by the information, immediately dispatched him with their arrows; so furious were they, on hearing of the sacrilege offered to their religious observances. He was the son of a captain, that is a prince, for only such could do penance in the Vanquech; others drank of the intoxicating mixture.

Having undergone the ceremonies described, they placed upon the poor Indians a brand, which was done in this manner. A kind of herb was pounded until it became sponge like; this, they placed, according to the figure required, upon the spot intended to be burnt, which was generally upon the right arm, and sometimes upon the thick part of the leg also. They then set fire to it, and let it remain until all that was combustible, was consumed. Consequently, a large blister immediately formed, and although painful, they used no remedy to cure it, but left it to heal itself; and thus, a large and perpetual scar remained. The reason alleged for this ceremony, was, that it added greater strength to the nerves, and gave a better pulse for the management of the bow. Besides, Chinigchinich required it of them, that they might be more formidable in war, and be enabled to conquer their enemies. Those who were not marked in this way, which was called *"potense,"* were ever unfortunate, easily conquered, and men of feeble capacities.

They also were obliged to undergo still greater martyrdom to be called men, and to be admitted among the already initiated; for, after the ceremony of the *"potense,"* they were whipped with nettles, and covered with ants, that they might become robust, and the infliction was always performed in summer, during the months of July and August, when the nettle was in its most fiery state. They gathered small bunches, which they fastened together, and the poor deluded Indian was chastised, by inflicting blows with them upon his naked limbs, until unable to walk; and then he was carried to the nest of the nearest, and most furious species of ants, and laid down among them, while some of his friends, with sticks, kept annoying the insects to make them still more violent. What torments did they not undergo! what pain! what hellish inflictions! yet, their faith gave them power to endure all without a murmur, and they remained as if dead. Having undergone these dreadful ordeals, they were considered as invulnerable, and believed that the arrows of their enemies could no longer harm them.

The young were not allowed to approach the fire to warm themselves, that they might learn to suffer, and become connaturalized with the changes of temperature—a severe deprivation, indeed, to the Indian! whose greatest luxury was to lie basking in the sun, or to enjoy the comforts of a blazing fire. They were forbidden also to eat certain kinds of seeds, and meats, until arrived at the age of manhood, and were even parents of two or three children. Should they eat of such, clandestinely, "*El Touch*" would know it, and chastise them in various ways; and Chinigchinich, also, would be very angry. Their faith and belief in these instructions were such, and the fear and terror produced therefrom, so infused among them, that, rather than violate them, they would suffer death.

Thus far, I have explained the education given to the boys. Now I will proceed to that instilled into the minds of the females. Besides the general instructions given to the males, to observe the commandments of Chinigchinich, the girls were taught to remain at home, and not to roam about in idleness; to be always employed in some domestic duty, so that, when they were older, they might know how to work, and attend to their household duties; such as procuring seeds, and cleaning them,—making "*atole*" and "*pinole*," which are kinds of gruel, and their daily food. When quite young, they have a small, shallow basket, called, by the natives, "*tucmel*," with which they learn the way to clean the seeds, and they are also instructed in grinding, and preparing the same, for consumption. Those who are industrious in their youth, are flattered with promises of many admirers when they grow up to be women—that they will be generally beloved, and receive many presents. In this neighborhood, and as I have been informed, as far south as Cape St. Lucas, the girls were tat-tooed in their infancy, from their eyebrows, down to their breasts; and some from the chin only—covering the arms entirely, in both cases—but, the execution of this was not generally complied with, until they reached their tenth year; and varied in the application and style. The usual method of effecting the same, was by pricking the parts with the thorn of the cactus plant, until they bled, and then they were rubbed with a kind of charcoal produced from *mescal*, so that a permanent blue color remained.

The particular reason for thus tat-tooing their females, was, that it added to their beauty, and when well executed, would insure them many admirers—but I think, besides this motive, it signified something more, and was a necessary kind of distinction. As the devil invented the branding of the males, so he may have ordered the painting of the females, and *Chinigchinich* required its performance; so that both might have their particular mark. Who was the inventor of the singular ceremony, I could not ascertain, but presume it must have been the famous *Ouimot*, who instituted the burning, or branding of the males.

A very novel, and rare custom, that these Indians had, was one that the parents invariably advised them to adhere to, after arriving at the state of womanhood, and it is this. In their excursions for the collecting of seeds, or for other purposes, should they unfortunately meet with one of the sorcerers, or eaters of human flesh, they were to comply with any desire which he might express, without manifesting the least reluctance on their part; not even if in company with their mothers, or if married, and attended by their husbands, should they command their protection. Both mothers and husbands were obliged to submit to his requests, through fear of the many inflictions, which they believed would be the result of their refusal; so, that whenever they discovered any of this detested race, if possible, they concealed themselves, so as not to be seen by them.

On arriving at the state of womanhood, a grand feast was made, and conducted with much ceremony and witchcraft. They made a large hole in the ground, in shape resembling a grave, about two feet deep: this they filled with stones and burning coals, and when sufficiently heated, the latter were taken out, and upon the former they laid branches of the "*estafiarte*" (a kind of perennial plant), so as to form a bed, which the natives called "*Pacsil*." Upon this, they placed the young girl, and for two or three days she was permitted to eat but very little; thus continuing until the accustomed term for purification had expired. In the meantime the outside of the hole was adorned with feathers of different birds, beads, and many other baubles. Several old women with their faces painted like devils, were employed in singing songs in a tone so disagreeable, that one could hardly tell whether they were crying, or laughing; and the young women danced around her, at intervals, every day.

28

Chapter VII
On Matrimony

THE USUAL CUSTOM OF THESE INDIANS IN SELECTing and obtaining their wives, was as follows:—When one of them was inclined to marry, and having seen one with whom he was particularly pleased, he kept loitering about her place of residence, until opportunity offered to communicate, in secret, the wish of his heart: generally, after this style: "I wish to wed with you," or, "We are to be married;" and the reply of the fair one, invariably, was, "It is well." "I will inform my parents, and you shall know." The girl then gave the information to her father and mother, and if the proposal were agreeable, the suitor was admitted to the house as a visitor.

Others proceeded after this manner:—They employed a third person to ascertain from the girl, if the proposal would be agreeable to her, and if so, the assent of the parents was solicited. In many cases the old men or women of the town made up the marriages, and after communicating with the parents of the girl, she was summoned to their presence and addressed as follows—"You are to marry so and so: you will be happy, because he is an excellent young man, and will have plenty to eat, and other things, for he knows how to kill the deer, rabbits, and other game." Others went direct to the parents of the girl to solicit their consent, and, if obtained, they were presented with some trifling gift as a token of the fact, and the daughter was informed as follows—"My child, you are to marry such a one; for we have given you away to him"—and the poor girl was obliged to submit, although, often-times, contrary to her wishes and feelings.

On the suitor's first visit to the house, he carried with him a present, either of some kind of fur skin, or of seeds or beads, or whatever else he had that was valuable; and from that day he considered it as his home, and the task of providing maintenance for the family, in part, fell upon him. During the time of their matrimonial promise, his obligations were to supply the house with fuel and game, and the girl attended to the domestic affairs—ever rising at the dawn of day, bathing herself, and supplying the house with water; after which, she put every thing in order, with the utmost precision, and prepared their customary repast. This task she was obliged to perform without any assistance whatever; thus, the wooer had an opportunity of witnessing the qualities of the girl, in regard to her acquirements in domestic duties, and for this reason, he was admitted to the house as a member of the family.

When the day was fixed upon for the celebration of the nuptials, the friends and relatives of each family were invited to attend, and every one in the town was expected to take part in the feast, which continued, always, for three or four days. In front of the house belonging to the lover, was erected a temporary shelter covered with the branches and leaves of trees, sufficiently large to accommodate a great number of people. The ceremony commenced by his sending one or two of the *Puplem* and a few of the old women, to bring the bride. In the meantime, he awaited her arrival, seated upon a mat or upon the ground. As soon as she appeared, adorned and dressed for the occasion, in all her gayest apparel, and before she entered the place prepared, already described, she was seized upon by the old women, disrobed, and thus, she was placed by the side of her husband. The dress and ornaments were never returned to her, but were considered by the women as "spoils," and each one present, secured as much as she could. This practice was universal, excepting at the marriages of the chiefs, who, while seated upon the mat, received the bride adorned with feathers only—her dress and trinkets having been previously removed. The *Puplem* then took her, and placed upon her person the dress of the "Capitanejas." While the feast lasted, the guests were employed in singing, dancing, and other diversions. It was usual on such occasions, before the separation took place between the parents and the bride, for the father to explain to her, her obligations and duties as a wife, and the instructions were as follows: "Reflect that you are the daughter of respectable parents—do nothing to offend them—obey and serve your husband, that has been given to you by *Chinigchinich;* be faithful to him, for if you are not, you will not only lose your life, but we shall be disgraced; and if your husband does not treat you as he ought, tell us, and you shall come back and live with us." This was the general custom among the Indians; and without any other ceremony, than the one here described, they were considered man and wife. Some parents, even, when their children were in infancy, by mutual agreement, would promise them in marriage, and the same was ever adhered to, and when the parties were of sufficient age, they were united with the customary ceremonies. During the period of their childhood, they were always together and the house of either was a home to both.

In the year 1821, in the Mission of St. Juan Capistrano, I married, in "facie eclesia," a couple who were thus betrothed. The girl was eight or nine months old, and the boy two years, when their parents contracted them.

There are other marriages, or modes, of taking a wife. For instance, whenever a captain, or a son of his, or a *pul* became enamored of one in another town, a messenger was despatched to solicit the *fair one*—if she declined, or if her parents were not pleased with the alliance, three or four armed men were sent to demand her in marriage, and to use any measures to secure her person. Others, when in the woods in search of game or seeds, if they met with one that pleased them, carried her off. These kinds of marriages, generally, were the cause of war, and severe conflicts between the neighboring towns.

Whether these Indians were lawfully and truly married, is a question. Apparently they were, excepting those who were united against their will and desire; and consequently, the contracts should be binding. Nevertheless, they did not consider the ceremony as binding, and they were at liberty to throw off the alliance, whenever they deemed it proper, or conductive to their convenience.

Quic noit noivam	"I go to my home,
Quic secat peleblich.	That is shaded with willow."
Ybicnun majaar vesagnec,	"These five they have placed,
Ibi panal, ibi urusar,	This argave, this stone pot,
Ibi ecbal, ibi seja, ibi calcel.	This sand, this honey," &c., &c.

The first time the wife became enceinte, it was the custom to give a grand feast to all in the town, and they passed the whole of one night in dancing and singing. This rejoicing was on account of the looked-for increase, and in their songs they asked of Chinigchinich, his clemency towards the unborn, for the female was good—having, in a short time, arrived to a state that gave hopes of her becoming a mother. They looked upon a sterile woman as being unfortunate—one who would ever meet with calamities. On the day of the birth of the child, they made no particular demonstration of satisfaction, except to exhibit the infant to the people. If it were a male, the grandfather named it, saying A. B., thus shall he be named. If it were a female, then the grandmother named it, and generally gave it her own name, or, that of the mother, unless some event occurred about the time of the birth, and then it was given a name which would serve to commemorate that event. Notwithstanding no observance was made of the birth-day, yet the day, on which the umbilical cord was removed, was noticed with many ceremonies. All the relatives and friends of the family were invited to assist in the superstitious performances, and they were conducted as follows. At the hour appointed, all the guests being present, several old women who were skilled in the operation, removed the superabundant particles from the child, and the same were interred, with many ceremonies, in a hole prepared either within, or outside of the house. Then immediately commenced dancing and singing; and even now, among some of the Indians, the same observances are retained.

The most ludicrous custom among these Indians, was that of observing the most rigid diet from the day of their wives' confinement. They could not leave the house, unless to procure fuel and water—were prohibited the use of all kinds of fish and meat—smoking and diversions; and this observance lasted generally from fifteen to twenty days.

One of the many singularities that prevailed among these Indians was that of marrying males with males, which has been spoken of by Father Torquemada. It was publicly done, but without the forms, and ceremonies already described in their marriage contracts with the females. Whilst yet in infancy they were selected, and instructed as they increased in years, in all the duties of the women—in their mode of dress—of walking, and dancing; so that in almost every particular, they resembled females. Being more robust than the women, they were better able to perform the arduous duties required of the wife, and for this reason, they were often selected by the chiefs and others, and on the day of the wedding a grand feast was given. To distinguish this detested race at this mission, they were called *"Cuit,"* in the mountains, *"Uluqui,"* and in other parts, they were known by the name of *"Coias."* At the present time, this horrible custom is entirely unknown among them. I was told by a missionary from the Mission of St. Domingo, in Lower California, that he once enquired of several Indians, from the plains of the river Colorado, if in their confines, were to be found any of the *Coias?* he replied that they were once very numerous, but a serious plague visited them, many years back, which destroyed them all—unfortunately the time when this great event transpired, they could not tell, as they possessed no idea, whatever, of chronology.

Chapter VIII
On Their Mode of Life and Occupation

AMONG THE NATURAL INCLINATIONS WITH which man is endowed, is that of defending, and preserving his own individual person. For this reason, he feels it his duty to consider how, and in what manner, he is to live, and how to procure the necessary means of sustenance. Necessity, "the mother of invention," has therefore revealed to him how to arrange the rustic implements, used for securing his food. No doubt these Indians passed a miserable life, ever idle, and more like the brutes, than rational beings. They neither cultivated the ground, nor planted any kind of grain; but lived upon the wild seeds of the field, the fruits of the forest, and upon the abundance of game. It is really surprising, that during a lapse of many ages, with their reason and experience, they had not advanced one iota in improving the things that would have been useful and convenient for them; for instance, in agriculture; in planting and cultivating those seeds which were most appreciated—also trees around their dwellings, bearing such fruit as they were obliged to bring from a great distance. But no! nothing of the kind; and in no part of the province was to be found aught but the common, spontaneous, productions of the earth.

It cannot be denied, that these Indians, like all the human race, are the descendants of Adam; endowed with reason, or in other words, with a soul. When we read of the ancients—of their having transplanted trees which were wild, thus increasing their abundance, and quality, and of

34

their planting seeds, which improved by cultivation, we cannot but wonder that a knowledge so important was unknown here until the missionary fathers came amongst them, and introduced the planting of wheat, corn, beans, and other grains, that are now so abundant every where. I consider these Indians, in their endowments, like the soul of an infant, which is merely a will, accompanied with passions—an understanding not exercised, or without use; and for this reason, they did not comprehend the virtue of prudence, which is the result of time and reason—of the former, by experience, and the latter, by dissertation. Although ripe in years, they had no more experience than when in childhood—no reasoning powers, and therefore followed blindly in the footsteps of their predecessors.

Their occupation consisted in the construction of the bow and arrow, in hunting for deer, rabbits, squirrels, rats, &c., which not only provided them with food, but *clothing,* if so it can be called. Their usual style of dress, was a small skin thrown over the shoulders, leaving the remaining portion of their person unprotected; but the females formed a kind of cloak out of the skins of rabbits, which were put together after this manner. They twisted them into a kind of rope, that was sewed together, so as to conform to the size of the person, for whom it was intended, and the front was adorned with a kind of fringe, composed of grass, which reached down to the knees; around the collar it was adorned with beads, and other ornaments, prized by the Indians.

They passed their time in plays, and roaming about from house to house, dancing and sleeping; and this was their only occupation, and the mode of life most common amongst them from day to day. The old men, and the poorer class, devoted a portion of the day to constructing house utensils, their bows and arrows, and the several instruments used in making their baskets; also nets of various dimensions, which were used for sundry purposes, such as for catching fish and wild fowl, and for carrying heavy burdens on their backs, fastened by a strap passed across the forehead. In like manner, the females used them for carrying their infants.

The women were obliged to gather seeds in the fields, prepare them for cooking, and to perform all the meanest offices, as well as the most laborious. It was painful in the extreme, to behold them, with their infants hanging upon their shoulders, groping about in search of herbs or seed, and exposed as they frequently were to the inclemency of the weather. Often it was the case that they returned home severely fatigued, and hungry, to cook the fruits of their toil, but, perhaps, there would be no wood, the fire extinguished, and their lazy husband either at play or sleeping, so that again they would be obliged to go out into the cold for fuel. When the brutal husband came home, or awoke from his slug-gishness, he expected his meal, and if not prepared at the moment, invectives and ill treatment were the universal consequence. Poor crea-tures! more unfortunate than slaves! They were in such subjection, that for the most trifling offence, punishment was the result, and oftentimes death; but, thank Heaven! since the introduction of the Christian re-ligion among this unhappy race, the females have received more liberty and better treatment. The most wonderful of God's blessings enjoyed among them, was the great facility with which they underwent their accouchement, when it would seem as if they endured no suffering.

Chapter IX
On Their Principal Feasts and Dances

AS ON ALL THEIR FEAST DAYS, DANCING WAS the principal ceremony, I will endeavor to describe many of the ludicrous customs attending it. Such was the delight with which they took part in their festivities, that they often continued dancing day and night, and sometimes entire weeks. Their whole heart and soul were wrapt up in the amusement, and hardly a day passed, without some portion of it being devoted to this insipid and monotonous ceremony. Chinigchinich gave to them as a religious precept, that they should adhere strictly to this custom, and once, previous to his death, whilst dancing, he was carried up among the stars. So this accounts for the enthusiasm universally observed among them on such occasions, and whoever did not take an active part in the festival, they believed would be chastised, and hated by him.

The costume used by them, called the *tobet*, has been already mentioned in a previous chapter, when describing the dress of the "capitans" or "puplem;" but perhaps, it would not be out of place to repeat the same, and in addition, to give a description of that generally worn by the females. In the first place, they fixed upon the head a kind of wig, called "*emetch*," that was made secure, by a braid of hair passed around the head, into which, they inserted various kinds of feathers, forming a crown, or as they termed it, an "*eneat;*" then, their covering for the body, was also prepared from the feathers of different kinds of birds, which were sewed together, and like a sort of petticoat reached down to their knees—this they called a *"paelt."* The parts exposed, were generally painted red and black, and not unfrequently, white.

The females painted their faces, breasts and arms, with a sort of brown varnish, imparting a glossy, and rather a disgusting appearance to their persons. From their necks, was suspended a variety of ornaments, such as beads, and pieces of shells. They never danced with the males, but each sex by itself, notwithstanding all danced at the same time, and after this manner. The males formed a file by themselves, and directly behind them, say two or three yards distant, the women were placed in like manner, and the musicians seated themselves upon the ground in front of all.

Many of their dances were very modest and diversified by a number of grotesque movements, so that for a short time one could look on, and witness their performances with some degree of pleasure; but they had no variety of figures, or songs, and kept on in the same monotonous movement. There were persons selected from both sexes to conduct the music, and for this purpose they had a kind of instrument, which they called *"paail."*

The most celebrated of all their feasts, and which was observed yearly, was the one they called the *"Panes,"* signifying a bird feast. Particular adoration was observed by them, for a bird resembling much in appearance the common buzzard, or vulture, but of larger dimensions. The day selected for the feast, was made known to the public on the evening previous to its celebration, and preparations were made immediately for the erection of their Vanquech, into which, when completed, and on the opening of the festival, they carried the Panes in solemn procession, and placed it upon the altar erected for the purpose. Then, immediately, all the young, married and unmarried females, commenced running to and fro, with great rapidity; some in one direction, and some in another, more like distracted, than rational beings; continuing thus racing, as it were, whilst the elder class of both sexes remained silent spectators of the scene. The *"Puplem,"* painted as has been heretofore described, looking like so many devils, in the meantime dancing around their adored *"Panes."*

38

These ceremonies being concluded, they seized upon the bird, and carried it in procession to the principal Vanquech, or temple, all the assembly uniting in the grand display—the Puplem preceding the same, dancing and singing. Arriving there, they killed the bird without losing a particle of its blood. The skin was removed entire, and preserved with the feathers, as a relic, or for the purpose of making their festival garment, "*Paelt.*" The carcass they interred within the temple, in a hole prepared previously, around which, all the old women soon collected, who, while weeping and moaning most bitterly, kept throwing upon it various kinds of seeds, or particles of food, and exclaiming at the same time, "Why did you run away? would you not have been better with us? you would have made pinole as we do, and if you had not run away, you would not have become a 'Panes!'" Other expressions equal in simplicity, were made use of, and as the ceremony was concluding, the dancing commenced again, and continued for three days and nights, accompanied with all the brutalities to which they were subject.

The Indians state that said "Panes" was once a female, who ran off and retired to the mountains, when accidentally meeting with "Chinigchinich," he changed her into a bird, and their belief is, that notwithstanding they sacrificed it every year, she became again animated, and returned to her home among the mountains. But the ridiculous fable does not end here; for they believed, as often as the bird was killed, it became multiplied; because, every year, all the different Capitanes celebrated the same feast of *Panes,* and were firm in the opinion that the birds sacrificed, were but one, and the same female. They had no evidence, however, of where she lived, or where she originated, and neither were the names of her parents known. The commemoration of the festival, was in compliance with the commands given to them by Chinigchinich.

The kind of dance common among these natives, was introduced by first preparing a large bonfire, around, and into which, the men promiscuously jumped, until all the fire was extinguished. The females stood a short distance from the scene, keeping up a continual screaming, and moaning, during the ceremony, and not until every particle of the fire was destroyed did the crying cease—then dancing commenced. Should it so happen, that they were not successful in extinguishing the flames, or if there should remain, and be discovered afterwards, any

39

sparks, the dancing did not take place immediately; but they remained silent and discontented. It was a bad omen, and signified the approach of some calamity. This dance was generally performed at night, but when introduced in their large feasts, and danced during the day, then, in addition to the ceremonies already described, they despatched one of the most active of the tribe in quest of water, which, invariably, was brought from a great distance, and from a place designated. When obtained, they emptied the same into a hole previously prepared within the Vanquech. Then all went up into the temple, each one in his turn, blowing with his mouth upon the water, and uttering expressions which were apparently designed to curse and not to bless; however, the latter was the interpretation given to me, and when this was done, they went up again in the same order to sprinkle their faces with the dirty water. The women remained some distance off, and on no account were they allowed to touch it.

Another dance equally ludicrous among these natives, was conducted as follows. The males commenced, first dancing alone, and continued to do so for a short time, when they formed themselves in a line, and one of the females came forward in front of them, with her arms folded upon her breast, and danced up and down the file with many graceful turns, and movements, which were several times repeated, when she retired, and the males resumed their part of the performances—and so they continued dancing, the males and females alternately, until it was time to change the monotony. They had another dance, very similar, with this exception—that the female was entirely exposed, and whilst she was singing and displaying her person in many disgusting attitudes, the spectators, men, women and children, all formed a circle around her. This immodest exhibition was also one of the teachings of Chinig-chinich, but was introduced twice, only, during the year, and then outside of the town.

They had another, which was introduced on the occasion of the son of the puplem, or chief's first appearing in public, adorned with the Tobet. Not only every one in the place was invited to attend on that day, but also many from the neighboring towns, and the arrangements were as follows. When all were congregated together, the youth was brought forward, and they put upon him the paelt, or robe of feathers, such as was used by Chinigchinich, afterwards the crown, and then the exposed parts of his person, they painted black and red. Thus arrayed, he commenced dancing, with the *paail* in his right hand, keeping time to the music of the singers, that did not cease until the lad was completely exhausted. If he were unable to dance, then, one of the Puplem was dressed in like manner, who, placing him upon his shoulder, danced before the assembly. After this was accomplished, one of the women rose up; a sister, an aunt, or some one nearly related to the youth, in all cases, however, a young person, who immediately disrobing herself, danced in presence of the multitude.

Chapter X
Of Many of Their Extravagances

SUPERSTITIONS OF A RIDICULOUS, AND MOST extravagant nature, were found associated with these Indians, and even now, in almost every town, or hamlet, the child's first education is a belief in their authenticity; and they grow up from infancy familiar with all their fabulous traditions. The effect tends to enervate their physical faculties, and weaken their mental, so that they naturally become a pusillanimous race of people, liable to be deceived, imposed upon, and of course easily influenced by the *puplem*, and old men, who are their sole instructors.

There are men, and also females, who are believed to possess the power of enchantment, to such a degree, that no one can withstand their powers; so that without resistance, all immediately acquiesce in their demands. The incantation is performed thus: Beneath the left arm, in a small leather bag, they carry a black ball, called by them *"aguet,"* composed of a plaster of *mescal*, and wild honey, or, as they term it, "quijotes," or "sejat." When they wish to make use of the same, to exercise its virtues upon any one, the right hand is placed upon the leather bag, and without any other ceremony, the sorcery is effected. Should the person appear indifferent to the presence of the enchanter, then a companion immediately announces the fact, that he bears the sacred charm, and their demands are complied with, without reply or opposition. The said "aguet," is a composition unknown to all but the sorcerers, and of course, only used by them. How it possesses so much virtue, I have never been enabled to discover. Nevertheless, they give up whatever is asked of them, under the impression that more calamities will attend them, if they do not.

They have an idea, that if the shadow of the *aura*, in his flying through the air, should fall upon them with their heads uncovered, they would become afflicted with sores and diseases, and on this account, whenever it so happens that a bird of this class approaches, they immediately cover their persons.

They believed when the *pelican* visited the inland population, that it was an omen of death to some one, and consequently, they persecuted the bird until it left their neighborhood. Another ridiculous belief among them was, that the deer hunters could never partake of venison which they, themselves, procured, and only of such as was taken by others, for the reason, that if they did, they would not get any more. And the fishermen, also, possessed the same idea with regard to their fish. More singular, however, than this, was the custom among the young men, when starting for the woods in search of rabbits, squirrels, rats, or other animals. They were obliged to take a companion for the reason, that he who killed the game, could not eat thereof—if he did, in a few days he complained of pains in his limbs, and gradually became emaciated. On this account, two went together, in order to exchange with each other the result of their excursion. This infliction did not extend to every one who partook of the game of his own taking, but only to such as were guilty of consuming it secretly. Neither was it incurable, for they had among them certain sorcerers possessing the power to reinstate them in their former health and contentment.

When the sun, or moon, was eclipsed, they appeared much frightened; and the men, women, and children, were heard crying and shouting, whilst throwing sand into the air, and beating with sticks upon dry hides, or upon the ground. This was done, as they said, to scare away a large and ferocious monster, who would devour the sun and moon, and if he were permitted to accomplish the entire consumption of either, that is, if there should be a *total eclipse*, all would immediately die, and the world would come to an end.

At the time of new moon, and on the first day of its appearance, it was usual amongst them to call together all the young men for the purpose of its celebration. A "correr la luna!" shouted one of the old men. Come, my boys, the moon! the moon! Immediately, racing commenced, and without order they ran about as if they were distracted, whilst the old men danced in a circle, saying the following words—"As the moon dieth, and cometh to life again, so we also having to die, will again live,"—thus manifesting clearly the resurrection of the flesh. How this was understood by them, I did not ascertain, for they could not explain it, and they merely observed the ceremony, on account of its having been practised by their ancestors.

Another belief, current with the younger part of the females of the community, was, that the meteoric appearances often beheld in the evening, were the *Tacuieh,* or children of the moon, and whenever they beheld them, they fell upon the ground, and covered their heads, fearing if seen by them, that their faces would become ugly, and diseased. They had amongst them certain individuals who pretended to be descendants of the "Coyote" eaters of human flesh—not as the cannibals and Mexicans—but their manner of proceeding was after the following disgusting custom. Whenever a Captain, or one of the Puplem, died, they sent for the *Eno,* who was thus called before he officiated in his duties, and afterwards *"Tacue,"* signifying "an eater." Having arrived at the place, where they had placed the dead body, he immediately cut off a large piece from the neck, and the back, near the shoulder, and consumed the flesh in its raw state, in presence of the multitude assembled to witness the performance. This was always done in commemoration of the feat performed by the "Coyote" upon the body of the great Captain *Ouiot,* as has been already recounted in a previous chapter. For this, *Eno* was well remunerated, and every one contributed for the purpose. The young of both sexes, were very much afraid of this *Tacue,* and looked upon him as a sorcerer.

These Indians were not entirely destitute of a knowledge of the universal deluge, but how, or from whence, they received the same, I could never understand. Some of their songs refer to it; and they have a tradition that, at a time very remote, the sea began to swell and roll in upon the plains, and fill the valleys, until it had covered the mountains; and thus nearly all the human race and animals were destroyed, excepting a few, who had resorted to a very high mountain which the waters did not reach. But the songs give a more distinct relation of the same, and they state that the descendants of Captain *Ouiot* asked of Chinigchinich vengeance upon their chief—that he appeared unto them, and said to those endowed with the power, "Ye are the ones to achieve vengeance—ye who cause it to rain! Do this, and so inundate the earth, that every living being will be destroyed." The rains commenced, the sea was troubled, and swelled in upon the earth, covering the plains, and rising until it had overspread the highest land, excepting a high mountain, where, the few had gone with the one who had caused it to rain, and thus every other animal was destroyed upon the face of the earth. These songs were supplications to Chinigchinich to drown their enemies. If their opponents heard them, they sang others in opposition, which in substance ran thus: "We are not afraid, because Chinigchinich does not wish to, neither will he destroy the world by another inundation." Without doubt this account has reference to the universal deluge, and the promise God made, that there should not be another.

WE CANNOT BUT BELIEVE THAT THE CALEN-
dar is one of the most important and the most necessary of inventions.
But theirs, if we may call it such, differed but very little from the natural
instinct of the brute creation, which possessed a knowledge of time, and
the seasons for their sustenance and procreation. We see that many
animals change their places, and even climates, at a time prefixed; either
on account of the temperature or want of food; and at the proper time
for their return they visit again the same locations. The Indians had the
same custom, as regards the changing from place to place; for in the
winter they resided in one place, and in summer in another. This was
general amongst them, excepting with those located on the sea-coast,
who seldom removed, because their maintenance was derived from the
sea; unlike the others who subsisted entirely upon fruits and seeds of
the fields. Their calendar contained merely the names of the months,
directing the times or seasons for the collecting of their different seeds,
and produce of the earth. Not all of them possessed this knowledge; it
being confined to the *Puplem* who were the criers that informed them
when to cultivate their fields, and observe other requisitions. In the first
place, they were destitute of chronology, by which to calculate the
period of time transpired; hence, the difficulty in giving any account of
their antiquities, as they had neither figures nor signs to preserve them;
and possessing no idea of the past, their thoughts were limited solely to

the present. On this account their calendar was confined to the months of the year, but as they reckoned these by the number of moons, they differed from the "sun's reckoning," having almost every year a less number of days—for at the conclusion of the moon in December, that is, at the conjunction, they calculated the return of the sun from the Tropic of Capricorn; and another year commenced, the Indian saying "the sun has arrived at his home." When the new year begun, no thought was given to the past; and on this account, even amongst the most intelligent, they could not tell the number of years which had transpired, when desirous of giving an idea of any remote event.

They observed with greater attention and celebrated with more pomp, the sun's arrival at the tropic of Capricorn, than they did his reaching the tropic of Cancer, for the reason, that, as they were situated ten degrees from the latter, they were pleased at the sun's approach towards them; for it returned to ripen their fruits and seeds, to give warmth to the atmosphere, and enliven again the fields with beauty and increase.

The names of the months were as follows:—

Aapcomil,	December and January.
Peret,	February.
Yarmar,	March.
Alasoguil,	April.
Tocoboaich,	May.
Sintecar,	June and July.
Cucuat,	August.
Lalavaich,	September.
Aguitscomel,	October.
Aaguit,	November.

In order to comprehend the manner in which they counted the months, it is necessary to know that their year commenced always on the 21st day of December, and upon the sun's arrival at the tropic—consequently, the days which transpired between the last conjunction and the 21st were not noticed—or, in their mode of explanation, "There was no day." The month "Aapcomil" always begun on the 21st, without any regard to the moon's age, and not only continued during the remainder of its term, but throughout the one following; thus including nearly two moons. Sometimes it so happened that the moon's conjunction occurred on the 21st or afterwards, in which case two entire moons were counted in the first month. Nearly the same occurrence took place in "Sintecar," with this difference only, that if the sun's arrival at the tropic of Cancer fell upon the day of the moon's full, then the month began; but the days previous to this were made use of, and annexed to the antecedent "Tocoboaich,"—that is, the month did not expire with the conjunction, but at the full; when the other began, and continued throughout the following moon. All the other months of the year commenced with the conjunction, therefore, they seldom agreed with ours.

Their calendar contained no more; and served, principally, to denote when to harvest the grain, celebrate their feasts, and commemorate the death of their friends. But of the number of days contained in their months, they had no knowledge whatever, and much less of those composing the year—so that the phases of the moon were their only guide, and these informed them when they were to observe their feastings, which never fell upon the same day in any other year. The way they ascertained when to celebrate them, was as follows. When the month arrived, one of the Puplem (to whom belonged the privilege of holding the feast) observed with attention the moon's aspect; and when its appearance denoted the time, he made known the fact to the public by sending a crier through the town.

In like manner, they proceeded, in regard to the anniversaries of the dead, although they were never celebrated on the same day in any other year, as that on which the person died. At the time of the decease of a captain, or of one of the Puplem, (for they paid no attention to others) a *Pul* observed the moon's aspect, also the month in which the death occurred; and in the following year, in the same month, when the moon's aspect was the same, they celebrated the anniversary.

Chapter XII
The Indian Wars

WAR WAS INVENTED BY MEN, AND FOR THE purpose of taking from each other, their estates and other property, or for carrying into effect their revengeful dispositions. Thus it was with these Indians, whose battles were frequent, and often declared from the most trivial causes. A consultation was not necessary to decide if the war were just or unjust, but to ascertain if their force were sufficient, and to provide measures whereby they might take advantage of, and surprise their adversaries. War was never waged by them for conquest, but for revenge; and in many cases for some affront given to their ancestors, which had remained unavenged. Their quarrels and disputes arose from trivial motives, for their wealth was trifling, and consisted merely of seeds, skins, or beads, which were universally esteemed amongst them as money. Also, when a chief neglected to return the customary present at their festivities, of which I have before treated, war was declared, and without even giving him notice. Again, if an Indian of one place stole anything from one of another place, although it might be so trifling a thing as a rabbit, a squirrel, or, ornament of some kind, it was sufficient among them to cause a war.

Whenever a captain determined to make war upon another chief, he called together the puplem, and revealed to them his desire to make war upon such a town, for reasons which he explained, and it was discussed by the body, whether they were sufficient of themselves to conquer. If

49

sensible of their inferiority, some other friendly tribes were invited to
join with them, to whom they sent presents of as costly a kind as their
treasury would admit; and if *they* acquiesced, then the day was fixed
upon to assemble for battle. All this was conducted secretly, but, nevertheless, the parties to be attacked were generally warned of their danger, and of course prepared for the conflict. The war being determined
upon, a crier was sent around during the evening, exhorting all the
people to repair on the following day, at an early hour, to the residence
of the chief, and when there congregated, he ordered them to prepare
their arms of bows and arrows; and to the females, he delivered grain,
for them to grind into flour, which they called *pinole*. But the reason for
such measures was not revealed. However, when the day was decided
upon for the marching of the expedition, then the crier went around a
second time, and commanded them to repair as before, to the residence
of the chief; and all went—the men with their bows and arrows, and the
women with their *pinoles*. Having assembled before the vanquech,
where the captain and puplem had resorted, according to the custom,
the crier explained to the people why such preparations were made—
why war was declared, and the young men were urged to combat and
revenge. Immediately commenced the necessary preparations—each put
on his dress, and uniform, corresponding to his rank. The women, in
like manner, adorned themselves for the occasion, and thus they started
off for the battle ground, old and young—the females carrying the provisions, and upon their backs their infant children. Their order of march
was as follows:—The captain, or one appointed by him, took the lead at
the head of the young men—in succession followed the older ones,
and the women closed up the rear, it being their duty to gather up the
arrows of the opposing force which were scattered around them, and
distribute the same among their own warriors. Should one of their own
party be killed or wounded, they were obliged to remove him to a place
of security, so that the enemy could not get at him. No quarter was ever
given, and consequently, no prisoners were ever made among the men,
excepting of such as were killed, or mortally wounded. These were immediately decapitated by some old men appointed for the purpose, and
the hair taken from the heads, together with the scalps, which were
dried and cured, after the manner of dressing their skins, and preserved

as trophies of victory. The women and children taken prisoners, were either disposed of, by sale, or detained by the captain as slaves.

When celebrating their grand feasts, it was customary to expose in public the scalps taken in war; and for this purpose they were suspended from a high pole, erected near the vanquech. Sometimes scalps were redeemed by paying largely; but the women and children were never released,—ever remaining as slaves to their enemies, unless fortunate enough to escape to the protection of their own nation.

Chapter XIII
Their Funeral Ceremonies

BEFORE TREATING UPON THE SUBJECT OF their manner of interment, I will just refer to the remedies used for their diseases. They possessed some knowledge of the virtues of certain medicinal herbs, and the external application of them to cutaneous disorders; but for internal diseases, such as fevers, &c., they always resorted to cold baths. For pains in the head, immediate application of cold water was the remedy. For external diseases, such as tumors, swellings, sores and rheumatic pains, they made use of various herbs, known to us, and called sage, rosemary, and nettle-plant—which were applied in a plaster. They made use of a kind of black rosin also, which was very oily, and manufactured from certain seeds. When attacked with pain in the stomach they inhaled the smoke of these plants, and if afflicted with any ordinary pain, a whipping, with nettles, was applied to the part affected, and frequently large ants.

For disease of the liver, fevers, and all malignant complaints, I have not discovered that they made use of any remedies but the cold water baths, before mentioned. Sometimes the patient, entirely exposed, was laid upon a quantity of dry ashes or sand, and at his feet blazed a scorching fire, without regard to the season. At his head stood a small vessel of water, and sometimes gruel, that he might partake of them, if he chose, but no persuasions were ever used on the part of his friends to induce him to do so, if he did not feel inclined. He was never left alone, being attended by many of his friends, both day and night; and thus he remained until either nature, or the disease, conquered.

As soon as any one fell ill, they immediately sent for the physician, who was one of the *puplem,* or soothsayers before spoken of. It must be understood that not all of the *puplem* possessed the necessary qualifications, but only those who received them by succession. When they appeared before the patient, it was always with an air of great mystery. A strict examination into the state of the patient, was the commencement of their performances, and divers infirmities were explained, and their causes—all originating from the introduction of certain particles into the body of the patient, such as the hairs of various animals, bones, stones, briers, sticks, &c., which produced the pain or infirmity. Before prescribing anything, they made use of many superstitious ceremonies. In the first place, the patient was examined from head to foot, and no part of his body remained untouched. Then the painful parts became the topic of discussion, and were represented as having within them something of a hard substance, such as a stone, splinter, or bone, and of course, their success in removing the disease was ever a matter of great uncertainty; but still, they would use all their skill, and endeavor to restore him to health. They placed feathers upon his head, and encircled him entirely with these, and other articles, such as horse-hair, grass, beads, and hairs of the head; blowing at the same time with their mouths towards the four cardinal points, and muttering to themselves certain low sounds—certain mysterious words—accompanied with antic gesticulations, of which no one knew the meaning. After this, one of them applied his lips to the part affected, and pretended to draw from it, by suction, the particles, which they had stated as being within, and exposed them to all present. The spectators, as well as the patient, placed strict confidence in the fact, and were satisfied, whether he recovered or died. When the patient did not recover from his disease, the *puplem* would say, it was because Chinigchinich had sent him the infirmity, as a chastisement for some act of disobedience, and that he must reconcile himself to death.

There were many of these impostors spread about the country, who, after being well fed and paid for their *services,* made all manner of ridicule of their too credulous companions. Wonderful as it may appear, oftentimes they performed cures, when the patients were apparently fast verging into eternity, and in the space of twenty-four hours, by their extravagances and witchcraft, they have enabled them to rise from a bed of sickness, and unite with their companions in their domestic employments. I will relate a case which happened in the mission of "La Purissima," A.D. 1809, which will serve to confirm the truth of the preceding statement. A young woman of eighteen years of age, had been sick for nearly a year, suffering from the effects of dysentery and fever, so that she had wasted away almost to a skeleton, and was to all appearances dying; having received the holy sacrament preparatory to her supposed departure. One morning, whilst walking in the garden of the mission, I saw her sitting with other females performing the task of clearing the grass; surprised at beholding her there, when I supposed her dying, I asked her how she felt? Her mother, who was at her side, replied to the question, and said that she was well, because such a one (naming one of the sorcerers) had taken from her some bear's hairs, which were the cause of her illness, and, immediately, she was restored. I inquired how they were introduced into her stomach, and how long she had had them? She replied, that when in childhood, and about eight or nine years old, one night, whilst asleep with other children in a room by themselves, a bear came and placed some of his hairs on her stomach. How he came there, or how the hairs got into her stomach, she could not explain; for all that she knew about it, had been stated to her by the sorcerer. This was all deception, of course, but still it happened from that day, that the girl improved in health, and, in a short time, was as robust and hearty as any one!

When the patient died under the attendance of these physicians, then preparations were made for his sepulture, or the burning of his body, according to a custom observed here, in commemoration of the last ceremonies rendered to the remains of their grand chieftain *Ouiot*. They did not put into immediate execution the solemn duties and funeral performances, but suffered several hours to elapse, that they might be assured of his death. In the meantime the pile was prepared, and the person summoned, who officiated on such occasions in applying the torch; for it was usual, in this neighborhood, to employ certain characters, who made their livelihood by it, and who, generally, were confined to particular families. As soon as every thing was prepared, and the time had arrived for the ceremony, they bore the corpse to the place of sacrifice, where it was laid upon the faggots. Then the friends of the deceased retired, and the burner (so called) set fire to the pile, and remained near the spot until all was consumed to ashes. The ceremony being concluded on his part, he was paid for his services, and withdrew. Every thing of use, belonging to the deceased, such as his bow and arrows, feathers, beads, skins, &c., were consumed with him, whilst his relatives and friends added, also, other articles of value to the sacrifice, but during the scene of burning they did not observe any particular ceremony, nor had they any; for as soon as the burner gave notice that he had performed his task, they all retired outside of the town to mourn the decease of their friend. The *puplem* sang songs, while the relatives wept; and the substance of their canticles was merely a relation of the cause of the infirmity—the location of the disease—when it first commenced, and its course throughout the body, until it attacked the heart, when he died, thus naming over all the parts of the human frame. These songs were generally repeated over and over for three days and nights, and then they returned to their homes.

The mode of testifying their grief by outward appearance, was by shortening the hair of their heads; and in conformity to the kin of the deceased, so they regulated the custom. For the loss of a parent, wife or child, the head was completely shorn; for a distant relative, they cut off merely one half of the length, and for a friend, only the extremity; but in all cases, however, they were governed entirely by the love and attachment for the deceased. The same custom is now in use, and not only applied to deaths, but to their disappointments and adversities in life, thus making public demonstration of their sorrow.

Chapter XIV
The Immortality of the Soul

HIS CHAPTER MAY CAUSE SOME PERPLEXITY, FROM the circumstance of its treating of that which is imperceptible to the senses; of a substance incorporeal and spiritual. Still, I can in a very few words make known the belief of these Indians, relative to the rational soul, and what they understood concerning its immortality. There are arguments pro and con, which are of particular interest, inasmuch as they involve the future destiny of man; I will be more explicit in my remarks here, than in the preceding chapter, and recount all that I have been enabled to acquire relative to the subject.

In their gentilism, they were undoubtedly materialists, for they believed that the soul was the *"espiritu vital,"* received from the air, which they breathed, and which they called *"piuts,"* signifying *"to live."* They possessed no knowledge, nor did they believe in the existence of any other substance than the material body. On this account they said, (and many believe it at the present time,) that man was composed of bones, flesh and blood only; for *"piuts,"* which is the breath, is another thing, like wind, that goes and comes. The body they called *"petacan,"* a term applied, to the brute creation as well as man, or rather, to all living or animated beings. To designate the soul belonging to the body from the *"espiritu vital,"* they possessed no term but *"pusuni,"* which is general in its meaning, and signifies a "substance within," applied to things animate and inanimate, and to the heart, on account of its location, and particular importance to the body.

They penetrated no farther than was perceptible to the sense, for the reason that the spirituality of the soul was incomprehensible to them; they only understanding the materials of the body. Thus they were materialists, for they said that when the body died, and was burnt, naught remained, for all was consumed. Death, they believed was an entity, real and invisible, who, when in anger with any one, took away by degrees his breath, until all was removed, and then the person died. I have observed, in a previous chapter, that the punishments they so much feared from Chinigchinich, were all corporeal, such as falling over stones, and upon the earth—the bite of the serpent, bears, &c.; and lastly, death—the termination, without reference to pain, punishment, or glory afterwards. I think this sufficient to prove that they were materialists; but as they relate a thousand novel accounts, relative to the immortality of the soul, which have proceeded from dreams or delirium, I will recount some of them, as they were related to me.

Materialists, as I have supposed them, (without adding other convincing reasons, such as the great insensibility manifested at the hour of their death—the little inclination for divine things, and desire for the unholy, which go far to show plainly their want of knowledge of the rational soul, and consequently of its immortality;) still, the words or expressions, made use of in the tenth chapter relative to the moon, are of opposing force—viz., "that as the moon dieth and cometh to life again, so we, having to die, will again live." But, as I observed in the chapter cited, I can not comprehend how they understood it—nor can I think that their ancestors believed in the resurrection of the flesh. They may have had such belief many ages back, and the tradition may have been preserved in songs. Other verses are used in opposition, and are frequently sung at their festivals—viz., "Let us eat, for we shall die, and then all will be finished,"—words similar in sense to the passage in the Holy Scriptures, referring to the expressions of the foolish young men.

Let us refer now to some of the accounts respecting the soul's immortality. It is affirmed by some, that "when an Indian died, he went to the abode of his God Chinigchinich, a sort of earthly paradise, called, 'tolmec,' applicable, more properly, to *hell*; for it implies a location below the earth, and since their conversion, the same word is made use of in the catechism, to denote the abode of Satan. They believed that Chinig-chinich "resided in that region—that there was plenty to eat and drink, and to wear—that there was constant dancing and festivity—that no one labored—no one was sorrowful; but on the contrary, all were contented and happy—every one did as they pleased, and selected the number of wives they wished." The reader will compare this belief with the doctrine of the immortality of the soul. It was taught by the moderns, undoubtedly, and since their conversion to Christianity; for the old men at the time of their gentilism, had no such idea; to confirm which, I will relate the following account, as it was given to me by a female, who had been many years a convert to Christianity.

In the year 1817, in the mission of St. Juan Capistrano, I visited this woman, who was recovering from a severe attack of malignant fever. When in the worst stage of the disease, and in a state of paroxysm, she said, that she died, and the Indians, her relatives, carried her to Chinig-chinich, where she beheld a great number of men and women. Some were dancing, some playing, and others were bathing in a stream of pure, transparent water. The "rancheria" was large and beautiful, and the houses were of different construction from those in modern use. Having arrived at the house of Chinigchinich, she was informed that she could not enter, to reside with them yet; that she must return to her home. Food was given to her, of delicious quality, such as she had never eaten before, soon after which, she returned without having beheld Chinigchinich; but she could not recollect if she came alone, or if she were accompanied by others. It is evident that this account was the result of delirium, for I visited her during the paroxysm, when she partook of a glass of warm water, sweetened, that I administered myself, and of which she drank the whole. This water may have been the repast which she referred to, as having been given to her in the house of Chinigchinich; it caused her to perspire profusely, and broke the fever, so that in a few days she recovered.

58 The ancients said, that when an Indian died, though the body was burnt, still the heart did not consume—(which must be the *spirit* or *soul*, for the heart of flesh, of course, would perish with the body)—that it went to a place destined by Chinigchinich. If a chief, or one of the puplem, it went to dwell among the stars, and like them throw its light upon the earth. For this reason, they said that the planets, and most luminous bodies, were their hearts, or in other words, they were themselves, in reality.

In the year 1821, there appeared in the N.E. a comet. The Indians believed, with undoubted faith, that it was a chief of a *rancheria,* who had died; and who, previous to his departure, had told them, that he should in time behold them again from the heavens. This idea they received from their ancient traditions, because, according to *Seutonio,* the gentiles believed, that at the hour of the death of any illustrious personage (as was seen at the death of Julius Cæsar), there appeared in the heavens some notable meteor, which was translated to the stars, and arranged among the Gods. The reason given why the chiefs and puplem, alone, went to the heaven of stars, and that the other people did not, is this: because *"Tacue,"* "the eater of human flesh," had eaten of them previous to their being burnt; and if it happened that he did not eat of them, in consequence of their dying in the power of their enemies, or on account of their being drowned, then they did not go to the stars, but to another place, to which they were destined by Chinigchinich. Others, who were not of noble rank, were doomed to the borders of the sea, or to the hills, mountains, valleys, or forests; and there they remained an indefinite time, while Chinigchinich held them doing penance for the faults they had committed, in not obeying his precepts, but after the performance of said penance, whether they returned to their former shape, or removed to any other location, they could not tell.

The Indians, when they saw any strange thing, or imagined that they beheld any extraordinary figure, said, that it was a ghost, and considered it a bad omen—the forerunner of misfortune. They believed, that if the dead appeared to any one, it was for the purpose of injury, and particularly so, if appearing to females, whom, weak and timid as they were, it required but little to terrify. On this account, there were villains, who personated such figures to effect their brutal purposes. This custom was not confined to the Indians in their heathen state, but prevailed also among those who had become christianized. I will relate an occurrence of the kind, which took place in this neighborhood.

On a certain occasion, two females, mother and daughter-in-law, went out in search of wild fruits, which they called *"naut."* When in the vicinity of a grove, they heard loud groans and lamentations—a breaking of the shrubbery, and limbs of trees—then followed a voice, calling upon the daughter, by her proper name, to come to the place, or she would be murdered. The poor girl, filled with terror, and believing it an apparition, went into the grove, where she beheld one, who appeared, dressed in feathers from head to foot, with his face covered. She was told that he was such a one, who died at such a time, and that Chinigchinich confined him there. He told her to inform his widow, that she must resort to a certain place at night. On her return home, she gave the message to the woman, who immediately went to the spot directed, to behold her departed husband, and to ascertain his wishes. At first, she could find no one; but in a little while, she heard a voice, which said to her that she must remain until night. Supposing that in reality it was the voice of her deceased husband, she rejoiced greatly, for, they had loved each other much in their youth. She remained with him three nights—during which time, he spoke to her but very little, and then in a low and disguised voice. She went about in the daytime in search of fruits, and he, on return of evening, would bring her meat, that she might eat. On the third day, in the morning, after separating, she went out upon a hill, and beheld the same person in conversation with another; she knew them both, and returned immediately to the Mission, where she gave information, and many of her friends went out to the place, and discovered them in a cave with three hostile Indians.

Others remained about the houses of widows, and the houses of their relatives, terrifying them and doing them injury; and on this account, it was the custom whenever the deceased were burnt, to burn also the houses, and rebuild in another direction, so that when the husbands returned in search of them, there would be nothing remaining to denote their existence, and thus they would escape their persecutions. The converted Indians of the present day, have the same idea.

There is another case which I witnessed in the Mission of St. Luis Rey, in the year 1813—a Christian died, and the Indians said that he was poisoned or bewitched, by another Christian of the same mission—that his death was the result of witchcraft. The deceased in his lifetime possessed a small garden, where he was accustomed to sow yearly, certain grain and seeds. This he left to a relative at a time when the plants were in blossom; but immediately everything dried up and was destroyed, so that nothing was harvested of either grain or fruit. The plants whilst young were fresh and fruitful, like the plants in the surrounding gardens, but the moment the blossoms appeared as if ready to produce seed, they died; so that, in the course of one night, nearly all were destroyed as if consumed by fire. The Indians said that the deceased was seen moving about at night in every direction of the garden, and that whatever he touched, perished. This was revealed to them by an old woman who owned the adjoining garden, and who related the story to me, also, so that I was induced to go to the place in order to witness the same, and found, as she had stated, the greater part of the plants dead, or in a perishing state; some, however, were still flourishing. These I took particular notice of, and on the following day I returned, and found seven of them, consisting of corn, pumpkins, and watermelons, dried up, and consumed to their roots. In this way the whole was destroyed. Said Indian died of *dysentery*, and not by witchcraft, nor poison as believed. They were superstitious in their belief that whoever died in this way, died of poison, and this accounts for the tradition of the death of their grand captain *Ouiot*. We have seen that the story of the garden was given by an old woman, and for this reason is entitled to but little credit, but that which has caused me some difficulty to explain is, why the plants were thus decayed. It was not from want of care, or from disease received from insects, or animals either, because, if so, there would have appeared spots about them, and they would not have been diseased to their very roots. This may excite wonder in the reader, and I have used every diligence possible, to ascertain the cause, but without success. What I conjecture is this—that the Devil did all this, that but few should escape from his hands, and the motive, I have for believing so is, that at this time, there were many gentiles in the mission, principally sorcerers, (some were catechumens, and others not) who night after night performed their heathen ceremonies.

What has been said, I think is sufficient to prove, that these accounts and stories relative to the immortality of the soul, are mere fables, frauds and inventions to deceive the simple: that the first, and original settlers in this region, had a knowledge of the spirituality of the soul, and, con-

61

sequently, of its immortality; that by tradition, they have preserved the same without believing it, and perhaps ages before, they had a totally different account. We often perceive that a history, by numerous editions and revisals, loses much of its originality; how much more liable to corruption, tradition must be, among an ignorant race like the Indians. But little respect is attached to their belief of the spiritual substance with which we are adorned, not only by the rule, and ignorant of the present day, but, by the wisest, and best instructed in our Holy Religion. To remove all doubt from the reader, that he may not think my ideas extravagant, I will relate two events which happened in places where I have resided.

In the year 1808, I was a missionary in the mission of "La Purissima," when a young man of the establishment became seriously indisposed. His age was 23 years, he had been reared from infancy by the fathers, and was instructed in every thing appertaining to religion; often serving as interpreter for them, and was almost always with them. When first attacked, he refused to take medicine, nor could he be persuaded to do so, by any advice of the fathers; but he went off in search of one of the quack physicians, who practised upon him all his diabolical art. The fathers, seeing that he became worse, daily exhorted him to confess, and prepare for death like a Christian; but he declined, with the excuse that he was weak, he required examination, and (as was the opinion of the quack,) he did not think he should die. But, alas! he was deceived; for when the *doctor* saw that his chicanery and witchcraft, had no effect for the better, he forsook him, saying, "that as he had always believed the teachings of the priests, his God, (or more properly his devil), was angered and sent him death as a punishment." Hearing this, the poor invalid concluded to confess—he did so, but not with that satisfaction to the fathers which they had desired, and very soon after, death followed.

In the year 1817, in the mission of St. Juan Capistrano, an Indian 35 years of age, who, like the one just mentioned, was well instructed, became afflicted with a dangerous disease, and died. No persuasion on the part of his friends, or exhortations of the priests, could prevail upon him to confess, and partake of the holy sacrament; at the bare proposal, he became frantic, and uttered expressions, which were contemptuous and blasphemous. A short time previous to his death, I called to see him, to give him that consolation, which the promises of our holy religion impart to the penitent soul, and I urged him, since he could do no more, to receive the extreme unction, to ask pardon for his sins, for God was infinite in his mercy to the repentant sinner. But all in vain! my words were ineffectual, and they were spurned with disgust. His limbs were extended—the froth came from his mouth—his eyes rolled back into his head, presenting a true picture of the appearance of one condemned to the torments of hell; and three persons were insufficient to confine him. These demonstrations seemed to me, the effects of the violence of the malady, but after a while his tranquillity returned, and some one exclaimed, "Why do you not confess?" "Because I will not," he replied, with anger. "If I have been deceived whilst living, I do not wish to die in the delusion!" These were his last words; for soon after, he expired, and there remained a corpse, truly horrible and revolting to the sight. Consider, what must have been my feelings! Such a spectacle before me, revealing to the letter the words of David, *"Pecator videbit et irascetur, dentibus suis fremet et tabescet, desiderium peccatorum peribit."*

I presume there may be some persons who will say, notwithstanding these accounts, that they are not satisfactory evidences of a total want of faith and belief; for rare occurrences happen every where, and God has permitted them to take place for his own inexplicable purposes, and for advantages resulting to others. To this I concede, but exceptions are few. These accounts generally conform to each other in substance, and he, who has perused them with attention, or is familiar with the character of these Indians, knowing that when they appear the most intelligent, and entitled to the greatest confidence, they are the least to be trusted; he will, I say, agree with me, generally, regarding their belief; as all their operations are accompanied by stratagems and dissimulation, they easily gain our confidence, and at every pass we are deluded.

Chapter XV

Origin of the Population of the Mission of St. Juan Capistrano

HAVING THUS FAR DWELT UPON THE USAGES, belief, and customs of these Indians, it may not be uninteresting to know the origin of those who first settled in the neighborhood of St. Juan, the account of which, will contain many absurdities, and some equally extravagant as those already related. The first, or earliest people, who populated this section of the country, emigrated from a place called *"Sejat,"* distant N.E. from the mission, seven or eight leagues, and in the middle of a valley, now known by the name of "el Rancho de los Nietos." Originally, the inhabitants were numerous, but the success, and influence of a holy conquest gradually eradicated their attachment to *"Sejat,"* and all, finally, became subject to the spiritual, as well as temporal, administration of the ecclesiastical missions. Their chief, named *"Oyaison,"* which name implies "wisdom" or "intelligence," and his wife, called *"Sirorum,"* signifying that which is noisy, (probably alluding to the noise made by the shells and beads attached to her dress), had three children, called *Coronne,* *"Vuiragram,"* and *Uiniojum.* *Oyaison,* after the death of *Sirorum,* separated from among the people many families, who accompanied him and his daughter *Coronne,* in a colonial enterprise; for, in consequence of the rapid increase of population, the annual production of seeds on his lands, were insufficient to maintain so great a number, and, accordingly, the colonists commenced their march. After travelling southwardly seven or eight leagues, or more, they arrived at a place called *"Niguiti,"* which is situated half a league only, N.E. from the mission. Here, they discovered a spring of fresh water, and from the favorable appearance of the neighboring country, they concluded that it was a place well adapted to the founding of a new colony. As soon as the erecting of their habitations was completed, and order had been established, the chief returned to *"Sejat,"* leaving behind, his daughter *"Coronne."*

Twenty summers had passed away, and still no feelings of love, or wish to marry, had ever been known to exist in the heart of *Coronne.* The Indians said that she was very coarse and fat—that they never had seen, or in fact, that there never was another of such proportions. The name given to the new establishment was *"Putuidem,"* which means "umbilicus projectura;" for *Coronne* was afflicted with an enlargement of that organ, and this was their notion for so naming the settlement. In course of time, owing to the scarcity of grain, many of the inhabitants separated; and, by permission of Coronne, located themselves about in different parts of the Valley of St. Juan; and in this way originated the many small villages, or towns, which were to be met with, in the route to Putuidem.

A custom was observed in all their new settlements, to appoint as chief or captain, the eldest of the families, and to him was given the name of *Nu,* and to the second in power, that of *"Eyacque."* Their wives were named also; the first *"Coronne,"* and the second *"Tepi."* These same appellations were given to a small insect, or fly, which was abundant in the fields and gardens, called by us the *lady bug.* The red ones were *Coronnes,* and the yellow, *Tepis!* The first was given to the wife of the chief, in commemoration of the *Capitana* of *Putuidem,* and that of *Tepi* to the wife of Eyacque, for the reason that the two names implied equality, as demonstrated in the character of the insects who varied only in their colors. These names are the principal distinctions of rank, known among the Indians, and there are many of the present day, who, on account of their appellations, are considered and respected as descendants of *Eyacque.*

A grand feast was given by *Coronne,* of several days' continuance, and all the neighboring tribes were invited to attend, and take part in the amusements and rejoicings. The feast commenced with dancing,

65

playing and singing, and all their accustomed games and usages followed; but as in this world there cannot be complete happiness, or joy unadulterated, it happened that after she had retired for the night, whilst asleep, her body swelled up prodigiously, and in an instant became a mound of earth; thereupon the people retired to their respective rancherias. In the place where the town was located, and where they celebrated the feast, there is a small rising ground, which was probably formed by the course of the water in a freshet; but the Indians say, and religiously believe, that it is the body of *Coronne*.

After having taken leave of their friends, who remained sorrowful, and disconsolate for the loss of their *Capitana*, the Indians on returning home, arrived and put up for the night at a place called *"Acagchemem,"* distant, from where the mission now stands, only about sixty yards; and from this time the new colony assumed the name corresponding to the place. "Acagchemem," signifies a pyramidal form of any thing that moves, such as, an anthill, or place of resort for other insects. Others apply the term to things inanimate; such as a pile of stones, &c.; but, the most correct signification of the word is understood as having relation to a heap of animated things.

The motive alleged by the Indians, for having dropped the name of their nation, and substituted that of *"Acagchemem,"* is that they passed the night before mentioned, literally piled upon each other; men, women, and children; and when rising on the following morning, they vociferated "Acagchemem," implying, that they had slept in a heap; and from that time the appellation remained as if to commemorate forever the event.

When the Indians came to settle in the valley of St. Juan Capistrano, they spoke a language somewhat distinct from the one now in use, and in a dialect, not dissimilar to the one used in St. Gabriel. They say the cause of the variation, originated with their chief *"Oyaison,"* who told them that as they were to change their place of residence, they were necessarily obliged to alter their mode of speech, as well as their customs, in order to become a distinct nation.

The name, *"Sejat,"* signifies a place of wild bees, and *"Sejar pepau,"* the honey. In this region there were to be found many hives, located in holes formed in the earth. The Indians search for them at all times, to extract the honey, and it is made use of in their food. The color is black, and it is rather bitter, but I have been informed that there are places, where it is to be found, of a kind, equally as good, as that which is extracted from the hives of the domestic species.

Chapter XVI
The Character of the Indian

TO COMPLETE THIS HISTORY, AND TO GIVE A RELA-
tion of all my observations during a period of more than twenty years'
residence in the province, it will be important to delinate the character
of the Indians, as I have been enabled to learn it. The undertaking will
be arduous, I know, and a curate of forty years' residence among them,
once told his bishop, "they were incomprehensible"—to which I agree;
but nevertheless, I will make the attempt. My idea is that the natural, or
Divine precepts implanted in the heart of man by his Creator, are by
the Indians observed in a retrograde manner, or in the opposite sense—
that is, the affirmative with them, is negative, and the negative, the affirmative; and this opposition appears innate among all classes of them.
An Indian curate of the Indians, appears to be of the same opinion, if
we may judge from his description. "The Indians," he said, "lead a life
of indolence, rather than devote themselves to the enlightening of their
souls with ideas of civilization and catholicism; it is repugnant to their
feelings, which have become vitiated by the unrestricted customs among
them. Their inclinations, to possess themselves of the property of others,
are unbounded. Their hypocrisy, when they pray, is as much to be
feared, as their insolence, when in tumultuous disorder. They are never
grateful for any benefit, nor do they pardon an injury, and they never
proffer civilities, unless to accomplish some interested motive. They are

ready to expose themselves to the greatest danger, to satisfy their pre-dominant passions. The future from them, is ever veiled by the present. Their inconstancy and want of confidence deprive them of friends, and he, who, by deception, holds them in subjection, may reduce them to almost abject slavery." Such is the picture of them drawn by this Indian curate, who was of Mexico, and I think, although referring to the Mexi-cans, it is sufficient to comprehend the general character of the Indian. Those of California are less curious, and in no wise so industrious; for the Mexicans, when in their gentilism, sowed and prepared the *maize*, as well as other grain for eating, and the females spun and wove a cover-ing for the body, out of cotton, which they also cultivated.

The Indians of California may be compared to a species of monkey; for in naught do they express interest, except in imitating the actions of others, and, particularly in copying the ways of the *"razon,"* or white men, whom they respect as beings much superior to themselves; but in so doing, they are careful to select vice, in preference to virtue. This is the result, undoubtedly, of their corrupt, and natural disposition.

The Indian, in his grave, humble and retired manner, conceals a hypocritical and treacherous disposition. He will deceive the most minute observer, as has been the case with many, or with all, who have endeavored to learn his character, until time has revealed to them his true qualities. He never looks at any one, while in conversation, but has a wandering and malicious gaze. For benefits received, he is never grate-ful; and instead of looking upon that which is given, he beholds only that which is withheld. His eyes are never uplifted, but like those of the swine, are cast to the earth. Truth is not in him, unless to the injury of another, and he is exceedingly false.

MYTHOLOGY

These Indians had the same belief as the Ancients, regarding the course of the sun, and believed that when he set, he went to repose in the arms of Thetis. He had twelve Palaces, which were placed at equal distances around the earth; in each of which, he was accustomed to pass a month. These twelve palaces were marked by a circle, called the zodiac, but with signs, which alluded to certain passages in the fable.

Characteristic Anecdotes

A CHIEF OF A RANCHERIA, OR VILLAGE, NOT far distant from the Presidio of St. Diego, who had observed, with much attention, the manner and authority with which the *"Comandante"* governed his officers and soldiers, as well as the inhabitants of the place, had heard, also, that the King of Spain was their grand chief, to whom, they all owed allegiance, and in case of disobedience were liable to severe punishment, and even death.

Desirous of imitating the domination of his royal master, he commenced a tyrannical use of his power, which gained him many enemies. However, it was of short duration. In 1822, when D. Augustin Yturbide was proclaimed Emperor of Mexico, and when his government was recognized, in due form, at St. Diego, there were many Indians present, who listened attentively, to the declaration that Mexico no longer acknowledged the Spanish authority. The king (or viceroy) had been deposed, and another placed in his stead, with the new title of Emperor. A few months afterwards, a grand feast was observed in the Indian village, to which all the neighboring Indians were invited.

To commence the ceremonies, they burned their chief alive! and elected another. The feast continued eight days, when the Indians dispersed and returned to their several homes. Those who lived in the Presidio, were censured for such inhumanity, which produced the following remarks:—"Have you not done in Mexico the same with the

King of Spain?" (meaning the Viceroy). "You say he was not good, and you killed him! Well, our captain was not good, and we have burned him. Should the new one be bad, we will burn him also!"

How little is the faith of these Indians in the teachings of the Catholic truths! A missionary, of the mission of St. Luis Rey, who had baptized several adults, the youngest of whom had reached his fiftieth year, attempted to explain, after the ceremony was concluded, the sort of life which they were to observe for the future; and he told them what they were to do to avoid the influence of Satan. By invoking the sweet names of Jesus and Mary, he said, and by the sign of the holy cross, well performed, we destroy the power of the devil, and drive out all unholy thoughts. A *satrap*, or governor, of one of the rancherias, smilingly observed to the others, "See how this pádre cheats us! Who believes that the devil will leave us, by the sign of the cross? If it were to be done by dancing, as authorized by Chinigchinich, he would depart; but that he will do so, by the means which *he* says, I do not believe!" The others united with him in laughter, and appeared unimpressed with the efficacy of such ceremony.

About the middle of December, 1823, a comet appeared in the north, which was visible until the latter part of January, of the ensuing year; and in September, 1825, another was seen. The latter appeared in the south-east, with its direction to the north-west, and was visible, though faintly, till the first of November.

The Indians, who had observed them, believing they were their deceased chiefs, consulted together, as to the cause of their appearance, and were all of one opinion, that they denoted some important change in their destiny; but how, or in what manner, it would be, they were ignorant. Some thought that they would return to their primitive mode of life; that it was *"Sirout,"* whom they had seen, he, who was the father of their grand captain *Ouiot;* and when *he* came, he ever brought good things, for their profit and happiness. Others said no! that it denoted that they were to live free, and do whatever they pleased, without being under subjection to any one; yet they would still remain occupants of the mission. The elder ones said, *Sirout* foretold, that another people would come, who would treat them as slaves, and abuse them—that they would suffer much hunger and misery, and that the chief thus appeared, to call them away from the impending calamity. Others said, that the comet was *"Tacu,"* the father of *"Ouiamot"* or *"Chinigchinich,"* which was generally assented to. These ideas have, undoubtedly, arisen from the fact, that when the declaration of independence was proclaimed in Mexico, the Indians were made to believe, that they would no longer be subject to the regulations of the missions; that each family, or person, would live separate, as colonists. But the government, considering them unfit for such a condition, has not made any innovation, up to the present time of November, 1825.

An Indian *"vaquero,"* of the mission of San Luis Obispo, who had been despatched on business, to some place not far distant, did not make his appearance until the day following, and then so pallid and trembling, that he could hardly speak. Upon inquiring as to what ailed him, he replied, "that being in a certain place, a phantom appeared before him, which prevented his progress; and his horse, though vigorous, remained immoveable at the sight. The phantom commanded him to tell his people not to travel in that direction, for if they did, he should molest them! Immediately, three of us, pádres, went out, with *"vaqueros,"* and other Indians, and remained all that day about the same spot, but nothing was seen of the phantom.

In a certain *"rancho,"* or farm, were several *Pima* Indians, and some *Sagues,* who were employed in erecting a building; he who directed them, was one of the *razon,* or native Spaniards. One day, whilst superintending the work, he discovered, concealed, in one of the apartments, a small wooden ball, which had around it, an unfinished crown of thorns. He enquired of a *"Sagui,"* what it was for. "Ah! Sir," he replied, "you have really escaped; with this ball you would have been destroyed. You were to be killed for having chastised the Pima Indian, and only two days more were required; that is, until the completion of the crown of thorns around the ball; then, immediately, you would have been attacked with pains in the head and heart, and would have died.

750

COPIES OF THIS BOOK HAVE BEEN
PRINTED AT THE GILLICK PRESS, BERKELEY, CALIFORNIA
DESIGNED BY BEN KENNEDY